The Shell
Book of Angling

Wales: the River Teifi (J. Barry Lloyd)

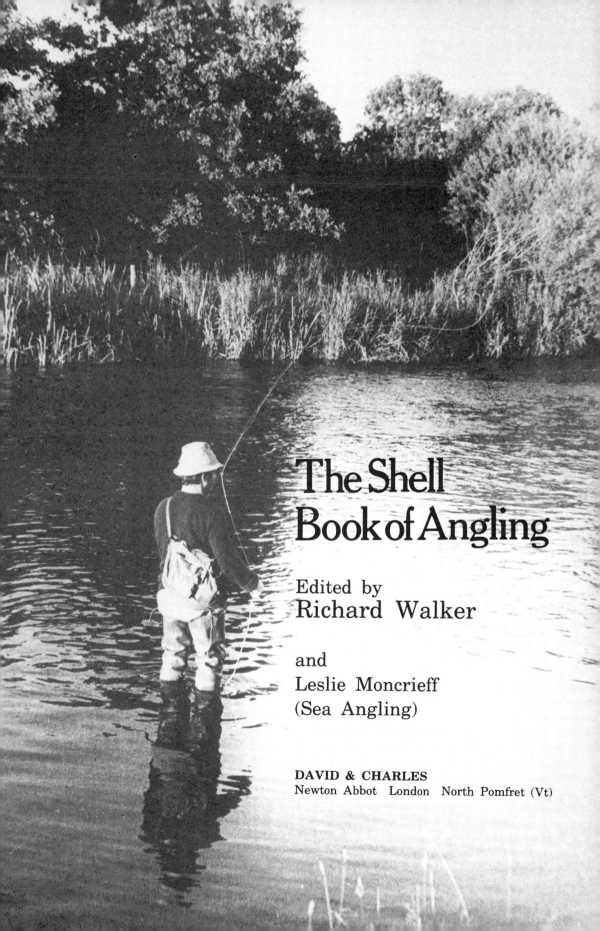

The Shell Book of Angling

Edited by
Richard Walker

and
Leslie Moncrieff
(Sea Angling)

DAVID & CHARLES
Newton Abbot London North Pomfret (Vt)

British Library Cataloging in Publication Data

The Shell Book of Angling
  1. Fishing
  I. Walker, Richard, b. 1918
  II. Moncrieff, Leslie
  799.1'2   SH439

ISBN 0–7153–7780–9
Library of Congress Catalog Card Number 79–53735

Photoset and Printed in Great Britain
by Redwood Burn Limited
Trowbridge & Esher
for David & Charles (Publishers) Limited
Brunel House Newton Abbot Devon

Published in the United States of America
by David & Charles Inc
North Pomfret Vermont 05053 USA

Contents

PART THREE SEA ANGLING
(Edited by Leslie Moncrieff)

PART FOUR THE SPECIALISTS

Introduction

In 1953, a book called *Still-Water Angling* which I had written, was published at the instigation of an importunate publisher. It said things about angling that had not been said before, and I am told that it initiated a new approach to the sport.

Now this same publisher (now at *David & Charles*) tries to bully or cajole me into writing another book, which I have refused to do because angling has, in the intervening years, become so specialised that no one man can treat it on a general basis. The best I could do was to write a few chapters myself and act as a recruiting agent in finding other accomplished anglers who could deal far better than I with the areas of angling in which they have specialised. I do not propose to provide biographies for these men whose names as leading exponents of their various branches of fishing are well known to readers of the angling press. I chose them because they practise very successfully what they preach, and are coherent in preaching it.

Introductions to fishing books often apologise for adding another volume to the tens of thousands already in existence. I make no such apology for angling continues to expand, every year producing thousands of recruits to the sport, unfortunately without a corresponding expansion in the facilities for pursuing it. The modern angler, especially if he is a comparative novice, needs all the advice he can obtain and, above all, the latest advice that will help him to make the best of the fishing available to him. This, I believe, is such a book. Its contributors are all fishing successfully now. I shall not single out any of them for special mention; if they were not among the best, they would not have been invited to contribute.

Richard Walker July 1979

Part One
Game Fishing

1

Salmon

Arthur Oglesby

Fishing for salmon is still something of a snob sport—it cannot shake off its associations with wealth and privilege—but those of us who are prepared to take the trouble can enjoy it at very reasonable prices. You might not have a large tract of water to yourself but such fishing can be had for as little as £1 per day—if you look for it.

The legal methods for taking salmon are fly-fishing, with either a floating or sinking line; spinning with natural or artificial lures; and fishing with the natural worm, prawn or shrimp bait. Many fisheries will allow all these methods at some time of the season, but there are others where some restrictions are imposed. Many ban prawn fishing, while others impose a fly-only rule for certain months or at certain heights of water. Undoubtedly, spinning is best practised in February, March and April when salmon are at the peak of their condition—then known as springers!

Spinning

Spinning for salmon requires a double-handed rod of some 9ft to 10ft; a fixed-spool or multiplying reel capable of holding 150 to 200 yards of 12lb to 15lb test monofilament or braided line; some ball-bearing swivels and a selection of spoon baits and devon minnows. Normally I prefer the fixed-spool reel, for this will cope readily with the very small spinning baits we might need later in the season. But, if you can afford it, get both and use the multiplier on such rivers as the Tay and Wye and the fixed-spool on the smaller, rock-girt streams. Long experience of a piece of

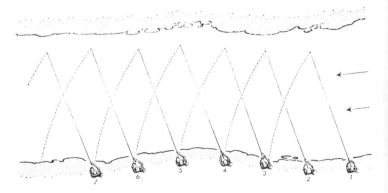

Spinning: move down the pool and cast the same distance every time

water is essential before the full potential of its fishing can be exploited. There is no substitute for local knowledge and if you do not know a piece of water and do not have a gillie, it will pay you handsome dividends to get a local angler to direct you to the most productive places. Even experienced salmon anglers are hard put to it to recognise the obvious places on a strange river.

Let us assume we are on a salmon river in February, there are salmon about and in our beat the river is running about 2ft above normal summer height with a water temperature of about 38°F. We have been advised to concentrate on the slower and deeper sections where almost any but the running salmon will, for sure, be concentrated. We may have to wade or be boated into a likely position to make the first cast although at this time of year it may be possible to spin from the bank.

We must always bear in mind that salmon do not feed in fresh water, but we know that there are occasions when they will take our lures and flies although the why's and wherefore's of salmon behaviour are not fully known; salmon in cold water do not, however, normally move fast or far to intercept a lure. It follows, therefore, that the angler with the best chance of catching a fish is the one who can make his bait move slowly, just above the bottom where the fish lie, and be able to assess the suitable weight of his bait. Devon minnows, for instance, are available in

Salmon fishing on the River Tweed at Innerleithen, Peebles-shire

Wood's method of leading the fly: cast a slack line and let the current tighten it

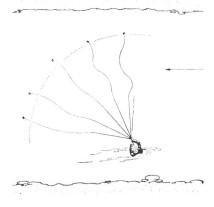

11

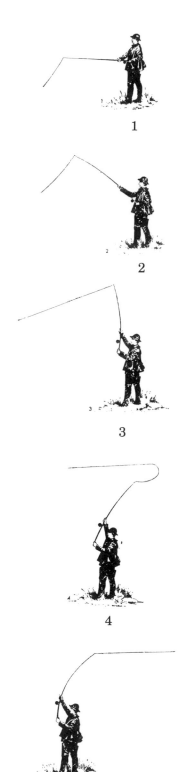

1

2

3

4

5

a wide variety of materials: the wooden ones almost float, but others, made of plastic and metal, even if they look the same, vary in weight. For our purposes, a 2½in metal devon minnow in either black and gold, or the popular spring colours of the yellow belly, should be about right. This might move well over the lies without additional weight, but it always pays to have enough lead wire handy to wind round the minnow flight to get it near the bottom. As we shall see, it is this assessment of weight which is the key to successful spin fishing for salmon.

Many a novice spinning for salmon on the bank will throw his bait out as far as he can and then wind it back quickly, or at any rate he thinks suitable. Then he takes a pace or two downstream to repeat the process and, doubtless, goes on doing so all day in the hope of catching a salmon. The experienced fisherman will throw his lure out in much the same way but when the bait alights he lets a few loops of line slip off the reel before closing it. He then tries to 'mend', or remove downstream 'belly' in the line, so that the bait gets well down in the water; he does this without winding the reel-handle but merely by letting his bait swing round in the current in much the same manner as would a wet fly. He is relying on the strength of the current to make his bait revolve or flutter and, by not winding the reel handle, he is hoping that the bait will move slowly, and at adequate depth, over the fish to induce it to take. Just occasionally, he may get his bait hung up on the bottom. In this event he will reduce the weight of his bait and carry on with the same tactic without getting hung up. The novice, on the other hand, often assumes that hang-ups can be remedied only by speeding up the retrieve, thinking: 'If I don't wind the reel the bait gets stuck on the bottom.' Of course, there may be semi-still water occasions when the bait has to be moved to make it spin, but these are rare in February; if necessary, this should only be done slowly to keep the lure near the bottom.

Ideally, therefore, select a weight of bait which, when cast out to the other side of the current, will swing round slowly on its own momentum just above the bottom, for any form of reel-handle movement will lift the bait in the water and bring it back too quickly to induce the salmon to respond. Differing strengths of current and heights of water obviously demand

Main arc of power with the fly rod

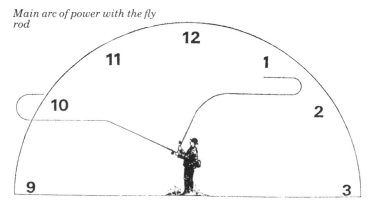

12

A 17lb salmon from the River Lune

appropriate sizes and weights of bait. But, and it cannot be emphasised too strongly, the successful spring fisherman must be ever-conscious of the paramount importance of allowing his bait to move as slowly and as deeply as possible, and he must carry a wide variety of baits to vary the weight permutations.

As the water becomes warmer it is, of course, possible to speed up the rate of retrieve. As the water temperature moves above the 50°F mark, the fish will be prepared to move quite far to intercept a bait; it may even be cast upstream and brought back just as fast as the reel-handle can be turned. But it may well be that at such times the angler should put his spinning tackle to one side and bring out his fly-fishing tackle.

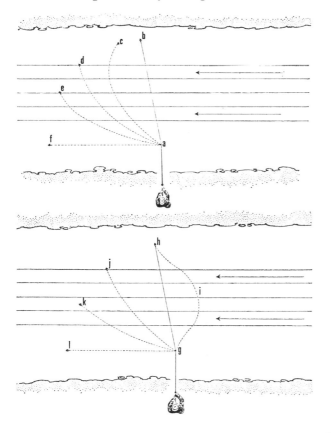

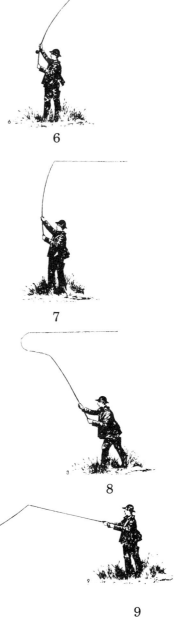

6

7

8

9

Sequence of a good overhead cast: the lift begins at 1 and continues to 3. A slight drift and pause between 4 and 5. Then the return power is applied between 6, 7 and 8, bringing the rod down to 9 as the cast straightens out

(left) If the line is cast as in a − b, some excessive line belly will be caused until it straightens out at f. Every attempt should be made to mend the line as in g − l

13

Fly-fishing

For those with a great deal of experience of salmon, fly-fishing will eventually become the epitome of the sport, particularly if you have access to the right river; on rivers like the Aberdeenshire Dee or the Spey, the fly, on either a sinking or floating line, is probably the best method of catching salmon anyway. Fifteen years ago, I suppose that as many as 90 per cent of my salmon were taken on a spinner; now I doubt if I catch 5 per cent and, in 1978, all the salmon I caught were taken on a fly. In times past, of course, all salmon fishing was done with some type of 'fly'. It is only since the development of the casting-reel that spinning has become popular. Before that, one fished with a size of fly to suit the conditions, and most lines sank; it was not until the late A.H.E. Wood found that greasing his line made it float and that in water temperatures above 50°F this was the best method, that we began to consider seriously the technique of fishing the small fly on the floating line. Nowadays, therefore, the angler who, like myself, genuinely prefers fly-fishing, can fish the spring and autumn months with a strong double-handed rod and a modern sinking line. Add to this the big, heavy tube fly—up to 3in long—and he has a type of tackle which gets the fly or lure well down to the fish and can move over it at much the same depth and speed as a spinning bait.

The author prepares to tail a 16lb salmon from the River Lune

There was a tendency until recently to select shorter rods for

their lightness. Since the advent of carbon-fibre, however, there has been a revolution in fishing tackle and techniques. Nowadays it is possible to fish with a 15ft or 16ft rod weighing no more than a 12ft rod in cane or fibreglass. Many ladies can now use a 15ft rod with ease—whereas with cane or glass it would have been virtually beyond them. The longer rods have given us that little thing, increased 'water command', without the earlier disadvantage of weight. The 15ft 'Walker' in carbon-fibre now being marketed by Bruce & Walker Ltd, for instance, is the most versatile salmon rod I have used. In February, March and April it will carry a heavy sinking line and the equally heavy tube flies; yet in May, June and July, it is just as much at home with a floating line and small flies.

The technique with either sunk or floating line is very much the same as that described for spinning. Unless the circumstances are exceptional there is little to beat the slow fishing methods advocated. In cold water the big tube fly may be cast out on a sinking, shooting head and allowed to swing round like the spinner. Only when the fly is on the dangle and out of the main current should some of the backing be hand-lined in and another cast made. The fly-fisherman on a normal stream would never dream of hand-lining his backing in during the swing through the current and, as we have seen, neither does the expert spin fisherman wind his reel-handle. In all cold waters, therefore, there is little to beat the slow and deep technique whether it be with spinner or fly. In former times this fly-fishing technique was the only one practised, but it was possible to vary the size of the fly with the seasons.

Nowadays, with the modern plastic lines which float without additional grease and after practice with a double-handed rod, fly-fishing in this style is just about the easiest of all forms of salmon fishing. Of course, it helps to be able to throw a long line and, in overgrown places, to be able to do the spey-cast. Many of the classic Scottish rivers are well suited to fly-fishing, although the Spey and Dee may be better suited to the floating than to the sunk line. Nowhere are these rivers very deep and, given a range of fly sizes, I would be prepared to fish a season through with nothing more than a floating line. This does not apply to all rivers—some in Norway for instance and many spate streams and rivers in the west coast of Scotland, England and in Wales.

Most of my own fly-fishing with the full, floating line starts about the end of April. This is when water temperatures are rising to the 50°F mark, salmon behaviour is in a state of flux and a fish might be taken on anything from a 2½in devon minnow to a small, sparsely dressed fly on a floating line. The fish in the Spey at this time, for instance, are still running, but they will frequently wait awhile in holding pools and only the luck of a collision course will bring your bait or fly over them in their brief residence.

The month of May used to be the premier time on classic rivers for sport on the fly but, sadly, there are not now many classic rivers in the United Kingdom. For the most part salmon rivers rely nowadays on spates to bring them into trim and

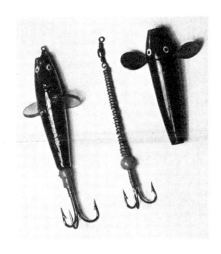

Devon minnows: the one on the right has been dismantled to show the lead wire round the hook flight

15

Castle Grant on the River Spey: playing a salmon to the net

many come into and go out of order with the rise and fall of the water level. In some of them good runs of salmon are not seen until the first spates of June or July. This is what I call 'opportunist' fishing, when the angler must be able to down-tools at a moment's notice and scurry off to the river whenever the local gillie or keeper telephones to say that the river is right. An appointments book is what the itinerant salmon angler has to ignore at this time of year, for the period of best salmon response will be confined to hours rather than days.

Most salmon rivers fish very badly when the water is rising. There may be a brief, good taking time on the first flush of the rise, but as soon as the level drops, you can start fishing. Maybe a bunch of lobworms legered in the quiet corners and eddies near the bank will produce a few fish when the water is still coloured, but as it clears it may pay to spin with a flashy Toby spoon or, depending on clarity, a 2in black and gold devon minnow. As being in the right place at the right time is such an important factor in salmon fishing, renting a stretch at the peak period on a classic river gives you much higher chances than taking pot-luck on some lesser known water.

The Strathspey Angling Association at Grantown-on-Spey administers one of the most inexpensive pieces of salmon water: here, for as little as £6 per week (1978), the visiting angler has access to a seven-mile stretch of the river Spey and its tributary—the Dulnain. The water does get well fished in the spring, but it yields its trophies nevertheless to those who persevere in getting to know it. In 1978 it produced over 600 salmon for the visitors and locals who took time to study its moods. I know it well for in April, May and September I run courses at Grantown-on-Spey (details from the Seafield Lodge Hotel) and many anglers go home from there with their first salmon.

Salmon fishing, you see, is not the exclusive perquisite of the privileged. In Scotland especially, it is sport for all—from every walk of life, in spite of a residual snob element. I have learned when to fish hard and when it is preferable to sit and watch the others. Nowadays, I spend the best part of three months a year on the Spey, but I may fish on only fewer than forty-five of those ninety days, and even then, for as little as an hour or two; and there is never a season when I do not learn some new aspect of catching Spey salmon, plodding away at one piece of water and learning its every mood and whim under all conditions.

The angler may travel thousands of miles to get the thrill of that magic moment when a salmon is on: it is the moment he has dreamed of, but alas! it may be a bitter disappointment. So very many anglers seem to lose their first fish, usually because of over-anxiety to get the fish ashore, or a too-timid approach which lets the fish have it all its own way. In the early stages a strong salmon has a few ideas of its own. Firm but gentle treatment is the rule, giving line grudgingly when the fish wants to take it, but always keeping the fish fighting the current and your tackle. The fish is best kept in the mainstream until it tires and can be brought near the bank. It will make several more excursions back into the current and the sensible angler should always be ready to let out the line when he has to. Play the fish firmly until it is lying beaten on its side; then it is simple enough to net it, gaff it, or merely lift it out by the tail. Many fish are lost through over-anxiety in these final stages of play, some merely get off the hook—a thing that can happen to anyone—but usually because you are, in the excitement, holding the tackle too hard.

Ten years ago I wrote a book about salmon fishing. Since then I have learned a lot more, and if I am spared for another ten years I shall still be learning. The outwitting of a fish which does not feed in fresh water and whose moods will never be fully understood—this is the fascination of salmon fishing.

Hand-tailing a salmon from the River Spey

2

Sea Trout

J. Barry Lloyd

Sea trout are not usually fished for in the sea and that is the first lesson about them—how much of an enigma they may be. The second is that they do not even behave like trout.

The main relevant characteristics of sea trout are their extreme shyness in the daytime and a willingness to take a lure more readily after dusk. Consequently, the majority of fishermen practise their art during the hours of darkness in the summer, and on rivers—where most sea trout are to be found. Although you can spin a bait or trundle a worm under these conditions, the most effective and for many, the aesthetic method, is fly-fishing.

Most of the sea trout are to be found within the pools, and an ideal one might have a steady current flowing down the run into a wider and slower middle portion with a depth of around 6ft or more. There should be a gradual shelving of this depth to the gliding water at the tail-end and, if the whole of one bank has overhanging trees to offer shade and protection, then so much the better. If, in addition, the pool is situated at the top of a long stretch of rough, broken and shallow water, then the sea trout will be more inclined to rest up here after running, and the potential for sport is excellent.

Before starting to fish an unfamiliar pool however, it is imperative to undertake a daylight reconnaissance in the interests of safety and efficiency. We need to familiarise ourselves with its layout as, during the hours of darkness, all the usual landmarks will be lost and, if we are not careful so shall we. Carefully wade down through the pool on the track

(right) The River Avon, tributary of the Spey

A 3lb sea trout

which you expect to take later on, and check for potential hazards such as submerged rocks and spits of loose shingle. Also, find out the length of line needed to cover the lies of the fish easily without hitting the trees in front or the bank behind. Note the way a floating line behaves in the fluctuating current and which type of sinking line reaches well down without constantly snagging the bottom. As it is undesirable to use a torch unless absolutely necessary, investigate any safe places to use when climbing down to the pool and returning up, and whether any shingle exists for beaching the fish instead of having to net them.

Such simple precautions increase efficiency quite considerably, especially if we wish to avoid the irritations of constantly becoming tangled up in the trees opposite, or of floating down the river just because we forgot that deep pot-hole. Apart from wasting valuable fishing time, one feels such an idiot sitting there on the river bank in one's shirt tail and wringing out a pair of sodden trousers.

Sea trout are very fickle creatures and seem inordinately susceptible to the weather, so much so that perfect nights for fishing are few and far between. Warm, settled conditions with little, if any, moonlight are what are required. Then we would probably start off by fishing with a floating line for the first hour or so until any activity ceased and then switch to a sunk line. You might as well miss out this first stage altogether on cold nights, when a wet, blustery wind blows, or thunder reverberates across the valley. However, the only nights when I consider fishing is not worth it is when a thick mist rolls down off the meadows and blankets the river, or the water is coloured due to a flood.

I suggest that you start to fish only when it has grown just too dark to tell the time from your watch, when you begin by carefully wading in without any noise to the top of the run and

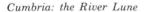

Cumbria: the River Lune

work your way down. Most of the sea trout will be in the slower and deeper section of the pool though they will spread out on favourable nights, especially into the glides, and so we should cover the whole pool to start with. Make your cast down and across, letting the current pull the flies round, but be prepared for a take at any moment. Sometimes the sea trout will tug fiercely at the fly and, before you have time to think, you are playing a mad creature which charges all over the pool and continually leaps out of the water with mighty flurries of spray. On other nights you may only feel the gentlest of 'knocks' against the fly and then you must try to tighten instantly. Do not be too disheartened if you miss most of these offers on such nights, as usually the sea trout will begin to take more freely later on. It does help, though, to keep the rod point up at an angle of 45° as this allows a belly of line to form and so cushion the resistance felt by the fish. This may make all the difference between success and failure.

A fundamental point is to make your fly travel at a realistic speed relative to the current. The word 'fly' is a misnomer here as it is not trying to imitate any insect life but attempting to re-stimulate the sea trouts' habit of feeding on small fish when they were at sea. So you have to try and make your 'fly' head into the current at the speed of a small fish and this will vary depending on the size of the fly being used. Also, do not forget that the sea trout will not be able to see quite so clearly in the dark and so the fly should be slowed down a bit to give it a greater chance of making some impact.

The most suitable size of fly to use has been a source of considerable debate, though there is more uniformity with the sunk-line fishing employed later on at night. Most fishermen would now prefer a fly from 1in to 2in long and a tube fly of this size is excellent for the treble hook used with it gives a firmer hold on the soft-mouthed fish. With a floating line I, personally, revert to a large fly when I know that the sea trout are fresh in from the sea. This might occur not too far from the estuary or, when extra water on the previous two or three days has allowed the fish to travel, well upstream. Under normal water height, the sea trout move more slowly, often at night, and the size of the fly has to be progressively reduced as the fish become more stale. Now you may find that, in the upper and middle reaches of the river, it will pay to use orthodox flies (size nos 8 to 12) and a lot of your ultimate catch will depend on an accurate assessment of the relative freshness of the fish in that part of the river where you are fishing.

The choice of a suitable pattern is not nearly so difficult to decide upon, despite the vast number available to tempt you with their beautiful colours. It must be obvious that sea trout will be unable to differentiate subtleties of colour after dark and therefore only the overall tone is of importance—allied, that is, with a correct shape to your fly. Put more simply, this means that you need a dark-toned fly when using a floating line because the fly will stand out more clearly when seen from underneath by the sea trout against what little light remains in the sky. Conversely, on a sunk line I would suggest a light-toned fly so that it shows up well against the darker background of the river-bed. A final touch of a roughened silver body to create some glistening in any available light and the choice of pattern is greatly simplified.

If you decide to try the traditional team of three small wet flies, then you could hedge your bets by using a dark, medium and a light-toned fly on the same leader—such as a Black Pennell, Golden Olive, and Teal Blue and Silver. However, I would not recommend this style to the novice unless his casting is of a fairly good standard. The only time when I can guarantee that the sea trout will come on the take, is if you are standing in the middle of the river, cursing loudly in the dark, while you attempt to unravel a dreadful bird's nest in which your leader has become mysteriously entangled. If you must use three flies, then make sure that your backward and forward casts are in slightly different planes as this will help to avoid some of these tangles. Needless to say, with a large tube fly and its associated big treble hook, you are apt to be more of a danger to yourself than to any sea trout—so do take the greatest care whilst night fishing.

I can well understand the impatience of sea-trouters waiting until dark before starting to fish, so you might like to be on the lookout for the following. On a few rivers such as the Spey in Scotland, the Lune in England and the Welsh Teifi, there is a sufficient volume of fly life to support a resident stock of brown trout as well as the young of the migratory fish. What may happen, as the light begins to change in the late evening, is a large enough hatch of fly to tempt the sea trout to feed—especially the 'school' sea trout returning to the river for the first time. Although this is not true feeding in the accepted sense, nevertheless the sea trout will take these flies and so could fall a victim to a well presented artificial fly. Use the same tactics as you would for brown trout and fish either wet or dry with an imitative or general pattern, but keep well clear of the main pools so as not to disturb the 'serious' sport to be had later on. Chances of this type of fishing are infrequent, to be sure, but keep a lookout for them, as a powerful sea trout taken on a dry fly can cause many heart-thumping moments.

Most of the remaining sea trout fishing in rivers during the daytime takes place in flood conditions except, perhaps, in Scotland where the wider rivers and rougher currents can provide more camouflage from these shy fish. A coloured water brings out the worming enthusiast who uses two or three lobworms legered in a known resting lie, or, perhaps, keeps the worms on the move by allowing them to bump along the bottom in likely spots. Spinning, also, is quite effective and there is a wide choice of baits such as quill and devon minnows, and various wobbling spoons. I have found the last to be most effective, especially in a gold or silver colour, from 1in to 1½in long. Cast down and across the current and make the bait move faster than you would for the more ponderous salmon. Again,

try the high water resting lies, such as a shingle bank on the
inside of a bend, and try to tempt a running fish as it comes into
the tail of a pool from the narrow neck of the run below.

Once the colour has gone, I like to make the most of this
opportunity of extra water to fly-fish during the daytime,
preferring a team of three wet flies on a leader of 5lb breaking
strain. A sink-tip or slow sinking line allows these flies to travel
just beneath the surface, where they seem to be particularly
attractive to the sea trout if you do not make the mistake of
using too large a size. A no 8 will be about right at the height of
the flood, but you will need to be using a no 12 by the time the
water has fined off almost back to normal and you are seeking
the fish in the runs.

Unlike during the hours of darkness, colours can now be
easily seen by the fish and this becomes important when
deciding on the best pattern. I have not solved this particular
problem to either my own, or the sea trout's, entire satisfaction
and I fall back on a good working compromise, ie to have a gold
bodied fly (Dunkeld) or silver body (Butcher) on the point with a
Mallard and Claret and Golden Olive on the droppers. This
seems to suit most conditions and the sea trout can pick out
which colour they want.

Fishing in the sea for sea trout is rarely practised in the
British Isles except in the Voes (sea lochs) of the Shetlands and
the nearest most of us get to the sea will be the estuaries. This is
a rather specialised form of fishing with the advantage of
having fresh fish to try for, but a knowledge of the tides is all
important. Most success comes with fishing the tide as it ebbs

Wales: the River Towy

and a spinning rod may be required with a flashing bait to cover a wide river adequately. As the tide ebbs further, and the river falls within recognisable channels, a streamer type of fly proves attractive and will often do so until low-water itself. Things usually go dead then, so take a well-earned rest as you will need all your energies when the tide starts to flood again. An especially good time is just when it hits each pool, as the change from brackish to salt water wakes up the fish, but be prepared to move fast to keep pace with the tide as it surges up river.

Lake fishing for sea trout is more popular in Ireland and Scotland which have an abundance of suitable waters, the best of which are connected by a short river to the sea—so allowing the fish to arrive in a fresh condition and be willing takers. However as most of these waters suffer the disadvantage of their best lies being difficult to locate, fishing from a boat is more productive and you should, if possible, obtain the services of an experienced local ghillie. Failing that, try the area surrounding the outlet into the river or shelving banks around islands.

Ideal conditions are a constant, gentle breeze with bright periods of sunlight shining through the well-broken clouds—then fly-fishing works well. The traditional method varies little from that used for brown trout except that the flies are a little larger, ie size nos 6 to 10. Usually the boat's broadside drift is slowed by means of a sea anchor or drogue, and the fisherman casts a team of two or three wet flies on a short floating or sinking line, downwind in front of him. The flies are not allowed to linger there for long as the boat comes down on top of them and they are quickly worked back by pulling in line or by raising the rod top. There is little room for experiment except for slightly altering the direction of the cast but there is one trick which is worthwhile. As the flies are worked back towards you, change their direction by sweeping the raised rod tip sideways and across your front so that the top-dropper fly skates along the surface. This often seems to stimulate a take. Suitable bushy flies which you might care to try in this top-dropper position are the Zulu, Soldier Palmer, Red Palmer or Invicta. Other flies which I can recommend for the remaining positions are Teal Blue and Silver, Butchers (various), Black Pennell, Mallard and Claret, and the Alexandra.

Many of the tactics perfected for the trout in the new English reservoirs would pay handsome dividends if they were used more often; for example fixed rudders or lee boards—a plank temporarily fixed to the gunwale which acts as a keel. In this way the boat can be made to travel both down and across the wind, consequently increasing the options by way of various directions in casting, the depth at which the fly can be sunk, and allowing the fly to be brought across the front of the fish. Now the use of a streamer type of fly comes into being and is a worthwhile addition to the tricks up your sleeve if you can cast with a shooting head.

The tactics mentioned above of skating the top-dropper across

Wales: the River Dovey

the surface are made even more use of in 'dapping'—a method originally employed to present a natural or artificial Daddy Long Legs, May Fly or Grasshopper to the trout. Now a large, heavily palmered dry fly, sizes from 4 to 8, is allowed to skip about on the surface, first resting here and then skating along the top of the waves; this seems to have a strong attraction, especially to the larger sea trout. A long rod of 15ft or more is needed to hold the fly well away from the boat by means of a special blow line of floss silk which is carried out by the breeze. Only a short leader of 2½ft is used as the blow line must be kept dry and off the surface at all times; it goes without saying that the fly needs to be well greased too.

This is a particularly fascinating form of sea trout fishing: you see these mighty fish break the surface just in front of you and, in turning, take down the fly before your very eyes. At all costs you have to try and control your bubbling excitement and not tighten until the pull of the fish is felt, or the hook will not hold and the sea trout will be gone.

I have yet to find a more exhilarating way of taking any game fish and no gamer fish ever swam than the sea trout.

3 Chalkstream Trout

Gordon Mackie

Chalkstreams generally flow more smoothly than rain-fed rivers, over a relatively even bed. The water itself issues from springs in the river-bed. It has been thoroughly cleansed in its passage through the porous chalk, and is thus entirely free from impurities at source, and absolutely clear. The springs ensure that a fairly constant level of water is maintained throughout the season, and even very heavy rainfall is mostly absorbed into the hills, so that the stream is seldom likely to rise or become discoloured, and then only briefly. Rarely will you see a rock or even a stone of any great size. Any areas of broken water are most likely created by beds of water plants, such as ranunculus, starwort and water celery which are so abundant in many stretches.

Trout are less inclined to congregate in clearly defined areas, such as where the current sets against a bank or in the numerous backwaters found on streams with many stickles and pools, or in those which meander in different directions. Here they are more evenly distributed over the whole river, and each usually has a larger territory. The trout are able to feed in a more leisurely manner, seldom finding it necessary to compete savagely for food, save for the occasional 'seeing-off' of grayling where they are present in numbers.

Nor are chalkstream trout continually on the look-out for food. For much of the time they lie away from the main flow of the current in some quiet pocket, yet in a position to take advantage of any meal which may become available. Trout must conserve energy, always endeavouring to secure sufficient food for as little effort as possible, and the food availability on most chalkstreams is such that they can afford to remain inactive for long periods. A few shrimps, or a crayfish, represent a very hearty meal for a trout, and it is easy to see how fish reach ample proportions yet often appear to feed in a rather unconcerned manner.

Of course, food availability is what survival is largely about, and from the angler's point of view the ability to judge when and where the fish are likely to find it is most important in terms of results. Just as trout feed well at certain times and rest at others, so the fisherman will enjoy periods of activity and others when 'nothing is doing'. Some are content to wait until trout come on the feed, sometimes for hours, while their more active colleagues are either searching likely places or trying to induce

26

The author on the Kennet at Denford, near Hungerford

non-feeders to start feeding. It is often the case that the angler who waits, and watches for the rise or the sight of a fish hovering beneath the surface, is the one with the heaviest basket at the end of the day. But having said that, it is also true that on some days, especially during July and August, if the angler waits for a rise he may wait all day in vain.

In terms of fly life, there are highly productive waters and those which are less so. The best daytime hatches usually occur at the start of the season until mid-June, and again from about the third week in August until the season ends. At these times there is likely to be a period of considerable feeding activity on most days, and on such rivers as the Test, Itchen and Avon, and on many tributaries, this activity is often to be seen at surface level. You see the upwinged flies, known as duns, sailing down on the current, and trout in position taking them one by one. There is little question then as to which method is most likely to be successful. A reasonable imitation of a dun, cast to a rising fish so as to float over him on the surface as the natural insects do, will be accepted in many cases, provided that the angler has given the trout no cause for alarm. The period from mid-June to mid-August is seldom as productive for daytime fly hatches, but a good rise will often occur in the late evening, and sometimes for an hour or two before mid-morning.

At times, although no rise-forms are seen breaking the surface, there will be a lot of activity under water. A fly fished dry, on the surface, then ceases to be of value, and a nymph

27

Landing a two-pounder from the Kennet above Kintbury

Missed him! The author strikes too soon on the Itchen, near Winchester

imitation, which represents the sub-surface stage of the insect before hatching will prove more profitable. Nymphs are often 'weighted' by using lead or copper wire in the tying process in order that they sink to the required depth. When fish are 'nymphing' immediately beneath the surface, say at a depth of just a foot or less, it is clearly best to use a relatively lightweight nymph, for trout generally feed at or above their current level, seldom below. Again, if a fish is seen lying deep down near the river-bed, a heavier nymph will be required.

Chalkstream trout have a reputation for being most selective as to the pattern of fly they will accept, and many anglers new to these rivers find this whole subject of flies—which pattern to use and in what conditions, and which artificial represents what species—highly confusing. They can take heart, for most of us who have fished here for years find it confusing too! Personally I believe, and to my own satisfaction have proved, that fly pattern is seldom of great importance. It should be about the same size and outline as the natural insect, and roughly the same shade. The species of duns you will see are actually quite similar in appearance, and each varies to a degree in both size and shade, so that in truth only a small proportion of experienced fishermen can tell you the names of all the flies they see, and even then it may be necessary to study them closely in the hand.

I would advise looking at the natural flies from a good vantage point, such as a footbridge, and selecting the one from your stock which you think most nearly resembles them. A handful of weed from the river margin will usually give a clear idea of which nymphs and other animals are available under water. There is no need to be familiar with the individual names of these species, but many do find the subject a fascinating one. There are excellent books available for those wishing to learn

about their life cycles, hatching seasons and characteristics, and the one to which I mostly refer is *Trout Fly Recognition* by John Goddard (A. & C. Black 1966).

A good cast with a dry fly on Mrs Dean's rod-letting stretch on the Wiltshire Bourne at Gomeldon

Having found a fly which seems to suit the occasion, it is a mistake to assume, if it is not taken at once, that the fly is at fault. There are many other factors to consider—factors which to my mind are often of greater importance. Has the fish seen you, or has it been frightened by the fall of the line or the sight of your rod? If it continues to feed without a pause it is unlikely that this is the case. Is the fly drifting naturally with the current just as the newly hatched insects are? If the flow is causing the fly to drag across or against the current, even fractionally, this may be enough to make the trout refuse your offer. It pays to cast a slack line rather than a straight one to overcome this problem.

I learned from Oliver Kite to cast at an imaginary point well above the surface, perhaps from 4ft to 5ft above, over-pitching to some extent in order to get the correct distance, and then allowing the line to fall in loose coils on the water. With practice, this is not difficult, and it works. The longer the fly has to drift before reaching the trout's position, the more likely it is to drag, so the closer the fly falls to the fish the better, within reason. I normally try to place mine between 12in to 18in upstream of a trout, but it is surprising how often he will take it eagerly if you land it right on his nose. Fish are usually less wary of a dragging nymph than of a dry fly which moves unnaturally. Indeed, the intentional lifting of a nymph in the water, accomplished by a slight raising of the rod tip, is a very

29

useful ploy on occasion. This technique is called the 'induced take' and simulates the nymph rising towards the surface to hatch. An artificial nymph or shrimp, of course, should be pitched further upstream so that it may sink to the correct level. This distance may be anything from perhaps 1yd to 5yd depending upon the weight of the fly and the pace of the current.

If you seem to be doing everything right, but the trout still refuse to take, perhaps the leader point is too thick. I find trout are seldom put off by nylon of 3lb to 4lb breaking strain, but if you are using heavier nylon than this it may pay you to change down—or try fishing at a slightly different level. Sometimes trout which appear to be rising to duns, for example, are actually taking nymphs in the surface film immediately prior to hatching.

Again, the fish may be taking some other kind of insect which you have not seen, such as black gnats or ants or tiny midges. Have another look at the water. They may be taking spinners— which are the final stage, the egg-laying stage, of those duns mentioned earlier, and since they often lie flat on the surface they can be difficult to spot. The spinners will have changed colour to a red or ruddy brown hue, with shiny transparent wings, and their tails are somewhat longer. A standard Pheasant Tail pattern is the only one I use to represent all these spinners.

You will not need to carry a large number of different fly patterns. A selection to represent the great majority of natural insects to be found on chalkstreams might be: Gold Ribbed Hare's Ear, Greenwell's Glory, Tup's Indispensable, Iron Blue, Pheasant Tail, Black Gnat and Sedge. Dressed mostly on size 14 hooks (the Sedge on sizes 10 to 12) these dry flies would certainly see me through a chalkstream season, although Mayflies would be needed in late May or during June on those stretches where this fly appears. Nymphs such as the Pheasant Tail and Grey Goose would also be carried on sizes 12 to 14 in a variety of different weights, and you may wish to use a shrimp imitation such as Frank Sawyer's 'Killer Bug'.

If you start at the bottom of your stretch and work upstream, you will approach each fish from behind and are thus less likely to be seen. Normally I like to search for rising fish and cover each in turn, at the same time looking out for trout poised beneath the surface which may accept a nymph. Sometimes trout can be extremely difficult to locate, and polaroid glasses help in certain light conditions by reducing surface glare. For rise-spotting though, you may find you see better with the naked eye, and you are likely to see your fly on the surface better too.

You do not need expensive tackle to be a successful chalk-stream fisherman. If you are buying a new outfit, try it out on water or grass if you can before making your choice. The 'feel' of tackle is a matter of personal preference, but most use a middle to tip action rod of between 8ft to 9ft in length which carries a double-taper floating line of between sizes 5-7. Thigh waders are useful, if only to keep your legs dry in long grass or when

Fishing dry fly on the Test at Sheepbridge Shallows

30

Keeping well back. High summer on the River Wylye

kneeling. You need a fishing bag large enough to carry your gear, a plastic bag for your fish which does not leak, a couple of spare spools of nylon, some fly floatant such as 'Permafloat' or 'Gink', a landing net which opens easily if it is a folding one, your flies (comfortably housed in a fly box), and you are ready for action. Some now dispense with the fishing bag in favour of one of a number of excellent waistcoats which are available. Mine has nine pockets, including one large enough for my catch, and numerous other useful items, such as fly 'pads', scissors pocket and net ring.

Finally, I would beg those coming to the chalkstreams to treat them with respect. If we view them simply as places to kill fish we may miss much of the joy and beauty which they can offer. These rivers are the finest in the world, for those who like to hunt selectively, kill sparingly and handle trout humanely. In character they are unique, in tradition unsurpassed. In years to come, looking back on your chalkstream days, you may find as I do that it is those little incidents aside from actually landing trout which you remember with the greatest pleasure. Above all, we should resist most strongly those who threaten our chalkstreams, whether by development, pollution, land drainage or water abstraction, so that the next generation too may enjoy our glorious heritage.

4

Rain-Fed River Trout

Brian Morland

Four good trout each weighing over 1lb. They were taken within an hour from the shallow margins at the end of a hot summer day

Rain-fed rivers, or spate rivers as they are frequently called, can provide very interesting and exciting trout fishing. Although a few rainbow trout are introduced into spate rivers, it is the native brown trout which provide sport for the angler.

A spate is a sudden increase in the river level caused by heavy rain near the source of the river. To be successful at catching trout from a rain-fed river, it is important to have some understanding of the river itself. The level and colour of a rain-fed river can alter drastically overnight so it is essential to keep a check on the weather forecasts prior to any fishing trips. Most rain-fed rivers whether they are in Wales, Northern England or Scotland have their sources in the hills and mountains. These hills usually have a high average rainfall and it is this which feeds the rivers. The moors and high fells are littered with hundreds of tiny becks and drains which in dry weather have little or no water running down them. When it rains on the high ground all the rain-water cascades down the steeply sloping hillsides along these becks and into the main water course.

Modern farming practices of reclaiming heather-clad moors for sheep pasture have necessitated more efficient draining of the land. This means that even more rain-water runs straight into the river. The effect of a heavy downpour near the source of a spate river can be quite alarming. I have been at the side of a river which has changed from being low and clear to a raging brown torrent 7ft above normal level in less than an hour. These sudden changes in level not only affect your fishing but they can be very dangerous to the unwary angler. The initial surge of floodwater can occur very quickly indeed and I have timed a river which rose 3ft in five minutes. In the upper reaches, this floodwater is almost in the form of a bore which surges down the river. There are several instances of anglers being drowned and many very lucky escapes.

When fishing a spate river in times of heavy rain do not cross on to islands, and if you are wading make sure the banking behind you is accessible in case you have to get out in a hurry. Going to the other extreme, spate rivers in dry weather can shrink to such a low level that the river becomes just a trickle between the rocks and boulders. It is these extremes which make rain-fed rivers rather difficult to come to terms with. When you learn to take into account the weather and river conditions, trout fishing in a rain-fed river can be very rewarding.

Trout fishing in a spate river is usually confined to the middle and upper reaches where the flow is faster and the river-bed consists of gravel and rocks. The flow of the river can fluctuate a great deal along a short stretch of river; a series of cascading falls and rapids may have deeper willow-lined glides immediately downstream of them. These constantly changing features make most interesting fishing and it is possible to learn quickly which are the best trout holding areas. The scenery surrounding the upper reaches of a rain-fed river can sometimes be rugged and picturesque but it is seldom boring. Fishing pressure is such these days that most rivers rely on restocking with hatchery reared trout to provide a reasonable level of sport. Even so, trout in a rain-fed river soon settle down to a wild existence and those which have been in the river for any length of time are beautiful fish. The coloration of brown trout can vary a great deal, but many river trout become yellow bellied with vivid markings along their flanks.

A fine spate river trout weighing 1½lb, taken on leaded shrimp

The trout season begins in the last week of March or the first week of April, depending on the areas in which you fish. The weather at this time of year can be rather wintry, and it is usually well into April before the best trout fishing can be enjoyed. The rules on some stretches of river allow only fly-fishing, but many clubs and estates also allow worm fishing for trout on rain-fed rivers. This enables you to fish for trout when the river is above normal and coloured and fly-fishing would be utterly fruitless.

A fly-rod suitable for use in conjunction with an AFTM 5 or 6 fly-line is ideal for most conditions encountered on a rain-fed river. On most rivers, a floating fly-line can be used for both wet and dry fly-fishing. The most versatile fly-line to use is a double-taper floating line. Fly-lines can be very expensive and are easily damaged so it pays to take a little care over how you treat them and store them after fishing. It is very rare that you have more than half a fly-line off your reel at one time, so a money-saving idea is to cut a double-taper fly-line in half and you have two for the price of one.

During the early weeks of the trout season, wet fly-fishing is the most productive method for catching fish. When wet fly-fishing using a floating line, the nylon leader should be de-greased with fuller's earth, to enable you to present flies to trout lying in deeper pools. It is possible to present flies at various depths by simply de-greasing the appropriate amount of the nylon leader. Flies and nymphs can be made to sink more quickly by incorporating a little lead onto the shank of the hook when dressing the fly.

A traditional way of fishing spate rivers for trout is to use a team of three wet flies on a cast. The anglers who use this method successfully argue that they are able to present the fish with a choice of three different patterns, and also the flies fish at slightly different depths thereby covering more fish. Personally, I prefer to use the single fly, and having used both methods I

33

have not noticed any difference in the number of trout I have caught. Flies tied to droppers are always prone to tangles and by sticking to just the one fly this is avoided.

The leader used for wet fly-fishing should have a stronger breaking strain point than that used for dry fly-fishing. In fast broken water, the force with which a trout grabs the fly has to be experienced to be believed, and I advise a point breaking strain of at least 4lb; where the average size of the trout is high then this should be increased to 5lb or even 6lb. When fishing directly downstream in fast water, the trout usually manage to hook themselves with the ferocity of the take and there is no need to strike. The pattern of fly is not nearly so important as the presentation. Most anglers have their own favourite fly, and all of these seem to catch plenty of trout. It has to be said that trout are not the most difficult fish to deceive, and fish in a spate river seldom become preoccupied with single food items as do trout in a rich chalkstream. Most patterns of wet fly will catch trout, but some notable north-country patterns are Snipe and Purple, Waterhen Bloa, and Partridge and Orange. During the early weeks of the season I have more success using flies tied to slightly larger hooks.

A fly worth mentioning is the leaded shrimp tied to the pattern devised by Richard Walker. Being leaded, the shrimp quickly gets down to where the fish are lying and is an excellent early season imitation. The lead is built up on the back of the shrimp so that it fishes point upwards. This is how a shrimp naturally propels itself through the water, but just as importantly the artificial shrimp can be tweaked along near the river-bed without the hook point catching on stones or bits of weed.

Leaded shrimps will catch trout throughout the trout season, but they are especially useful during the opening few weeks when the water is still cold and the trout are lying deep. Another useful time for fishing leaded shrimps is when trout are taking advantage of coarse fish spawning. The upper reaches of a rain-fed river will hold very few if any coarse fish, but further downstream towards the middle reaches coarse fish will be more evident. In Scotland there are very few if any coarse fish in the spate rivers, but in England chub and dace will be frequently

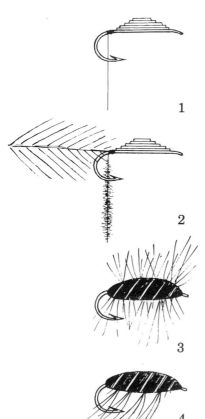

1

2

3

4

Leaded Shrimp *(Devised by Richard Walker)*
The hook is a size 10 or 12, the shank of which is covered with a binding of silk. A narrow strip of lead foil from a wine bottle top is bound on from just behind the eye to a little way round the bend above the shank. On top of that, another strip is bound which is a little shorter and a little wider.
This process is repeated with each strip progressively wider and shorter until five or six strips have been bound on. This gives the shrimp its weight and humped back appearance (see 1 in diagram).
The silk is then dubbed with some pale buff khaki or olive wool at the back end, and a big buff hackle is tied in by its point at the same place (see 2 in diagram).
The dubbed silk is then wound on to behind the eye giving a nice fat woolly body, then the hackle is wound over it like a palmer fly and secured behind the eye (see 3 in diagram).
All the hackle fibres are then clipped off on the back and sides, whilst those pointing downwards are cut so that what is left projects a little further than the hook point. The back is then given successive coats of clear varnish until it is smooth and shiny (see 4 in diagram).

Aysgarth Falls during a spate

encountered. Chub spawn in the fast gravelly shallows. When spawning, the chub will waft at the gravel with their tails sending clouds of disturbed silt downstream with the current. Trout will often gather in numbers immediately downstream of the chub to intercept the nymphs, snails, shrimps and even chub eggs which are dislodged by the frantic activity of the chub. I have taken some really good bags of trout by locating spawning chub and then fishing a leaded shrimp or nymph downstream of them.

The traditional method of fishing a wet fly for trout in a spate river is to wade to the edge of the river at the head of a pool, then cast across and let the current swing the fly downstream in an arc until it ends up directly downstream from your position. This works fairly well and in fast water the trout will give the forceful takes already described. It is surprising how many takes do not occur until the fly-line has tightened up immediately downstream of your position. I have watched many trout follow the fly across the river as the line swings round. As the line tightens in the current the fly will be drawn towards the surface, and it is then that the trout finally lunges in to grab it.

When using a wet fly on a greased line, so that the fly is fished just below the surface, I have watched trout chase the fly across the current and create a big bow wave. As soon as the line has tightened and the fly stops moving, the trout have grabbed hold and created a tremendous surge as they hooked themselves on the tight line. During the low water levels of summer and when fishing the slower glides, I prefer to fish a wet fly, casting upstream and across. The takes when they occur are signalled by the line suddenly stopping or the floating part of the leader slightly twitching forward.

The most difficult time of year for catching trout in a rain-fed river is during bright hot weather during the summer. Lack of rain soon has an effect on a spate river. The slower reaches will have hardly any flow and the rapids will shrink to a trickle of

35

A leaded shrimp

water over the rocks and between the boulders. To make things even more complicated, the water will be very clear making a careful approach extremely difficult. It is in these conditions that the clumsy angler, who does not consider himself to be fishing unless he is paddling up to his knees in water, will fail to catch many fish. Worse still is that one of these characters splashing from pool to pool will spoil the chances for anyone who has the ill luck to follow on after.

Surprisingly, trout will sometimes feed from the surface in the middle of a hot day with the sun beating down from a cloudless sky. I have watched trout cruising around in slack water picking off flies trapped in the surface film. A method which I have used with deadly effect in these conditions is to fish a Snipe and Purple on the surface. As most anglers will appreciate, the Snipe and Purple is a traditional wet fly, but fished in the manner I shall describe it is deadly especially in hot weather. I find the most effective hook size is a no 14. I tie the fly with slightly more hackle than is normal, and immediately behind the hackle tie in a few turns of peacock herl to give the fly a bit more bulk and better floating properties. The peacock herl makes the soft hackles stand out a little more which again helps the fly to float. I grease the leader all the way along, then fish the fly as if dry fly-fishing. The fly wants to either float or just settle in the surface film. If the fly sinks below the surface film it is nowhere near as effective. A Snipe and Purple fished this way will also catch trout under normal conditions, and to those who are interested it is also a deadly way of catching grayling during September and October.

During hot weather, there is little doubt that the best time to catch trout is in the evening. In a rain-fed river there is seldom what is traditionally called the evening rise, but the trout do become very active. From the middle of June onwards, the shallow margins will be full of minnows and coarse fish fry on which the trout feed. Trout will also fall back to feed at the tail-end of pools where the water begins to become shallow. In these conditions, trout will frequently chase anything that moves either on the surface or below it. A large sedge or bushy dry fly buzzed across the surface can provoke the most violent reaction from a feeding trout. I have caught a few larger than average trout by fishing a small reservoir lure, such as a muddler minnow, on a greased line and twitching it along just below the surface. I have often arrived at the river late on a hot summer's evening, when all the other anglers have retired to the pub or television set, and caught some fine trout as it was getting dark.

Dry fly-fishing is by far my favourite method of presenting a fly, but unfortunately it is not the best method for catching the larger trout in a spate river. Small trout will rise readily to a dry fly and occasionally some of the larger fish will be caught by this method. There can be few experiences in angling so rewarding as seeing a fat trout hanging in the current, casting a dry fly upstream of him, then watching as he moves up to intercept. Spate rivers lack the big hatches of fly which occur on

36

chalkstreams and there are seldom enough flies hatching together to induce trout larger than a pound to the surface. Once again I am confident that the pattern of fly is not as important as the way it is presented. Two dry flies which will nearly always catch trout in a spate river are Greenwell's Glory and Pheasant Tail.

Part of the skill in presenting a fly to a trout is in thoughtful wading. I have mentioned how an angler wading noisily from pool to pool will not catch many fish. On rain-fed rivers which are rocky and shallow, wading is sometimes necessary to reach a position from which to cast a fly to a rising trout. It is often possible, however, by carefully observing the actions of a rising fish, to find a position from which to cast a fly without having to wade into deeper water and risk scaring other fish. I was once able to watch the reactions of some feeding trout to the disturbance created by a wading angler. I had spotted some good trout lazily rising to intercept flies on a smooth glide about one foot deep, and I climbed a bankside tree so that I was looking directly down on these feeding trout. My companion then very gently stepped into the river some twenty yards downstream. Almost before any ripples had spread over the smooth surface, the trout became visibly agitated. The fish stopped feeding and began to slowly move round in circles. As my friend carefully took two steps forward the response from the fish was immediate. They milled about in utter confusion for a second or two before scattering at full speed in all directions across the river. Since that episode, I only wade when it is absolutely necessary and I am not likely to scare a lot of fish.

A rainbow trout caught on a leaded shrimp

Worm fishing for trout is allowed on many stretches of rain-fed rivers for the simple reason that the river is sometimes too high and coloured for fly-fishing to be practicable. I prefer fishing for trout with a fly, but I use worm tackle when conditions dictate it. Some anglers float fish with worms using converted fly tackle but this is not very delicate. I prefer a 12ft float-rod used in conjunction with a free-running, centre pin reel. Long-casting is seldom necessary, and often you can position yourself at the head of a pool, trotting a worm directly downstream on delicate float tackle. In recent years I have changed over completely to barbless hooks; for trout fishing especially they are superb. Fish can be returned easily with no damage whatsoever to their mouths. Small worms of any description will catch trout but the ones I prefer are gilt tails. These are the small stiffish worms which inhabit the fringes of a compost heap. The head end is a reddish colour and the tail is a light yellow. Another good trout worm is the small greenish worm which can be collected by turning over clay soil. When fishing, the worms can be conveniently kept in a cloth bag hung round your neck. Some excellent sport can be had from fishing small feeder streams when they are carrying extra water. These streams are often very rocky and during low water conditions the trout hide away under the boulders. When these streams are in spate, the trout will feed avidly and can often produce some surprising results. One small tributary I fished used to produce several trout over a pound with many smaller fish, but in low water conditions there was not a fish to be seen. This stream was so small that in some places I could stride across it.

The average size of trout in rain-fed rivers is not very big, but what they lack in size they more than make up for in appearance and fighting ability. A trout of one pound is a nice fish in most spate rivers, but there are enough two- and three-pounders to make the fishing interesting.

Spate river trout fishing does not have the attraction of limit bags and monster trout, but it does have a charm and fascination which is pleasing to many anglers.

How dry summer weather can reduce a spate river to a relative trickle between the boulders. Trout have then to be winkled out of the small pools

Reservoir Trout

Bob Church

Still water fly-fishing has enjoyed a growth explosion unparalleled in any other branch of the sport. So much has happened in the past decade that to describe it otherwise would be a gross underestimate. As more and more new trout fisheries open, the banks are as quickly filled with new anglers. Unlike the criminally meagre stocking policies of twenty years ago, today's fisheries, in the main, carry by comparison massive stocks of trout. Two hundred fish in an angler's second season is regarded as a reasonable target, an unthinkable figure for even the very best still water angler of not so long ago.

It is thanks to such fishermen as Dick Shrive, Tom Ivens, Cyril Inwood and their contemporaries that the catches are so big today. Such men devised or improved methods to catch the new breed of fast-growing trout which, unlike their upland cousins, are less eager to dash at anything slightly edible.

For the beginner, the new world of trout fishing must appear utterly confusing. He must quickly learn the difference between a wide variety of insect life, how it lives, when it is important and so on. Then he is faced with the mumbo-jumbo of tackle: sink tip, slow sink, fast sink, shooting heads, and the AFTM numbers must seem to be designed to but one purpose—to dissuade anyone from ever taking tackle seriously. In reality, a satisfying standard is not too difficult to achieve. The approach to the sport is probably more easily defined and understood if we go through a season period by period. Certain methods will

(left) *Bob Church and a fine limit catch (3−4¼ lb) from Blagdon near Bristol. It fell to a Black Chenille lure.* (right) *A superb 4¼ lb rainbow from Grafham at sedge time to a small Amber Nymph*

Tandem White Muddler

Appetizer lure

catch trout in, say, April and September, while others are more likely to succeed in June and August.

Much depends on the temperature of the water and a basic understanding of trout behaviour. In the cold months, the trout is disinclined to feed much as the low temperature has slowed down his movements to a crawl and he needs less food. As the water warms, his appetite returns and he begins to wander in search of food. In high summer, the rainbow in particular will chase his food freely on the surface or down in the deeps. The native brown trout is a territorial creature and does not have the wanderlust of his immigrant American rainbow cousin. By autumn, the cooling water warns of the onset of winter and the time for spawning. To cope with these rigours the trout, and the brownie in particular, homes in on the fry-filled shallows, losing to a marked degree the caution which has kept him alive through the season. Strangely enough the rainbow, normally a less cunning fish, does the reverse and is less easy to deceive than he was a month previously.

There are obviously overlaps in the feeding habits during the loose periods we have discussed so far, and therefore the angler must never be a slave to one style when a variation of an old method or an adaptation of a newer one makes more sense.

So first to the early spring. Unless March has been kind, fishing will be confined in the main to the bottom or close to it. Early-season fish have a very marked preference for a meaty black or a white-based lure. If one fails, so almost certainly will the other. Another factor to remember is that apart from the dark and unwanted rainbow cocks, who are now very aggressive and willing to snap at anything which enters their domain, the bulk of the trout will require a lure moving past them at eye level. Waters up to 20ft deep can be easily coped with from the bank or boat with a sink tip line. It has the distinct advantage of allowing you to fish slowly yet deeply without the fear of your lures being dragged into old rotting weed as they tend to when presented on a faster sinking line. Chief on my own lure list for April would be the Black Chenille lure, the Sweeney Todd, Missionary and the Baby Doll.

Black Chenille lure

You can often spot an experienced hand fishing the first days of the season with both coloured lures on the same leader and the trout will show which they prefer. The lure can be retrieved in the figure-of-eight style (more easily done than described) or with the more normal slow pulls with the left hand. The latter method is very often the better as the slightly longer and jerky action seems to give the lure more life.

The first take comes and is often missed by novice and expert alike, for the long lay-off in the winter months has allowed the quite natural instinct to strike strongly at a pull in the opposite direction to be less easily controlled—and controlled it must be. The next take comes, but the fish fails to stick. No strike is made and the lure is kept moving on the same path and at the same speed. The trout may snap at it three or four times before eventually making up its mind that the lure is worth the eating. The strike is made against the now solid pull and the fight is on. An hour later and no more pulls are forthcoming, so we have got to rethink our tactics. The natural thing to do is to move. This is often the best course of action but before doing so it will pay first to change the lure colour, the depth and speed of retrieve, as this may well bring a fish or two who by now are 'wised-up' to your initial offerings.

So much for early-season lure fishing. It has become very marked in recent seasons that nymph fishing is becoming very popular. The lure is replaced by a large and perhaps weighted nymph and crawled across the bottom. A nymph fisherman can often score heavily in April and early May when, with a bursting through of the watery sun, comes a sudden hatch of chironomids or 'buzzers' as they are now better known. It is almost certain that these will be the black variety.

What is equally certain is that the fish we see rising will be in better condition than those down in the deeps. The sight of a trout sliding porpoise-like through a nice gentle wave is a sure sign that the hatching black buzzer is on top of the menu for the day. High feeding trout can pose difficulties in that with their vision being concentrated to an inch or two of the surface, artificials must be fished so that they remain in that narrow zone for as long as is possible.

An effective method I often use is to put two black buzzers on 6in droppers, tying a small Black Muddler onto the point. All the grease is removed from the leader itself with mud or a mixture of fuller's earth and detergent, and then cast across the waves. No retrieve as such is made. Sometimes the inert Muddler is sucked under, but more often than not it will skid across the water just like a float as the trout makes off with one of the buzzers. This simple but effective style works the season through, not only with buzzers but with other nymphs, when to be accepted they have to be fished in or near the surface.

Although black is the predominant early colour it really does pay to make as sure as is possible to use the correct colour of artificial later on in the year. Very fussy at times about their buzzer colours are trout! Later on it will be pale green, claret, or even a striking silver and orange kind. A point also worth

Missionary as used by Dick Shrive as a fast retrieve lure

Whisky fly

(above) *Cinnamon Gold* (below) *Invicta*

41

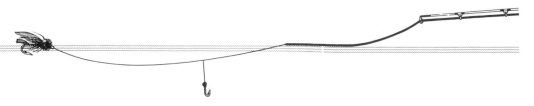

A method that works well throughout the season, provided fish are close to the surface. The muddler (centre) is acting as a controller, presenting the nymph quite perfectly

A 3lb Grafham Brownie caught on a lure and fast-sinking line. It came from deep water close to the dam

remembering is that it pays to work on the little boy and big red apple theory, and to give the trout a size larger artificial than the natural. The buzzer can also be fished on the same cast as a black or a white lure, as trout don't by any means confine their buzzer-chomping activities to the surface.

I have often stressed the importance of fishing into the wind during the early season. You may impress your companions by hurling your flies into the next parish when fishing off the easy bank, but what is the point when the fish are on the other side of the lake? It is the man brave enough to fish with the wind in his teeth who will take the early-season fish. A short line of perhaps only ten yards may be the most he can manage, but he will be the man who will go home smiling at the day's end.

Still water fishing is really a misnomer, for no sheet of water is ever really still. It has currents and drifts just like the sea or a river, although obviously to a much less marked degree. The

food is swept along in these currents and the trout with them. In big waters, it takes quite a long time for the currents to change direction after moving in one path for a day or two. This means that the bank bearing the full brunt of the wind on the fishing day may well, if there has been a rapid wind change in the night, have been the calm shore for a week or more. A chat with the bailiff will tell us all this and the choice of fishing spot will be that much easier.

By the middle of May and into June the water is being stirred into life, quickened by the strengthening sun. Trout are now very much more inclined to wander in search of their food, and we can begin to move our lures at a quicker pace, although by no means at the breakneck speeds often necessary in high summer.

June should provide the cream of our fishing. While buzzers are still accepted freely, the rainbows tend to concentrate on their favourite food which is a tiny water flea called daphnia. These tiny creatures congregate in reddy-green clouds and where conditions are good they will multiply at a phenomenal rate. Daphnia are the key to rapid rainbow growth. Too tiny to be intercepted singly, the rainbows merely charge through the jelly-like clouds swallowing daphnia, water and all. Oddly enough, the lure is the best means of attack. It must be that while scooping up the protein-rich daphnia the rainbows are susceptible to something far larger swimming through the daphnia masses.

Daphnia are highly sensitive to strong sunlight. On a bright day they sink down into the lower layers. Conversely on a dull warm day, they will be very close to the surface. This knowledge then helps us to determine the zone in which to concentrate our own attack. A white-based lure like the Missionary or Appetiser is always worth its first place on the starting-grid at daphnia time, and orange lures such as the Whisky Fly or even brilliant lime green lures should be kept firmly in mind as alternatives.

It was the rainbows' liking for daphnia and their fatal weakness for a lure moving across their path which led Dick Shrive to devise a style which has since been responsible for the downfall of many thousands of trout. This involved the use of a sink tip line and a rudder device to steer the boat across the wind, married with an adaptation of the traditional Missionary lure. Instead of the normal wing, Dick's had a pale grey mallard feather positioned like a flat roof so that it would hover and flutter down in the water.

The full importance of the thinking behind this intelligent approach should surely silence all those who claim that lure fishing entails nothing but hurling out a lure and stripping it back until a trout stops it. The boat is taken to the top of the wind, and positioned so that it will move down a bank, passing as many headlands as possible at about 70yd from the bank. Each angler then casts at right angles to the moving boat, allowing the lures to swing around in an arc.

The boat may well have drifted half-a-mile or even more before the first take comes. As with all methods, it is all a question of first finding your fish. If the takes arrive almost as

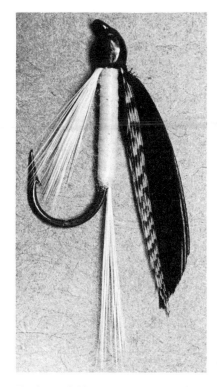

Traditional Missionary

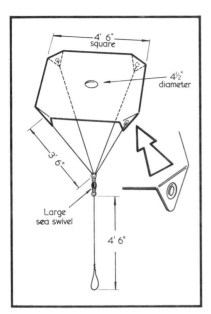

A drogue such as this is most important when you are going to drift. Trailed behind the boat, it acts as a brake when winds become unpleasantly strong

A drift control rudder helps you to control handling of the boat, enabling you to cover far more water and to steer in and out of bays. The numbers indicate the fittings and screws for adjustment

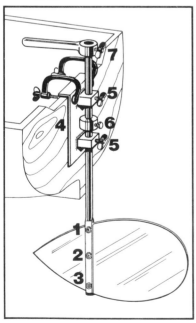

soon as the lure hits water, then the rainbows are feeding high in the water. The further the lure swings before it is taken tells us at what depth the fish are feeding. To save wasting fishing time—and we can only be actually fishing over a shoal for a short time—we can, by taking note of where the takes come, switch to a more or less dense line so that our lures are fishing in the correct layer for as long as is possible. The same technique can of course be achieved when fishing from the bank. If, when fishing the style from a boat, no takes are forthcoming, then the chances are that the fish are lying deeper than was at first thought. The boat should then be slowed down by attaching a drogue from the stern. This slowing down of the boat will allow the lines and lures to sink that much deeper before becoming affected by the forward movement of the boat.

Lines do not sink anywhere near as quickly as is often thought. Even a high-density line like the metal-cored Aquasink will only sink a few feet if the retrieve is begun fifteen seconds after the cast. Knowing this, the more dedicated boat anglers sometimes carry a stopwatch so that they can find out accurately how long the line must be allowed to sink before the retrieve is begun.

This swinging lure method is best achieved on most days when the boat is steered by a drift control rudder. The catching of a limit of rainbows using this style was usually a matter of course at Grafham until the rudder was banned there last season. Where rudders are allowed, I would urge all boat anglers who don't own one to get one made as soon as they can. The difference in results has to be seen to be believed.

Despite the undoubted effectiveness of this style there are times, towards the middle of July and for the next few weeks, when only the very short-sighted pass up the chance of taking fish feeding on the now freely hatching sedges. These large roof-winged insects beginning to crawl from their stick and stone tube homes, provide us with some of the most exciting and to be honest, the most frustrating fishing of the year. Like us, the sedges are creatures of comfort and prefer the more sheltered and sun-warmed shallow bays. Hobbling about the bottom, the sedge larvae are highly vulnerable, and the trout who eat the larvae know it, stone home and all.

A Stick Fly crept along the bottom in the daylight hours before the fish begin feeding on the ascending pupae has a very good chance of being picked up. The takes when fishing the Stick Fly are best described as being solid rather than savage. But it is during the late evening and into darkness that sedge fishing is at its very best. But be warned. Although the trout may seem to be feeding frantically on the newly hatched adult insects resting on the surface, I firmly believe that the trout's attention is fixed on the ascending pupae rather than on the more obvious adults. A dry sedge left in the area of the most activity is sometimes taken, but the use of pupae imitations is by far the most productive method.

The traditional Invicta takes some beating when put in the prime top dropper position. One of my favourite leaders at sedge time is the Invicta with a Brown-and-Yellow Nymph in the middle position with an Amber Nymph on the point. The Green-and-Brown Nymph is always held in readiness for when the trout are taking the greener sedges rather than the amber or brown sort.

The speed of retrieve is most important. I have found that a quick (but not too quick) speed with the flies travelling just under the surface is best, although as always it pays to experiment. Smash takes are the order of the day. This being so it pays not to fish too fine a leader. The rod should also be held at an angle to the line to provide us with a degree of elasticity which we would not have if the rod were pointed straight down the line.

During June and July, the majority of brown trout have sought the safety of the depths, but even these naturally cautious creatures will venture to the surface in the gloaming to feed on the easily available sedges. Rainbows are now suckers for a Muddler ripped back at breakneck speed through the waves. What they believe it is I do not know, but chase it they do! This is lure fishing at its very best. It involves casting a greased-up Muddler Minnow on a floating line downwind. It is allowed to settle for a moment, then is brought back to the boat or bank in long, fast pulls. First comes the V-shaped wake of the chasing rainbow; very often this undoubted interest will come to nothing, as the high-speed chaser veers away at the last moment. On some days the method brings follow after follow— although none or very few actually take hold of the Muddler. On other days, there will be few follows but every fish will be well hooked. A good rule of thumb to follow is the bigger the wave the bigger Muddler you can employ and the faster it can be pulled.

This exciting method can be used right through until September or even later, but we have now entered the last period of the season. Where they are available, the small coarse fish fry are on top of the menu for the day. But be warned—even though the brownies and rainbows are clearly seen harrying the shoals of terrified fry, they can be very fussy about accepting the

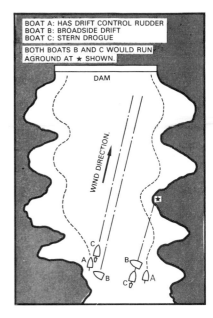

Note how boat A keeps you in the area of the reservoir shelf where the depth is 15–25ft. This is where the fish feed for much of the day

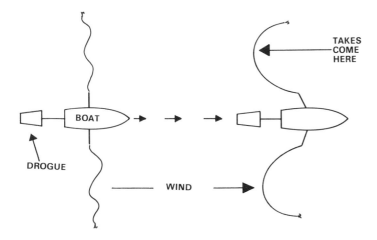

When we regulars swing a lure in this fashion, we call it 'round the bend'. It is the best way of using a lure from a drifting boat. In light winds the drogue is replaced with a drift control rudder

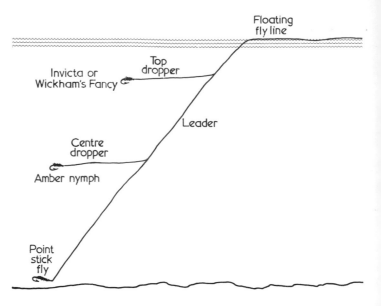

Floating
fly line

Top
dropper

Invicta or
Wickham's Fancy

Leader

Centre
dropper

Amber nymph

Point
stick
fly

*A deadly tackle when set in
June and July, especially when
sedges are hatching*

right lure size, just as they are when feeding on a certain size of insect.

After watching fry-feeding trout for some time, I have come to the conclusion that they have a definite plan and style of attack. The shoal of fry found, the fish crash into the small fry, lunging this way and that, crippling far more than they actually eat. Then, after making this ferocious attack, they return to mop up the floating dead and the cripples attempting to make for the weed-beds and safety. While the lures can be fished to imitate the fry fleeing from the marauding trout, it often pays to cash in on the habit described by laying down an ambush.

A lure designed to float, by building up the body with buoyant material in a Baby Doll shape, is cast into the area of intense activity and left lying still. Very often, the returning and now feeding trout can be seen picking up the maimed fry. The lure is then twitched to imitate the dying fry. The actual take can be deceptively gentle, the trout accepting your floating lure for the real thing. As the hook is driven home the trout, and remember that this may be the time for the very biggest fish we are likely to catch, realising his mistake hurtles for the horizon.

This has been a simplified breakdown of what the still-water trout fisherman may expect during the six-month-long season. Perhaps, you may realise now why it has proved to be such a booming sport.

Trout from Small Lakes

6

Alan Pearson

Let us consider basic principles one by one. The very best of the small lake fisheries have clear water and the angler who slowly walks the banks will be able to see many more trout cruising than if he remains in one place and waits for the fish to come to him. Fish-spotting is much easier if polaroids are worn, and it also helps if a fishing hat has a good wide brim that can be pulled down to protect the eyes from light coming in between eye and lens. Since the water is clear, the trout can see the angler too, and become alarmed by him. This risk is minimised if drab clothes are worn.

The man who moves too quickly will probably miss seeing more than half the trout that he passes, and this apart, sudden movements are more likely to be noticed by a fish. The slow mover will have plenty of time to spot his trout without being noticed, and he should not tread heavily for a trout can hear sounds such as low voices, and there is no doubt at all that the vibrations of stamping feet are very quickly picked up by fish, alarming them.

Once you have located a trout you wish to catch, it is wise to survey the water a little longer. Is the trout feeding? If so, what is it taking and have you a good imitation? Is there another trout in the vicinity that might be frightened by the casting of a fly and, if so, is it likely to scare the one that you wish to catch? Are there submerged or bankside obstructions that might interfere with the successful playing of the trout if you hook it, and is there any way to avoid these obstructions? Finally, it is always worthwhile taking a look over your shoulder before making that first cast for nine times out of ten there will be a tree, a bush, a fence, a clump of giant nettles, or a cow; and nine times out of ten you will hook that obstruction on your back cast. By the time you have freed your fly and re-checked your leader, you will almost certainly have scared the trout off.

Choosing suitable tackle for the particular fishery is not difficult, yet too many anglers use something hopelessly wrong, so wrong that they have no hope at all of landing a biggish trout unless they are extremely lucky, and successful trout fishing has little to do with luck! The reason probably is that many anglers have started trout fishing on reservoirs where long distance casting is all important, so they start off with a long rod which is usually quite stiff over most of its length, with all the action concentrated near the tip. Combined with a matching

Bob Church watches Alan Pearson netting a giant rainbow trout (Bill Goddard)

line or shooting head, a fairly heavy leader and a lure, they have tackle well-suited to reservoir fishing, but for small lake fishing you have to start working out your tackle from the other end. Remember that many of the small waters ban lures or large flies, so that you will normally be restricted to imitations of natural good items tied to hooks as small as no 18 and possibly no longer than no 10. In clear water conditions small dressings cannot be tied to powerful leaders—you might need to use one as light as 2lb breaking strain for a no 18 hook, and up to no more than 5lb to 6lb for a no 10 hook.

As you may well encounter plenty of trout around the 6lb mark and more, it is obvious that these light leaders will break unless they are cushioned against the worst effects of sudden jerks and pulls: the rod must bend nicely all the way down its length—not just at the tip. Such a rod is described as 'easy actioned', or having a 'soft action'. You can easily test it by setting it up with a leader of the required strength, tying on a fly and then sticking the fly firmly into a tree. Then, some ten or fifteen yards away and holding the rod well up, try to break the leader by pulling firmly. You will be amazed how much force you can apply without breakage, and that is the balance you are

48

aiming for—a soft-actioned rod that does not transfer too much pressure to the leader and does not break under the strain.

Next, the line. This is not so important as the rod, so you merely purchase a line of the correct rating. The best profile for short, accurate casting is the double-taper and, as you need only half of it, try to find a friendly tackle dealer. Colour does not matter much because, even if you have bought a white, or brightly coloured line, it can always be dyed brown or green—any dark colour—with Dylon dye. White or brightly-coloured lines reflect light which scares fish. Dye them dark colours so that they no longer flash, and you will catch many more trout.

You need backing line too, and this is another argument for using just half a fly-line, because it takes a good many yards of nylon monofil backing to equal the volume of half a fly-line and quite a small reel will take, say, 80yd of backing plus the half-line. Small means light and that is better.

A fly-reel should be as small and light as possible, commensurate with holding the desired amount of line, for it is only a line *holder*! I never use the reel when playing a trout, for to do so when fighting a really big specimen will soon lose it.

Now let us return to the subject of leaders. To start with, I always needle-knot a 2ft length of 18lb nylon monofil to the end of the fly-line, and attach my leader to this. I do not use leaders made from short lengths of monofil knotted together—only rarely a single, level strand of monofil. I much prefer one-piece tapered leaders, without droppers, made in a variety of tip strengths. To attach them to the extension to the fly-line, I take the loop which the manufacturers kindly provide at the heavy end and cut this off! Then I use a bloodknot to fasten the two lengths of nylon together. This makes a far neater junction than a loop. Generally, these tapered leaders are 3½yd long, and with the extension piece, a pretty good leader-length is created. If, however, a longer leader is needed, I add an extra length of heavy nylon between the tapered leader and the extension piece. In this way, all knots (a potential breakage risk) are restricted to the heavier gauge nylon, where knot strength will be greater than tip breaking strain which can make the difference between success and failure. Most nylon monofil, being bright and flashy, can scare trout, so I either dye it or immerse it in a solution of silver nitrate.

I am not sure whether the rod should be built-cane, hollow glass-fibre or carbon-fibre. Good built-cane is hard to find, expensive and rather heavy. This narrows the field to glass-fibre or carbon-fibre. I have caught a great many big trout on glass-fibre rods, and the sort of action that I described as 'easy' can be found readily enough, particularly within the ABU range which, to my mind, is ideally suited to small lake fishing. Carbon-fibre is a little different in that many of the earlier rods were rather too stiff and needed heavier leaders than I like to use. Although later models have the required easy action, they are expensive. However, if money is no object, select a carbon-fibre rod.

Small still water trout fisheries are becoming popular with the women as well as the men—a welcome innovation

The 'best' length of rod depends upon the fishery. I use rods varying from 8ft to 10ft to suit my convenience. The shorter rods are ideal for close-quarters casting, the longer ones for roll casting where the back cast is obstructed, but if I had to pick just one standard-length rod for all use, I would settle for something around 9ft, while another angler might select a rod 6in longer or shorter. Whatever length is comfortable to use is the right choice.

I do not believe that one needs an enormous selection of flies to fish small lakes, for presentation is more important than pattern. The only exception is when a trout is seen to be feeding exclusively on a specific natural bait and will look at nothing else (usually when it is profusely available), and the probability is that it will be a chironomid pupa that is being taken, just sub-surface. So I always carry a good selection of these so-called 'buzzer' pupae. Black is the most common colour, but there are common varieties which may have claret, crimson, green, brown, grey, yellow or orange bodies. Sometimes when the trout is taking the black variety, it will refuse all black imitations but may be induced to accept a hot orange pattern tied as small as no 16 or even no 18. Whatever the colour or size of buzzer pupa offered it must be fished at the depth where the trout is feeding, and this is achieved by greasing the leader for part of its length, leaving the rest ungreased so that it will sink to the designated depth. Normal retrieve technique is to wait until the required depth has been reached, and then tweak the pupa back very slowly, allowing a considerable pause between tweaks. Remember that since the water is clear, you can keep both the fly and the trout under observation and actually watch the take.

Some fisheries are blessed with an abundance of sedges, and trout can become preoccupied with sedge pupae at times. The actual pattern may vary from water to water and according to the time of year, so again it is advisable to carry a fair selection. Just as in the case of buzzer pupae, one is casting to an observed trout, and the actual method of retrieve is subordinate to getting it into a position where it can be seen by that trout, and then giving it only enough movement to impart the impression that it is alive.

Excellent leash of rainbows from Damersham

Other useful patterns are Shrimp Fly, Corixa, Damselfly Nymph, Pond Olive Nymph—all imitative patterns. However, every fishery varies in the life forms that it contains, so apart from these few basic patterns, you will eventually collect more based upon your personal experience and observation.

Generally speaking, the larger trout seem to concentrate on submerged life forms and it is usually a waste of time fishing the dry fly. Nevertheless, for the rare occasions when they are on the move taking dry fly, it is worth having two or three patterns available. The Red Sedge is the most important dressing, and the White Ghost Moth can occasionally be a killer at dusk. During late summer and autumn, the Crane Fly (or Daddy Long Legs) may help you complete your limit, and in high summer, that Drone Fly can prove invaluable. It never does any harm to carry some alternative sedge patterns, and I suppose the Cinnamon Sedge is the best of these but as always knowledge might indicate another.

There are a few specialist nymph patterns which should be carried for really big rainbow trout: the first is the Richard Walker Mayfly Nymph which has killed more trout over 10lb than any other. Then there are my own Green Beast, a good killer on its day, and a large version of the Damselfly Nymph. There is also Bob Church's Westward Bug with which he caught his 16½lb specimen; and there are other, less important

The catch of a lifetime from Avington, Hampshire, a UK record at the time: (from left to right, weights refer to the fish) *Alan Pearson (18lb 7oz), Bob Church (15lb 8oz), Peter Dobbs (11lb 12oz), Dick Shrive (13lb 8oz)* (Bill Goddard)

51

patterns too. All these have points in common: they are correctly tied to a no 8 long shank hook, have a number of strips of lead tied on the back of the hook shank before the body is applied, and none of them is other than sparsely hackled.

Because these patterns are large and heavy, the angler unused to their weight will find them coming through very low from the back cast, hitting his rod, or even hitting the back of his neck! Nevertheless, with practice they can be cast with great accuracy at short range, and their weight enables them to sink quickly to a chosen depth. Most rainbows over 10lb in weight have been caught on these big, leaded nymphs, and this leads us on to the best ways of catching such whoppers.

If you visit a small lake fishery which is stocked with very big trout, it is worthwhile to try to locate one of them. Remember to keep quiet, and be persistent. In many cases, the trout will be moving slowly at 6ft or more. If it is swimming fast, it will not be feeding and uninterested in a fly, but as long as it is not hurrying around, you have a chance. Now, a big trout will rarely chase after food, so somehow, you have to put your fly right in front of it and this is where the leaded nymphs come into their own. With experience you will be able to drop one right on the trout's nose, but if such accuracy is beyond you, the best thing to do is cast beyond the fish, and then work the nymph back until it is within a few inches of the trout, at exactly the same depth.

What happens next is unpredictable. Sometimes the trout will take the nymph as it drifts down past it, sometimes it will ignore it unless you give a twitch or two to the line to make it jiggle about; or you will not get a take unless you let the nymph sink to the bottom, and then lift off sharply so that it zooms up past the trout. It may even not be taken whatever you do! But persevere for I have sometimes offered a nymph a dozen times or more before it has been taken. When you see those thick white lips open, then close and your nymph has vanished inside, pull the line tight with the left hand and lift the rod smartly with the right (or vice versa if you are left handed). What you are aiming to do is pull that nymph firmly home without jerking it, because that could result in a broken leader. Once the hook is set, the battle begins.

Although every trout fights a different fight, broadly speaking big trout fall into two categories: some will speed off at a great rate when they feel the hook, and may strip up to 100yd of line on their first rush, while others will behave like a giant tench, staying deep and boring away with immense power but rarely moving far in any one direction. In either case, you must fight back hard, keeping the rod well bent, not giving line unless you are forced to do so and try to overpower the trout as fast as possible. This is why your tackle must be correctly balanced, and why you have tested your tackle by sticking the hook into a tree and pulling like mad for a break. You now know just how much it will stand up to, and can exert maximum strain on your big trout.

In my early days I used to conduct the battle with much more delicacy, taking anything up to fifty-five minutes (timed, not guessed) to land each fish. This was wrong because I was risking the leader wearing out or the hook-hold giving. I have now learned just how much pressure my tackle will stand and I keep it up all the time, never giving line unless I am forced to and retrieving it at the slightest opportunity. The result is that my 19½lb rainbow, which took the UK and World Records in 1977, was in superb condition, and yet it took me just eleven minutes to kill on a 5lb leader. My boast is that few anglers I know could have landed it on a 10lb leader! So, after you have hooked into that big one, keep the pressure on. Your back will ache, your arm will ache, you will get spots before the eyes and you will suspect you will die before you land that fish, but, I assure you, you will survive!

Finally there is netting your big trout. If you have played it correctly, it will be very tired when you lead it towards your landing net. Just be sure that the net is big enough, for too many trout nets are only suitable for straining tea! You cannot fold big trout up and I do not recommend trying to beach a whopper, even if the margins are suitable. Remember that you are using a fine leader and the direct weight of the trout on that leader is certain to break it. Use a 'specimen hunter's' net because, if it is large and deep enough to take a giant carp, it will do very nicely for big trout.

I think the prospect is good for the small trout lake angler. Rainbows will get bigger—there already are a few around over 30lb—and we are rapidly approaching the time when there will be American Brook Trout at weights over 10lb—maybe over 20lb. During the early 1980s two hybrids of the Brook Trout, which are capable of exceptional growth, should be freely available. And for those with more modest tastes, many small lake fisheries will continue to offer superlative brown and rainbow trout fishing with stock varying between 2lb and 5lb.

Fishing from the rocks at a trout fishery

7 Scottish Loch Trout

William B. Currie

It would be a mistake to think that Scottish loch trout are unique; they are the same fish as we catch in rivers and still waters in many parts of the world. They are the same as the brown trout of England. Yet the feeling one often gets is that Scottish loch trout are different. They behave in distinct ways; they have a character and an appeal of their own. I have often fished for fatter trout elsewhere and longed for Scottish lochs. There is no doubt an element of homesickness in some of that longing, but there is also a good angling case for upholding Scottish loch trout as among the most rewarding and enjoyable fish to catch on the fly.

The key to understanding loch trout, and that means to fishing well for them, is undoubtedly the environment, and it is because the Scottish environment is different—better and worse—than other trout environments that Scottish loch trout seem Scottish and tactics for fishing them seem national. Having said that, it should be stated that those who think least clearly about Scottish loch trout fish for them in a rather

Setting up tackle for a day on Loch Vaa, near Grantown-on-Spey. Rainbows have been introduced into this Highland loch

inflexible, mindless way, claiming that it is traditional, that wet fly-fishing in a wind before a drifting boat has centuries of authority behind it and is virtually a fixed art. I find it impossible to hold this view. Good Scottish loch fishing is the result of thinking about the fish, its environment and its characteristics; it is also the product of thinking about ourselves as intruders on the natural scene, launching our boats and waving our rods in the air.

Scotland has Highland and Lowland waters, but that classi-fication, based on a generalisation about terrain, can be misleading. In terms of colour coding, there are brown lochs and green (or clear) ones. The brown ones are those which are peaty and the green ones are not. Brown lochs have a chemistry related to decaying vegetation and, thus, are usually mildly acid waters. Green lochs are often neutral, or with luck, are slightly alkaline, though there are precious few of these in Scotland. For example, Loch Leven is a green loch on fertile Lowland territory, over glacial silt with traces of ancient sea shells in it. Loch Leven will produce fish or two, three or four pounds. I fished it one evening a couple of seasons ago and took three trout, the smallest was just under 2lb and the largest was 3lb 2oz. This illustrates what I may call the English type of loch in Scotland—green or clear water which can grow good fish rapidly.

Some Caithness lochs show green characteristics too, and again it is a matter of the chemistry of the loch-bed. Lochs in the Hebrides and on the West Coast, lying over shell sand on the grassy raised beaches (the machairs) are often alkaline waters with tremendous trout in them. They are excellent anglers' fish. Here and there throughout the country, lochs may lie over bands of limestone and produce green (or clear) waters of the highest quality.

Now I cannot, obviously, go on to give you a detailed list of all the green lochs of Scotland, implying that limestone is all, and that waters lying over it are the cream of our fishing. This would be misleading. Green waters are often the home of coarse fish, or of small numbers of large trout, because they are often, ironically, waters with poor trout spawning resources. They may make good put-and-take fisheries, because they give good growth rates, and can yield good rod fishing in reasonable quantities. Interestingly, not every angler in Scotland wants fat, well-stocked fisheries. There is a great value placed on wildness in loch trouting. Wildness, of course, is something which human beings perceive; it is part of an attitude to landscape and its enjoyment. This brings us nearer to the truth about Scottish loch fishing. People want to fish the romantic, peaty lochs of the Highlands and Islands; they want to feel that the heather nearby is full of grouse and stags and above all, they want to feel that the trout they are catching are wild fish, hunted and caught in an unspoiled place.

The brown lochs of the Highlands exist in abundance, and they provide trout fishing which is wild, often lonely, magni-ficent in setting, spiritually uplifting—and often quite poor. I

A 2½lb trout from Loch Glutt, Caithness

say 'poor' because I am thinking of size of fish. In many unmanaged Highland waters a half-pounder is not a bad fish at all. I can think of lots of smallish lochs in the Hebrides, in the western Highlands and elsewhere, where you have multitudes of quarter-pounders. Press me, and I will remember some which have yet more fish of still smaller size. Often these waters respond well to the local hotel putting a couple of boats on and increasing the rod pressure. Many Highland lochs need to be fished hard, if they are going to produce worthwhile growth at all. It is really impossible to control spawning in areas rich in shingly hill streams. Thus, the indigenous stock competes for the food available and you will have old fish of quarter-of-a-pound in weight.

A Scottish loch is likely to be windswept, since many of the hill waters are in treeless country. Wind and wave are critical to the fishing. This is one thing I noted with interest when I was almost two years in Suffolk, fishing trout in still waters there: wind did not matter so much. On flat English still waters one could catch trout on nymph, or on well sunk flies and lures in calm conditions. On Scotttish lochs it may happen occasionally, but for a reasonable chance of sport you need ripple, or wave. How much wind do we want on a loch? Lochs fish from the slightest ripple, which merely corrugates the surface, to high waves with ripples running too. What will ruin your chances of sport is that unwelcome kind of ripple which we call 'scud'—a blackening of the surface by cold gusts of wind, often cutting across steady wave. My ideal day is one of high even cloud, mild atmosphere (that is, you can fish in the boat without a waterproof on and a steady gentle breeze making an even, low wave, often with flecks of bubbles patching the ripple as it moves. Trout will rise into such a wind, feeding, for the most part, on the nymphs of flies as they gather at the surface film and go through the final stages of hatching. Where there is ripple, flies can puncture the film and hatch successfully; where there are calm patches, flies will hatch less successfully because

56

the surface film there is too strong for the nymphs to penetrate.

There is a splendid phenomenon called *slicks* on windy lochs, which I have known and exploited all my fishing life, but I still do not really understand them. Slicks are those avenues of comparatively glassy water making something like roads over the windswept surface of the water. These calm strips, which may run for hundreds of yards, trap hatching nymphs and trout cruise up and down them, usually concentrating on the sides where the calm and the ripple meet. These are superb places for trout. They are particularly good in the evening when a general hatch is on. Slicks give trout feeding lines full of trapped nymphs.

What we try to do on a loch is present the trout with a reasonable imitation of hatching flies. The particular stage of hatching which loch fishers are most interested is is the nymph—the fly in the last of its underwater stages before it breaks through the surface film, and sheds its final nymphal skin emerging as a winged insect. If you look carefully at the surface of a loch, you should be able to see the empty shucks, or skins, of flies which have hatched. Wet fly, that is sunk fly, fishes better on most Scottish lochs for most of the time than dry fly—floating fly. You do see lots of trout taking insects from the surface of Scottish lochs, and from time to time I have found a floating fly does well; but even when the trout do rise to the surface fly, they will also rise to the wet fly fished in the top 6in or so of the loch.

There is a far more important distinction in loch fishing between flies fished near the surface, say in the top 6in or so, and flies fished deeper. In recent years, influenced partly by the rapid development of sunk fly-fishing which has overtaken the

Coire Na Mang, a Sutherland hill loch, is one of the excellent waters on the Badanloch Estate, Forsinard

English reservoirs, and undoubtedly influenced by the availability of fly-lines which sink in a controlled way, Scottish anglers have experimented with flies at different depths. My own experience of this field has brought me some fascinating results.

Fly-fishing on a Scottish loch does largely represent hatching flies when they are fished on a floating line, or a line fished just below the surface. But even there, who is to say what a trout sees in a fancy fly such as a Hardy's Gold Butcher, or my favourite, a Dunkeld? It is not very profitable to draw rigid lines and say this is fly-and that is lure-fishing. I have, for example, fished ordinary wet flies on a deeply sunk line and have taken trout on them. Indeed, in an even more extreme set of experiments, I have taken trout on flies which appeared to be lying inert on the bottom at the time of the take. Why not leger flies, in the right conditions? I've done it, and it works. Further, it takes sea trout well in slack deep pools on rivers. Do the fish stir up the flies with their tails as they forage for food deep down, and thus take a fly put into motion by their own efforts? I don't know, but that would be just as wise a piece of fly-fishing as surface (or just sub-surface) presentation.

I remember a day on a Lowland loch when I was faced with one of those bright, high-pressure skies in May—I was fishing under a hard blue heaven with the odd puffy white cloud in it. Trout would not rise to my surface flies so I changed to a sinking line—a nice slow sinker—and fished two no 8 nymphs—old sea trout flies pruned down to nymphal shape. I had a splendid day with fish up to 1½lb, well above the class of trout I would have expected to rise to my ordinary wet flies there. The deep nymph may work well. In these circumstances deep lure fishing might also work well. Fly-fishing embraces both surface and deep extremes on a Scottish loch, but having said that, by far the most productive way to fish a loch, and, for me, by far the most

Loch Ard, near Kinlochard: a shallow bay at the mouth of a small burn

entertaining way to take trout is with wet flies worked just under the surface.

I do not fish three flies: I fish two. The tail fly is often specifically chosen as a nymph seen hatching, or likely to be hatching. The bob fly is usually a spider pattern—that is a fly dressed without wings. Palmer-style dressings are also excellent for bob flies—that is, flies dressed with hackles wound up the body in a spiral. Let me give you some of my favourite combinations for different times of the year and for different types of loch. I fish Gladhouse (a Lowland reservoir near Edinburgh) one day a week through the season and one of my favourite tail flies there is a Greenwell. The Greenwell's Glory is a remarkable fly. It is quite like an Olive, but just misses it; it is quite like a whole range of ephemerids and it even looks reasonably like some of the larger chironomids. What a fly! it comes in light and dark dressings; some local variants give it a yellow tail, a split-wing dressing or a wingless (spider) dressing. I greatly favour it dressed as a nymph, with a wingless body, a fat thorax and no hackle to speak of, but with the body teased out a bit to give the impression of legs. The Greenwell is not a fly: it is an experience. I hardly ever have a cast on without one on the tail.

An excellent tail fly in the earlier months of the season—say April to June, is the Blae and Black. This fly fishes well in Lowland and Highland waters. You probably know it well with its blae (greyish) wing, its black body ribbed with silver and its red tail. Now this fly looks like a fancy fly, tricked out with red tails and silver ribs, but it is in fact an imitation of the dark midge (chironomid) which hatches in great numbers in the earlier season on Scottish lochs. That fly has a reddish nymphal shuck which it struggles out of as it nears the surface. Thus the trout's eye-view of the fly is of a black fly with wings trailing a reddish shuck at its tail. Try it.

In the Highlands, in the brown lochs of the moors, I find bright flies a boon. Gold bodies seem to work well in brown water. Thus the Dunkeld or the Hardy's Gold Butcher or a similar bright-bodied fly is taken well by trout. In these waters trout seem to like flies worked fairly quickly through the water, and I am under no illusions that we are appealing to the pursuit principle in trout with our technique. I like searching the water with a longish line out, say 15yd or more, running the line over the index finger of my rod hand, hand-lining in yard by yard, and using the rod angle to make the bob fly surface and play attractively in and out of the surface film. It is important to get the right speed of retrieve .

The bob fly plays a very important part in loch fishing. It fishes quite differently from the tail fly. To begin with, it is higher in the water than the tail. It comes to the surface first and can be made to break through the surface film, scuttering around the surface in a way which has earned it its name 'bob'. It is, in my experience, responsible for something like two-thirds of all offers during loch fishing, and in certain conditions it seems that the bob fly is all the trout want. Now, there is a touch of illusion

Dunkeld

Greenwell's Glory (dry)

Black Pennell

Pennell's Claret

Loch Mackaterick, a hill loch in Ayrshire: the ripple has died away and trout are proving hard to find

about this. You can see the fish which move to the bob fly far more readily than you can see those following or moving to the tail fly. Again, the action of the bob makes the fish take one or two wild splashes at the fly and in the process, often miss the fly completely. But, spectacle aside I have no hesitation in asserting that the bob fly, properly chosen and properly fished is the best fly on the cast.

What do you choose for such an important position? My list is short, because they work so well I don't need to ring the changes on the bob very much to get the results I want. Broadly, the bob flies I use on the brown lochs—the Highland lochs with some peat in them—divide into the reddish spiders and the blackish spiders. Typical of black bob fly would be that great favourite the Black Pennell. That fly, with or without its yellow tail, is a splendid example of a palmer-style spider which works excellently on the bob and is wasted on the tail. Usually Scottish loch flies are tied in rather bulky dressings, and some of the Pennells I have used have looked like chimney sweeps' brushes. On working the fly properly, you should see this action of popping in and out of the surface film. Sometimes the fly drags, making a tiny wake on the surface; sometimes the fly daps on the surface, opening out like a little parachute as it enters the water. The bob fly gets that 'wet look', as one of my Sutherland friends describes it. It is not a dry dancer, but a very bedraggled one, given bulk by the water and not by the air.

On the honours list for best bob fly in the conditions I describe we must also include the ginger-red equivalent of the Black Pennell—the Soldier Palmer. What a fly that is above Inverness! I recommend it in a size larger than your Lowland sense would choose it. Windswept lochs and big flies go well together. My other great favourite for this position is a Dark Mackerel. This fly is in the Claret range, reddish, but dark. It looks rather like a Mallard and Claret, with two important modifications; it has a palmer-style hackle wound up the body and in the version I like best, the body is of red lurex—that special tinsel which, in small quantities, works so well for trout and migratory fish in Highland waters. I have turned to the Dark Mackerel after years of using it as a sea trout fly, and in its smaller sizes, say no 12 and no 14, it kills well throughout the Highlands and in several Lowland reservoirs. The lurex gives it some of the appeal of a silver or gold-bodied fly, which can be tremendously important in some brown waters.

One could go through a gallery of flies, but in fact a Scottish loch fisher is well equipped with a small range of natural looking flies such as Blae-and-Black and Greenwell's Glory, together with a few well-tied spider or palmer dressings, like the Pennell style, and two or three gold- or silver-bodied patterns. The nymphs are exotics, but are well worth trying when the wind drops.

One of the great arts in loch fishing is knowing where to find trout. It is very difficult for a newcomer to a water, even quite an experienced fisherman, to know where to try initially; the loch looks inscrutable, slightly mysterious. This feeling of dealing with a mystery is somewhat alleviated when you consider that the key to good loch fishing—apart from your own skill—lies in the bed of the loch and the way the wind affects the water over that bed. Let's hold the wind element constant for argument. You have a gentle, southerly, steady breeze over the new water. What you look for first is how the bank is shaped. That may sound Irish—judging the water by the dry land, but it is eminently logical. The contours of the bank are directly related to the underwater contours of the loch. Thus a gentle, natural bay with a semi-circular margin and easy slopes behind is almost certainly a reach of water with a shallow, and normally earthy bed. Crags beside a loch are usually matched by rocks and crags below water. Those spectacular lochside cliffs are always associated with sudden deeps. Islands should be seen as the bottom breaching the surface, not as land somehow dumped in the loch. From bankside features like that, one can build up the more important map of how the depths run and where you will find shallow water. Water under 10ft deep, particularly over shingly or silty beds, is where fly life thrives best and, thus, where trout find their best feeding and congregate. You will find that trout rise well on some occasions over deep water, but then the food which is attracting them is airborne, and that is a special case.

It can happen on any Scottish loch! This trout of over 2lb came from a peaty hill loch in the West Highlands

I have written so far largely about the natural environment, of depths and types of water and peat, and of the trout itself. But the other end of the formula is the angler and his tackle. Let me give, in manifesto form, what I would require as sound, basic equipment for loch trouting.

Rod: Not too short. 9ft to 9ft 6in good glass, or carbon-fibre (if you can afford it) or cane. I still fish cane for much of my trouting, but that is obviously a carry-over from the days when cane was the standard material for rods and glass was the newcomer. Cane is heavier, slower and somewhat more forgiving than glass. I find that it rolls lines nicely and when I do hook a big sea trout or a salmon on my loch rod (it happens not infrequently) my cane rod seems to take the challenge without too much difficulty. Some of my glass rods would bend forever and hardly cope. I have not had the chance of trying a carbon-fibre rod on a salmon hooked in this way, but I believe it would bend excessively and have little control. My advice is thus not to fish a tooth pick rod, fish a competent glass reservoir or loch rod (every catalogue lists several) and leave cane to me. My Sawyer Still-water rod (9ft 6in) and I are probably inseparable anyway.

Reel and Line: Get a reel with enough capacity to take an AFTM 6F line and 50yd of braided terylene backing of 20lb breaking strain. In practice, a 3½in reel of modern design will be right. A perforated drum helps to keep line and backing from becoming mouldy—although modern materials have a tremendous resistance to rot. The best all-round loch trout line is a double-taper design—that is the line has a tapered end and a level middle. The double-taper allows you to reverse the line when one taper shortens or cracks. Modern floating lines are plastic covered, shoot well, roll nicely when you want to use this form of cast and are versatile—they float in and not on the surface and fish flies nicely just under the surface film. Forward-taper lines, listed as wf on the code on the box (as opposed to DT) have their heaviest section forward, and this is backed by a thin shooting line which allows you to cast in an overhead style and achieve greater distances than would be normal with a double-taper line. This has its advantages in certain types of bank fishing, but this line design is less versatile than the double-taper for rolling and mending (altering the lie of the belly). Why not have a reel with each, or a spare drum with WF and DT? Take it further; why not have a reel with a slow sink line on it and one with a fast sink line too? It begins to multiply doesn't it? Yet I find myself with just that array of reels and rods to match them in the car when I go out for serious loch fishing. In fact I have yet another line assembly—a shooting head tied to nylon monofilament running line for really long overhead casting. This reel dates from my experience on English reservoirs, and in fact I use it very seldom in Scotland. My main line is the DT 6F.

Leaders or Casts: Tie your own, using one of the good knots like the Blood, the Grinner or the Fisherman's. I like the first; I know the second is technically better and I don't seem to need to use the Fisherman's much at all. You need only level casts for most Scottish loch fishing, and my favourite size for fishing a good wave is 6lb bs. Lighter casts are good for fine conditions, but I would not advise you to go below 4lb bs except in ultra-light dry fly points.

I am conscious that in this chapter I have written more about brown lochs, the Highland variety, than I have about Lowland reservoirs. This reflects something I said at the beginning, that loch fishing is somehow wrapped up with our expectations of Scotland. We expect hill and mountain scenery and there is certainly plenty of that north of the border. Further, there are vast numbers of brown lochs and far fewer clear or green lochs. Again, tactics for hill waters will give you a means of fishing all lochs, but the clear Lowland waters will be more demanding, in terms of fly-matching and tempting trout. The fish are less hearty in the Lowlands, and of course are much more fished. Loch fishing is singularly satisfying. It has all the elements of the wild in it, and that implies inclement weather, excess of wind and the wettest of wet rain. Yet what I remember most clearly of my years of fishing the lochs of Scotland, from the Borders to Caithness, is a sport with constant surprises, and a feeling of being in touch with the unspoiled land. But it is not all luck; careful study and planning shows up in the bags taken. Happy is the man who can read the details of a loch and act accordingly.

Part Two
Coarse Fishing

Barbel

Richard Walker

The barbel is a fish that prefers to live in rivers; while it can thrive in still waters, it does not breed in them. Built to hold position with ease in rapid currents, it is a very powerful swimmer indeed and consequently becomes a strong fighter when hooked, able to continue fighting for as long as any fresh water fish, not excluding the carp or the salmon.

As its general shape and the position of its mouth would indicate, it lives and feeds mainly on the bottom, though it often feeds at the surface among dense weeds on warm summer nights when it is possible to hear quite a chorus of sucking and croaking noises. This is encouraging to the angler in that he knows plenty of barbel are present, but discouraging as well because no one has found a way to catch barbel that are feeding like this.

Although barbel shoal mainly in deep fast water, there are exceptions. On heavily fished waters, they may move into slack areas where anglers' ground-bait has accumulated, while after dark they often occupy very shallow stretches. While they are well able to stand very fast currents, they will assemble behind obstructions in the river-bed, such as boulders, ridges, water-logged tree-trunks and the like, probably less to avoid the force of the current than to exploit back-eddies where food is trapped.

When the river is running high and muddy, they move into shallower water nearer to the banks; and in many rivers, a good deal of movement of barbel shoals takes place, so that a place where fish are seen in the daytime may hold none after dark. Consequently, the angler needs to observe the movements of the fish as much as possible, as well as their whereabouts at a particular time. As well as seeing the fish themselves, it is sometimes possible to see a flash of gold as a barbel turns on its side, or to observe places where gravel and stones have been disturbed by feeding fish.

Little information is available about the food of barbel, but it is known that they eat a wide variety of aquatic animals such as insects, crustacea, molluscs and other creatures. The appearance of cleaned stones in areas of bottom otherwise covered with algal growths leads one to suppose that algae are included in the diet. So are small fish, specially in the early weeks of the coarse fishing season.

Barbel are particularly prone to preoccupied feeding and are thus very susceptible to extensive and generous ground-baiting.

The business end of a barbel

The look of the fish. Colonel Crow holding a 16lb 1oz barbel

Among the more successful and popular baits are worms, maggots, stewed seeds of various sorts including hemp-seed, tares, wheat and sweet-corn. Small fish like minnows and loach make useful baits at times, but perhaps the most deadly of all baits for barbel is a small lamprey or lamprey larva, for which no ground-baiting is necessary. Wasp grubs will catch barbel, as will pieces of sausage, cubes of luncheon meat, cheese-paste and other pastes made by mixing cat or dog foods or soaked trout pellets with bread. Peeled shrimps, prawns and crayfish are also useful baits.

In practice, the basic choice is between relatively small baits accompanied by fairly extensive ground-baiting, or larger baits that may be sufficiently attractive to need no preliminary ground-baiting—or relatively little of it. On heavily fished waters, it helps to know what other anglers are doing; where very large quantities of small particle baits, such as maggots or seeds are constantly being thrown in, it may be necessary to use such baits oneself because the barbel are preoccupied with these foods.

In the angling literature of the last hundred years, we find frequent reference to long-trotting with float tackle as a good method of catching barbel. I have no doubt that it can be successful in certain places and at favourable times, but my own

A good day's work: a catch of barbel from the Severn

experience leads me to think that in general, legering is much more successful if carried out correctly. By choosing the right weight of lead for the swim, it is possible to search large areas of river-bed until the fish are located.

A great variety of means for detecting bites when legering is now available, but no fish demands the use of touch-legering more than the barbel, because this species can produce bites that are completely undetectable by any other means. Often enough, the bites from barbel on a leger tackle are very violent, and any kind of bite indicator cannot fail to detect them. When barbel are producing that kind of bite, it suffices simply to put the rod in a rest and be ready to grab it before it is snatched into the river.

Equally often, however, the only indication of the bite is a tremor or vibration of the line which can be detected only by holding the rod in one hand and the line, between the reel and the butt-ring, by the tips of the fingers of the other hand. The sensation one feels when a barbel takes the bait, when the fish are feeding in this peculiar way, has been variously described as a high frequency vibration, a physical buzz, a feeling like wind

66

The River Severn at Atcham, the well known barbel hotspot

in telephone wires sounds, and so on. Once one has experienced it, it will always be recognised, and when it is, a quick tightening of the line seldom fails to hook the fish. No one seems to know what the barbel do to produce this effect, but it is important to know that they do do it, since if it is not detected, an angler may be unknowingly getting bite after bite from barbel and catching none.

The usual practice in legering is to cast down and across the current, using sufficient lead to hold bottom when the rod is held still, but not so much as to prevent movement of the end tackle when the rod point is lifted. By this means, the bait can be moved across the river-bed in a series of arcs, extending the search by casting a yard farther at each throw. Because fine adjustment of weight is possible, a string of swan shot on a sliding nylon link is usually the best choice of lead, but in very fast water an Arlesey bomb of appropriate weight may prove preferable.

There are, however, circumstances in which it is better to leger by casting upstream, in which case tremble-bites must be felt in the usual way, but positive bites will nearly always be

67

indicated by the line suddenly falling slack, in which case it must be tightened at once by a sweeping strike far back over the angler's shoulder. Obviously, the longer the rod, the easier this is to accomplish, and while a rod as short as 10ft is adequate for legering down and across, one of 13ft or 14ft has clear advantages for legering upstream.

When should one leger upstream? Well, there are sometimes runs of water between dense beds of ranunculus weed that can be more easily reached by an upstream cast, and from which a big fish can be pulled down with the current helping the angler. Other swims can be reached only by casting upstream due to obstructions on the bank; or the geography of the river such as where two currents meet at the tail of an island, or because of the disposition of weed-beds. It is really a matter of applying common sense after assessing the position, but I stress its importance because many anglers fail to realise how often the upstream leger can succeed.

Two auxiliary items of tackle have their uses in barbel fishing. The first is the bait-dropper, of which the tackle shops offer several kinds. These devices enable small particle ground-baits to be placed very accurately on the bottom, within a limited range.

The other is the swim feeder, at its best in relatively open water since it is all too easily caught on weeds or snags. Although certain types of swim feeder can be used to distribute inert small particle baits, the main use of these devices is for putting in maggots; other baits can be placed by mixing them with stiff cereal ground-baits, or clay, and simply throwing them accurately by hand or catapult.

As stated earlier, the barbel is an extremely powerful fish, and except in open water relatively free from thick weed and snags, fine tackle is inappropriate. Barbel are not particularly shy of tackle and I have never found it necessary to use a finer line than 4lb breaking strain. Usually my line is 6lb bs; occasionally where there are severe snags, a line of 8lb or 9lb bs becomes necessary, used with a rod stiff enough to make full use of the extra strength, which means a test curve of about 1½lb—a similar rod to one which would be used for large carp. Otherwise, a lighter rod with a test curve of about 1lb will suffice.

Even when using quite small baits, there is no need to use tiny hooks. For some odd, unknown reason, barbel will tolerate a great deal of visible hook; they have been caught by anglers fishing a single grain of hemp or wheat on a hook as large as no 6. I do not recommend quite such extremes, but there is no bait for barbel that requires a hook smaller than no 10, on which a fish of perhaps 12lb or more—possessed of great strength—is much more likely to be landed than on the silly little no 14 and no 16 hooks that some anglers use and advocate.

Opinions on reels are divided; I favour a fixed-spool with a modest recovery ratio of about 3¾ to 1, and an effective roller in the pickup. This minimises friction and effort when it becomes necessary to maintain heavy pressure on a fish while recovering

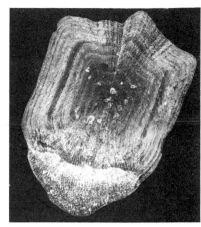

(left) *Removing a scale* (shown above) *from a 7lb 1oz Severn barbel. The scale was read as 11 years old by a Severn River Authority biologist, which means that it is a first generation Severn barbel* (Norman Worth)

line. This is important when one has to pull a fish upstream in a swim that contains weeds or snags.

Barbel vary considerably in their behaviour from one river to another, and specially in respect of their feeding times. On the Hampshire Avon, night fishing was relatively unproductive and most fish were taken during the period from one hour before to one hour after sunset. This was also the case on the Kennet, but on the Thames and its tributaries, many more fish were taken through the night. On the Great Ouse, early morning proved most productive, but there are no very hard-and-fast rules; if an angler can put a suitable bait where there are barbel, he has a chance of bites at any time of day or night.

At one time, it was supposed that barbel hibernated in the winter. We now know this to be untrue, but in common with most species, barbel feed less in cold water after the end of November; fishing for them is seldom productive except when there is a noticeable increase in flow, and usually in coloured water combined with mild winter weather.

Barbel have been caught on rod and line in Britain, albeit accidentally and out of season by salmon anglers, as large as 16lb and 17lb, and it is probable that a few reach 20lb. However, any barbel over 10lb may be regarded as a very big one, and even a fish of half that weight will give an angler a stiff fight. It is only the fact that its capture requires more knowledge and skill than most other species which prevents it from being more widely appreciated.

69

9 Bream

Graham Marsden

Bream are more popular today than they have ever been, particularly with match-anglers who know that bream can provide the winning weight more often than any other species; but more and more anglers are choosing between big bream or big catches of smaller bream and are seeking them in every water that holds a shoal or two. At the same time the bream is becoming more educated, demanding a greater sophistication in approach, bait, tackle and techniques.

Bream are not renowned for their fighting qualities, but if we had to fish for the big ones with heavy lines, there would be problems. There are four classes: first, bream up to 1lb, popularly known as 'skimmer' bream (probably because you can skim them across the surface like a flat stone when they're hooked). Skimmers are usually found in poor waters, short in natural food, and with few predators to keep the numbers down. Then we have bream up to 6lb, found in fairly good waters with good stocks of other species competing for the available food.

Bream from 7lb to 9lb are found in waters ideal for the species, where they have very little competition for the plentiful natural food. Double-figure bream are found there too, but there are usually few, if any, good spawning sites, and so the numbers are kept to a minimum. For the same reason other species are scarce too, but the natural food is rich and abundant because there are comparatively few mouths to feed.

Each class of bream, as it increases in weight, is more difficult to catch, partly because bigger fish have a greater awareness of danger and feed less often than smaller fish, but mainly because big fish are usually rare and therefore much more difficult to locate.

Locating the bream is the first task. No matter how competent an angler is in the use of tackle, to be successful he must know about the bream's behaviour before he can choose a swim and exploit his knowledge to the best advantage. Bream are basically bottom feeders but, fortunately for anglers, they often advertise where they are feeding by rolling on the surface. This peculiar habit is commonly known as the pre-feed roll but, make no mistake, bream indulge in this activity during, as well as before, feeding. More often than not the roll is a smooth, quiet, slicing motion, but occasionally they will slap their tails on the surface with a resounding smack. The roll is always in one direction. If ever you see bream at the surface heading in more

70

Roger Harker nets an 11lb 1oz bream for the author from a Cheshire mere

than one direction, then you are not seeing true feeding activity.

Locating bream is, then, mainly a question of observation. The best time to watch for the feeding roll is in the early morning and late evening; and except for skimmer bream you will usually find them at least 20yd from the margins. There are, unfortunately, a few waters where the bream rarely, if ever, show at the surface. It may be that for some unknown reason they have forsaken the habit on these waters but, more likely, they are rolling below surface without actually breaking it. Even on waters where they roll quite often, I have seen, on calm days, swirls and vortexes where they have rolled just below surface.

When you cannot locate bream by observation, choose a swim which has some character in the way of a shelf or basin, and preferably from a bank which is being hit by the prevailing wind. Some say that you can locate them by watching for the mud-clouds and bubbles they send up when feeding, but I have only seen this once. There were no bubbles, but the water became distinctly discoloured as the shoal foraged along the bottom; but, as the shoals are usually found far out from the margins, this type of observation is seldom possible.

When bream roll you will see them showing, off and on, along a stretch perhaps as much as 300yd long. The path they have taken is not necessarily straight: it may be a curve, a 'V' or an 'L' shape (page 72). Choose to fish at the point where they were last seen to roll, but only if you are the sole bream angler fishing along that 'beat'. If other anglers are ground-baiting and fishing

71

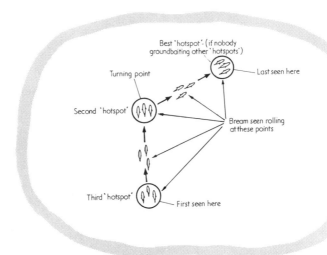

Best 'hotspot'- (if nobody
groundbaiting other 'hotspots')

Turning point

Last seen here

Second 'hotspot'

Bream seen rolling
at these points

Third 'hotspot'

First seen here

Bream hotspots

along the same patrol route, they will perhaps satisfy the
breams' hunger before they reach your swim. The terminal
point of a bream beat is invariably the best hotspot. Another is
where the bream beat goes off at a tangent, at the turning point
of an 'L' shaped beat. When my friends and I have an area of a
water to ourselves we often ground-bait the start, the turning
point and the terminal point of a beat, and move between the
three with the bream. With experience you can judge when the
fish will feed in each swim.

Once you've chosen a swim, you should feed it regularly for at
least two or three weeks. It has been said that pre-baiting is
unnecessary if a swim has been chosen wisely, and that the fish
will be visiting there anyway without the attraction of ground-
bait. This is true, of course, but ground-bait serves more than
just the purpose of attracting fish to a swim: it should consist
mainly of hook-bait samples and serves to teach the fish that
what you are offering on the hook is tasty, easy to get and safe.

Pre-baiting increases in importance the bigger the fish you
are after, and the bigger the fish, the greater are the stocks of
natural food in the water. When the fish are pre-occupied with
natural food, pre-baiting is needed more than ever to teach them
that your hook-bait is a tasty and safe alternative. After a
fortnight or so they will take the hooked bait as confidently as
the samples. They've become hooked on it, in both senses of the
word!

Their tastes vary from one water to another, although I think
the majority are caught on maggots. This is not because
maggots are superior, but because many waters become maggot-
saturated by anglers reluctant to try anything else because they
are so easy to buy and to use. Once bream have become
accustomed to this bait they don't respond quite as well to
anything else. On waters rarely fished with maggots, bread and
worms are usually the most successful bait, even when maggots
are fished on a second rod in the same area.

Float fishing for bream, particularly the larger specimens, is rarely viable owing to the great distance the patrol route usually lies from the margin, but where the beat lies no more than 20yd or so from the bank, or when a boat is available, a float can be deadly.

A match-type rod of 12ft or 13ft is ideal, coupled with a fixed-spool reel and line of 3lb to 5lb, according to whether the water is snaggy or open and the size of fish expected. For distance fishing a long zoomer-type float with a cork body low on the stem, works very well. For boat fishing, Peter Drennan's onion antenna floats are good. I equip them with Betalites for night fishing, and incorporate another, small cork body high up the stem to counteract the top-heaviness of the Betalite.

I 'shot' my floats by placing as much shot about 15in from the hook as is needed to hold bottom against the pull on the water, then sink the float to the required depth by adding more shot directly beneath it. If the water is more than 10ft deep I use the float as a slider and bunch all the shot about 15in from the hook.

Dave Ankers weighs a big bream

I use size 8 to size 14 spade-end, forged hooks, according to the bait I'm using. Lobworms and flake on a size 8 hook, maggots and small worms on sizes 14 and 12, and bunches of maggots and small worms on a size 10. I have used one or two maggots, or one small worm on a no 16, but only rarely, when the bream have been in a particularly finicky mood.

Although bream are basically bottom feeders it is not unknown for them to feed in mid-water or thereabouts. This usually happens when a huge shoal moves into the swim and there just isn't enough room for all of them over the baited area. Many of the fish then hover over the main pack and mop up the particles of food that swirl up from the intense foraging on the bottom. When this happens you can bunch most of the shot

A big bream goes into the landing net

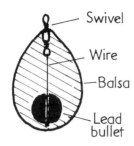

Balsa bomb

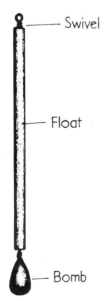

Stem-leger (or fleger)

directly below the float, leaving just one small shot to sink the bait slowly. The bait will often be taken while it is still sinking. This style is known as fishing 'on the drop'.

Bream bites are usually quite positive and the float will tilt slightly, then slowly move across the surface before being pulled directly under. Usually you will hook the bream by striking as soon as the float moves across the surface, but there are occasions when it is better to wait for the float to go under. It all depends on the mood of the fish that day and only trial and error will tell you when to strike.

Nearly all bream fishing is done on the leger because the distance involved makes it the most efficient method of bait presentation; also legering has become a very sophisticated and highly skilled technique in its own right. The days of chucking out a big bait on a big hook held down by a coffin lead threaded directly on the line and waiting for a pull on the rod tip are long gone. An experienced angler can do wonders with a leger rig and he will work with it constantly when he knows fish are in the swim. Patience for patience's sake has never been a virtue in angling.

I like a rod of 11ft, or just over, with a test curve of about 1¾lb for legering at long range. It should be of medium-fast taper which makes it capable of long and accurate casting and of picking up lots of line on the strike to set the hook. It goes without saying that a fixed-spool reel is essential. A line of 4lb test is ideal. This is strong enough, in experienced hands, to cast lead up to 1oz without breaking off, and is strong enough for the biggest bream at long range with lots of elasticity in the line to assist the rod's shock-absorber effect. A 5lb line is better for the inexperienced angler. Hooks are the same as for float fishing.

I use a fixed paternoster (above right) for most of my long-range legering. The bomb length is about a yard long and the hook length about 6in, but this can be varied according to the type of bottom—eg a longer hook length for fishing over soft mud or weed. Both the bomb length and hook length are attached to one eye of a small swivel and the reel line attached to the opposite eye. I use tucked, half bloodknots throughout. The bomb is ½oz for ranges up to 30yd, and ¾oz for greater distances. It may be necessary to use 1oz bombs for exceptionally long-range fishing and when a strong cross-wind is blowing.

Another rig for beating weed and soft mud is the balsa bomb (above left). This is a lead encased in balsa with a swivel attachment and you run it directly on the reel line. The lead and balsa should be balanced to sink slowly, coming to rest gently on the weed and mud. It is also a useful rig for fishing 'on the drop'. Then there is the stem-leger or fleger (left), which is a float with the appropriate weight at one end and a swivel at the other. This rig also runs directly on the line. The lead sinks to the bottom and the stem stands upright, holding the swivel and running line clear of weed and mud. The length of the float, or stem, should be an inch or so longer than the depth of the mud or weed. The fleger can also be balanced to fish 'on the drop'.

Another rig worth knowing is the well known link-leger

74

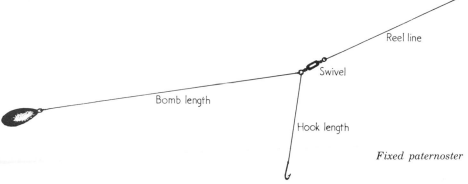

Fixed paternoster

(centre right) which can be made up by folding a piece of line over the reel line and pinching on the necessary number of swan shot. This type of link-leger is useful for fishing snaggy areas for the swan shot will pull off the link if the rig becomes fouled. And a swim feeder is very good, for the hook-bait is kept among a sample of free offerings. To beat soft mud and weed you incorporate a piece of cork or polystyrene in the cap of the swim feeder (bottom right) at the swivel end which runs directly on the reel line. This will hold the feeder upright and keep the swivel clear.

All in all, my choice is the fixed paternoster for its great asset is its accuracy in casting, and accurate casting, particularly for big bream fishing when you need to ensure the hook-bait is lying in what could be a relatively narrow beat, is of prime importance.

Indicators for legering range from the simple to the downright ridiculous. The simplest one of all is the dough bobbin, a small piece of bread-paste pinched on the line, usually between butt-ring and reel. This is fine for daylight fishing, but it means you need to use a torch for night fishing.

At long range, a dimly lit torch shining at right angles to the water is hardly likely to make the fish wary of your presence, but, if you can avoid using one so much the better and eyes soon grow accustomed to darkness. Indeed, you can bait the hook and land fish almost as well as you can in daylight, but if you use any kind of light at all, even a dim one, your vision never gets a full chance to adjust. I even close my eyes when I light a cigarette so that my vision never loses its night-sight, but king size cigarettes help to prevent a burnt nose!

The butt-indicators I recommend for night fishing are glow bobbins (page 76). These are Betalites encased in clear, protective plastic, which have a clip at one end for attaching to a loop of line between butt-ring and reel, and a length of thin cord at the other end which you fasten to the back rod-rest. This cord pulls the indicator free of the line when you strike and ensures you don't lose it. Lately, however, I have been using swing-tips more often with Betalites built into the end of the tip for night fishing. I have also fitted them with very stiff, angled rubber hinges which make casting easier (fewer tangles when the tip isn't flapping around when the cast is made). Another advantage of stiff hinges is that I hit far more bites when I offer the bream more resistance than normal.

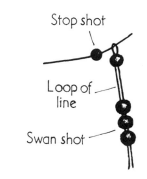

Link-leger

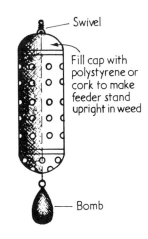

Swim-feeder

75

Landing a big bream from a Shropshire mere

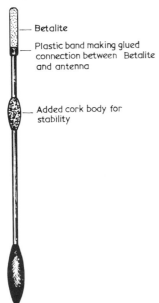

Betalite

Plastic band making glued connection between Betalite and antenna

Added cork body for stability

Peter Drennan onion float adapted for night fishing with a Betalite and extra cork body

Bream have a very annoying habit of picking up a bait by simply sucking it to the edge of their lips. They give a perfect bite but a strike simply pulls the bait and hook away. I experimented with different sizes and weights of bait, with the timing of striking (late and early strikes), and with different weights of indicator, because I was working on the theory that offering more resistance on the take would force the bream to grip the bait with their lips because a mere suck would not be sufficient. So far I have settled for my stiff-hinged swing tips, for they hang slack enough to enable the bream to suck the bait to their lips initially but offer increasing resistance as they move away with it. My swing tip will very often give a 1in or 2in indication and then fall back. This is when the bream has sucked the bait to the edge of its lips and the resisting swing tip has pulled the bait away again. A moment or two later the swing tip will straighten right out from a good, confident bite, as a result of the bream realising a suck wasn't enough.

Once a shoal of bream moves into your swim don't be content simply to cast and wait for a bite: I re-bait and cast at least every five minutes, not because I think the bait may have come off but because a moving bait is a certain attraction for bream. Those few moments following a cast, when the bomb has hit bottom and the bait is slowly settling, are the deadliest time of all for getting a take. During the five minutes or so the bait is in the swim I inch it along the bottom several times.

When you strike you should sweep the rod right back over your shoulder, quite rapidly, in order to set the hook at long range. You have a lot of line to pick up and a lot of stretch in the line which make the pull on the hook only a fraction of the pull you put into the rod. Nevertheless, the strike should be controlled and your reactions tuned to easing off the strike when the solidness of a deep-bodied bream is felt. If bream are going to break your line at all it is during the strike. Time it correctly and you'll lose very few fish.

As the bigger bream feed less often and stay for shorter spells in a swim, you must make the most of the moments when they are over your ground-bait. As soon as you land a fish, unhook it and get a bait back with all speed. Always remember, when you have sat for a long time waiting for a bite and are beginning to feel despondent, that bream can move into a swim and begin feeding in a flash. Remember too, that they can go off feed just as quickly!

A 9lb 3oz bream taken from a Cheshire mere on a no 14 hook and three maggots

10 Carp

Kevin Clifford

During the last ten years or so some snobbishness has developed about carp fishing and this has deterred some anglers, particularly youngsters, from taking it up. That is a great pity, for there is no reason whatsoever why anyone nowadays should not catch carp, given that they have the ability to catch other fish. It may entail waiting longer between bites than in most other types of fishing, and it requires, for consistent success, at least some knowledge of specialist tackle, techniques and baits, but all of this comes with experience.

I believe that a large carp of 10lb or more has all the attributes that make its capture a great and satisfying achievement, although the captor has no cause to feel superior. There is a tendency nowadays for some carp anglers to belittle the smaller sized carp, and usually the less successful the angler is, the larger is the size of the carp he belittles. In extreme cases of this malady, the anglers who have never caught a carp even approaching 20lb, belittle all carp under that weight.

'Any carp over 2lb is worth catching, one over 10lb is a big one, one over 15lb is a monster, and a 20-pounder ought to be big enough to satisfy anyone. Anything upwards of 30lb is not so much a feat of angling as a matter of biological interest.' Those are not my words, but those of Dick Walker, written over ten years ago. They are as valid as ever today and I have never lost sight of their importance, even after the capture of more than two hundred carp over 10lb, and not a few over 20lb. Any beginner to carp fishing would do well to commit them to memory.

In fresh water there is no more intelligent fish than the carp and, when hooked, it can fight as hard and as long as any other, and with more subtlety. It is one of the largest too: several over 40lb having been caught in Britain, with the largest rod-caught fish being a monster of 44lb captured by Dick Walker from Redmire Pool on 13 September 1952. The ultimate size of carp in this country is quite probably higher than the existing record, although circumstances rarely allow a fish to reach such a vast size. There are, indeed, authenticated details of a number of carp weighing upwards of 50lb and 60lb in countries where conditions, such as water temperature, are more suited to the growth of really big ones.

It is always difficult embarking on a new interest, and never more so than in carp fishing, because the protagonists keep their

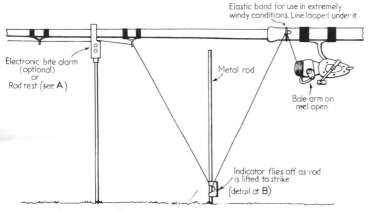

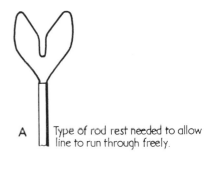

A Type of rod rest needed to allow line to run through freely.

A set-up showing an electronic bite indicator

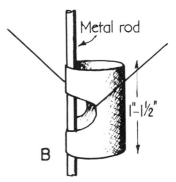

Rick Gibbinson indicator made from ¾" plastic waste piping (obtainable from DIY shops or plumber's merchants) with section cut out

knowledge under their hats. Some secrecy is understandable, but it can go too far: some beginners become discouraged and give up and (still worse) perpetuate this exaggerated exclusiveness. My own beginnings in carp fishing were enriched by the companionship of a friend and our shared successes and failures were a great help. In most areas there are usually some local specimen groups and they are worth joining, but they generally require prospective members to have had some experience in the capture of big fish. Information regarding those specimen groups, which are affiliated to the National Association of Specimen Groups, can be obtained by writing to Eric Hodson, 45 Long Croft Road, Dronfield Woodhouse, Sheffield S18 5XU (and enclose return postage). There are also two national specimen groups: the British Carp Study Group, and the Carp Anglers Association. They both have regional meetings and magazines, as well as social functions and 'get-togethers' which are extremely useful, especially for the beginner, for meeting other anglers with the same interests. Details of these organisations can be obtained by writing to Peter Mohan, Heywood House, Pill, Bristol BS20 0EA (and remember to send return postage).

There is no short cut to becoming proficient in catching carp. The road to disappointment is to believe that knowing the ingredients of some secret bait or the location of a private carp water are all that is necessary. Every successful carp angler has

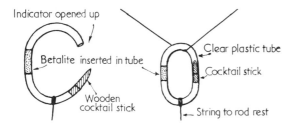

Alternative bite indicators

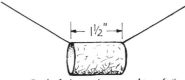

Coil of aluminium cooking foil (Not so effective in strong winds, has a tendency to spin and tangle line)

Len Arbery caught in the pose
known only too well by carpmen
on his way to his pitch for an
overnight session

(right) Very few carp anglers
have caught more than two fish
over 30lb. This is Bill Quinlan
with a 34-pounder, caught from
a Hampshire pool on sweet-corn
in September 1975 — his fourth
carp over 30lb (Len Arbery)

spent many years fishing: knowledge and skill come through
long practical experience. If there *is* a short cut it is reading
about carp fishing in angling magazines and books.

There is no better way of gaining experience than fishing
waters which have a plentiful supply of modest-sized carp, and
there are almost always local fisheries which fit this category.
My own start was made in a local gravel pit of about 4 acres
which at that time held a good head of about 100 carp,
averaging 6lb or 7lb. I could expect to hook one or two carp on
most visits and, because it was local, I was able to fish it
regularly and learn about the habits and behaviour of those
particular carp. Much of that knowledge was of enormous value
when in later years I travelled further afield in search of larger
carp. During those first few years I became aware that the best I
could reasonably hope for, from my local pits, would not be
really big by national standards. This did not influence me to
dash off to waters all over the country in search of 20-pounders.
It is true that many of my larger carp have come from waters
further afield but, in retrospect, I realise that I could not have
made a better beginning than concentrating on my local waters

most of the time, with just the occasional holiday spent at more exotic fisheries in search of much bigger fish.

If you begin by fishing small, shallow lakes with clear water and spend time just observing the habits and behaviour of carp, much can be learned about the varying characteristics of different waters, and the particular nature of their carp. Observation, for instance, can give valuable information about patrol routes, specific feeding areas and times, and reactions to various free offerings. To observe carp successfully, you must dress in drab-coloured clothes; wear plimsoles for creeping about rather than waders or wellingtons. Polaroid glasses or 'clip-on' attachments are invaluable, and best used with a wide-brimmed hat or eye shade. Binoculars with a magnification no greater than about 12 by 50 are also useful.

Not too long ago, before a suitable proprietary rod was manufactured specifically for carp fishing, anglers had to make them from split-cane, and the ideal type was devised by Richard Walker and called the Mark IV. Nowadays, we have a multitude of fibreglass models (a superior material in many ways) such as fast-taper, slow-taper, medium-taper, compound-taper, reverse-taper. Some conditions call for rods with special qualities. For instance, some carp feed at extreme long range and rods capable of hooking a fish at up to 100yd are needed. However, in most cases a fibreglass rod with a similar action to that of the original Mark IV is ideal. A general indication of the action of a rod is given by its test-curve, and for this type of rod, that would be 1½lb. The only improvement that could be made in the fibreglass version of the split-cane Mark IV, is to increase its length to about 11ft.

Most carp anglers use Mitchell reels, generally 300s and 410s. They are one of the more expensive makes and fixed-spool reels costing much less are quite adequate for landing the biggest carp. Those incorporating a roller pick-up in the bale-arm are the best for playing the large fish. A good sized landing net is a 'must', especially for fishing in the dark. One with arms of around 36in is about right, with a nice soft, knotless mesh to alleviate possible damage the netting of a big fish might cause. A small torch, taped along the top of the handle, is also useful if there is no one else about to help. Although fibreglass landing nets are excellent, the drawback is they break if trodden on! So do not leave them lying about on the ground. There are many brands of monofilament line, each with different properties, and I have not found one which completely satisfies me in every respect. I do not like the extra-thin lines because they are liable to break on the strike. The manufacturers' claims for breaking strains are often exaggerated. My own preferences are for Maxima Chameleon and Sylcast, but some of the cheaper bulk lines are quite adequate. Broadly speaking, spools carrying lines with breaking strains of 6lb, 8lb, 10lb, and 15lb are sufficient, but of course you must use a line capable of landing the biggest possible carp the water can hold!

The most important quality of any hook is that it is needle-sharp. None are sharp enough when new, so they must be sharpened on a stone or with a small file; don't just do it before a session but keep them touched-up. Before tying your hook on, always check the eye is completely closed up. For particle bait fishing, I use Au Lion d'Or hooks, model no 1534, in sizes between 2s and 8s, and for other methods of carp fishing, where it is not as important to use such a thin wire hook, I use the Jack Hilton carp hook by Partridge.

By far the most important development in carp fishing during the last ten years has been the vast increase in the range of baits. Carp have more ability to learn and remember than any other fish, and it would be difficult to devise a better way of teaching a fish to avoid a particular bait than by consistently sticking a hook into it. As carp fishing became more popular, and really 'took-off' in the 1960s, it became necessary to keep one step ahead of the carp by devising new baits. Today, the range is legion, and with all the permutations available, there is no need to imitate another's success by copying his bait. Of course, carp do eventually forget that a particular bait has been dangerous and after an interval it can be used successfully again. The time it takes carp to forget varies, but all fish, when presented with a particular bait which they regard with suspicion, are torn between the choice of an easy meal and taking a risk. Carp from 'hungry' waters are more ready to take that chance than those in water where there are ample natural food supplies. It has been said that carp can be educated by pre-baiting into taking just about anything that is edible. This is true but there are a great number of differences in the enticing properties of baits.

Bread baits

Although bread has long been used for carp fishing it is still effective—and cheap of course. Nowadays, it is best employed as floating crust, which can be coloured with vegetable dyes and flavoured by coating it just before casting with such things as treacle, Marmite, jam and peanut butter. Dying the crust has the advantage of making it less visible to birds who are tiresomely partial to it. For crust, use a stale loaf with a tough, rubbery crust, rather than a flakey one. Flake and bread paste are sometimes worthwhile baits, and again they can be coloured and flavoured. Flake is best made from a fresh loaf, but paste can really be made only from a loaf several days old. Flake is a good bait for stalking, especially when a few maggots are added. (See right.)

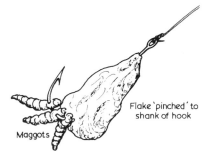

A good bait for stalking: flake with a few maggots added

Potatoes

I do not rate potatoes very highly. I know on some waters they are, or have been, very successful, but generally they are not particularly attractive to carp; their main asset is their virtual immunity to the attention of other fish, and this is why they have been used extensively in the past, particularly on waters containing bream or tench.

83

Idyllic setting: Waterways at Hemingford Grey, a Midlands gravel pit famous for big carp

Naturals

This term covers maggots, wasp grubs, meal-worms, casters, snails, slugs, caterpillars, shrimps, mussels, cockles, leeches, worms, crayfish, silkworms, beetles, tadpoles, dragonfly larvae, caddis-fly larvae, tubifex worms and fish eggs. The list may be long, but is not complete! All of these, and others like them will catch carp, and they come into their own when used for stalking and casting to feeding fish. Worms (and the best are lobworms and redworms) can be made to float by injecting a small amount of air into them with a hypodermic syringe, using a size 16 needle. Worms so treated can either be used in the same way as floating crust or legered at various depths, or just to get the bait above soft bottom weed. Maggots and casters have accounted for a great number of large carp in the last ten years.

In general, small baits tend to arouse less suspicion than large baits, and because a great number of individual bait samples can be introduced without over-feeding, carp are often attracted and feeding initiated. Once carp start feeding on particle baits in this manner, they often become intensely preoccupied. I well remember at Redmire Pool when, after a pre-baiting session with a small seed bait, spread over three days, about a dozen carp, all well over 20lb were concentrated in a tiny area, no more than 12ft square, very close to the bank. The normally clear water was churned a deep red as the carp dug into the bottom, frenziedly searching for the tiny seeds. From the branches of an overhanging tree I could watch them come swimming out from the billowing clouds of silt, leaving a mud trail streaming out behind them, only to take a wide arc, their gills puffing out the silt and rubbish as they sucked in clean water to wash the seeds before grinding them with their powerful pharyngeal teeth, and then gradually circling round before entering the foray once again.

This vigorous feeding seems to derive from the carp's competitiveness when numbers of them are feeding in close proximity on the same bait, and they are most effectively encouraged in this by the introduction of quantities of small particles. Of course there are drawbacks with small baits: small nuisance fish readily eat them, especially if they happen to be maggots or casters. Maggots can be used in various colours, which gives them an extended lease of life, when carp become wary of the conventional white coloured ones. Another tip is that a couple of floating casters put on the shank of a hook will offset the weight of a large hook, allowing it to react more naturally under close inspection by a carp.

The author with four double-figure carp up to 18lb 6oz taken on sweet-corn from a northern club water

Specials

There are many special baits used on their own or in mixtures such as sausage meat, pet foods, cheese, tinned fish roe, luncheon meat, tinned sardines and pilchards in savoury sauces, and a vast range of animal and human foodstuffs made into pastes. The list is almost endless, the combinations well-nigh infinite. Binders are usually needed to stiffen and hold the bait together and give it a paste-like texture. This can be achieved by adding combinations of plain and soya flour, cornflour, bread-crumbs, rusk, casein, gluten. powder, wheatgerm and ground trout pellets. Additives to enhance the attractiveness of the bait, such as liquidized liver, Oxo cubes, curry powder, meat extracts, maple syrup, coffee, molasses and Phillips Yeast Mixture can also be used.

Today, this trend has led to the use of more technical and, potentially, more dangerous, pure chemical additives. We now have bait additives such as monosodium glutamate which is used in minute quantities in some human foodstuffs because it activates the taste buds, although it has been banned in some western countries because it is suspected of being carcinogenic. Other pure chemicals which are being experimented with in carp baits, such as amyl acetate, which is used in the food industry to give that characteristic pear-drop smell, are possibly dangerous when used in large quantities.

There is evidence that fish use some amino-acids to locate and recognise their natural food, and some of these and other pure chemicals excite taste and smell responses in fish. Anglers in the last few years have been experimenting with such chemicals in their baits. It is a complicated subject and even amongst the scientists who work in this field, not a great deal is yet known about how these chemicals work, the exact nature of the feeding response and how it is triggered off. The smells and tastes which prompt fish into feeding are probably only rarely brought about by single chemicals but much more often by a mixture. If you become interested in this field of experimentation, it is imperative that any information on these chemicals is fully understood before they are used. It is important to remember on this subject that a little knowledge can be a dangerous thing for the well-being of the carp.

Seed and particle baits

These have caused a minor revolution in carp fishing and called for a major reconsideration of dogma that has been accepted for many years. They can bring quick, spectacular results, as sweetcorn has done on many waters, but they must be used thoughtfully. Many of the seed baits are by no means as 'instant' as sweetcorn, and in many cases anglers would get far quicker results using 'specials'. But when used under the right conditions, seed bait can be quite startlingly successful—as the results at Redmire, for instance, have shown. In certain cases, it is how they are used that is more important than the bait itself and this is true to some extent of all baits, but more so with seed baits. Some of the more popular seed and particle baits are: haricot beans, hemp-seed, maple peas, chick peas, sultanas, aduki beans, red and white dari seeds, currants, soya beans, trout pellets, raisins, black-eye beans, buck wheat, lupin seeds, lucerne beans, rape seed, wheat, barlotti beans, barley, red kidney beans, sunflower seeds, blackcurrants, tic beans, gunga peas and rice—and that is not the end of the list. The larger

A famous carp water: Ashlea Pool looking bleak in winter

beans, if they are hard, have to be boiled to soften them, but the small seeds can be stuck directly on the hook using 'Super Glue 3' or an equivalent, or 'Mystic' paste. Brittle baits, like trout pellets and 'Tasty Morsels', which tend to split when a hook is pushed through them, can either be made into a paste for use on the hook or holes can be bored through the hook-bait samples using a red-hot needle.

The following examples will, I hope, give an insight into the different ways particle baits can be used.

There is a small, shallow lake, surrounded by a great many trees, near my home. Its 2½ acres hold a good head of carp, weighing up to about 20lb, and nowhere is it wider than 30yd. It is a private syndicate water, but it has been fished in the past by a number of experienced carp anglers, and the fishing is not easy. Nearly all the carp have been caught either by stalking fish and casting 'naturals' at them or by pre-groundbaiting in one specific swim. A friend and I adopted a different approach and baited the whole lake with barlotti beans, very lightly. By this, I mean we tried to put just an odd one or two beans, every square yard or so, over the areas of the lake which were frequented by carp regularly and where we had seen them feeding. This was carried out four times, over a period of fourteen days, and we then reasoned that certainly some of the carp would have become accustomed to finding the beans almost anywhere and accepting them without suspicion. Since the topography of the lake made it an ideal stalking water, we dropped in of an evening for a few hours after work, quickly looked around the water until we found some carp, and cast the barlotti beans to them with a reasonable chance that they would be taken. It worked well and a good number of large carp over 10lb were caught.

When I was a member of the Redmire Pool syndicate, one of my favourite pitches was the 'In-Willow', which was the very next one along the west bank from the famous 'Willow' pitch where so many large carp have been captured in the past, including of course 'Clarissa', Dick Walker's record. I liked the 'In-Willow' pitch for a number of reasons: firstly it was a pitch which had not been one of the most popular in the past and it had been a difficult swim to fish before the large willow tree had

87

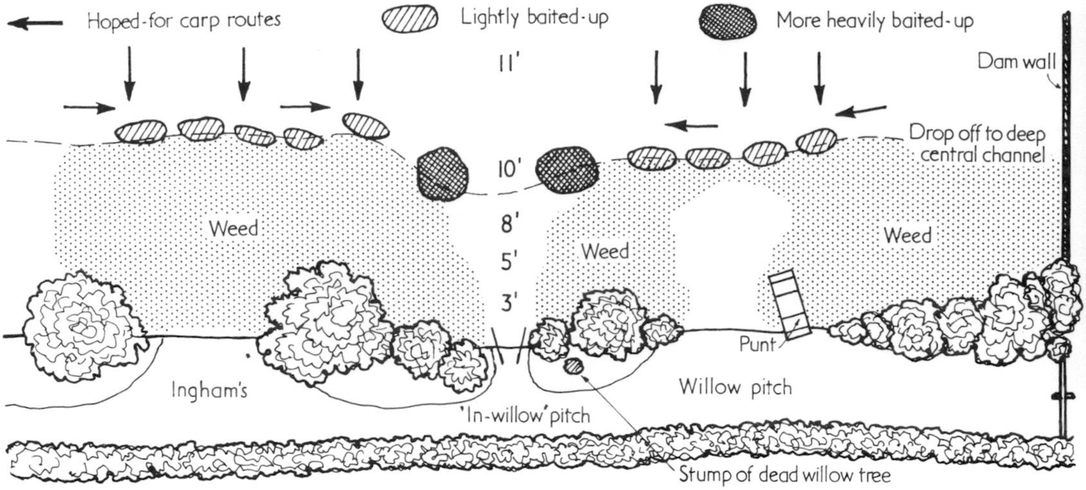
Hoped-for carp routes
Lightly baited-up
More heavily baited-up
11'
Dam wall
Drop off to deep central channel
10'
8'
5'
3'
Weed
Weed
Weed
Punt
Ingham's
Willow pitch
'In-willow' pitch
Stump of dead willow tree

'In-Willow' swim

died and been cut down. I knew that while the willow was alive, carp regarded the area under its branches as safe and felt secure enough to try an angler's bait. Directly out from the 'In-Willow' swim, the drop-off to the deep centre channel, where the bottom-weed did not grow because of the depth of water, came closer to the bank than at any other point along the bank. (See above.) Having learned in my early days at local gravel pits that carp would often be prepared to take a bait adjacent to weed-beds which they would not consider in open water, I knew the character of the 'In-Willow' was such that carp could pass along the edge of the drop-off without realising (I hoped) that the swim had been dragged clear of weed. I felt these reasons might make this an area where the carp might feed with a little less suspicion on a new bait than in other swims which had been highly productive in the past. I baited up heavily on either side of my pitch with red-dari seed, firing out about 3lb to 5lb of seeds with a catapult. From the 'Willow' pitch I fired some more seeds out, to cover the bottom lightly along the edge of the weed-bed, and this was repeated from 'Ingham's' pitch. This performance was repeated, usually in the middle of the day, when there was the least chance of disturbing feeding carp with the baiting-up process, and usually after a few days carp started feeding on it and getting caught. The result was I landed a number of carp over 20lb from the 'In-Willow' pitch, including a common carp weighing 27lb 4oz and a leather carp of 27lb 7oz.

Now no young angler reading this should dash out and start fishing with barlotti beans and red-dari seeds, believing that they will bring instant success! *No bait* in itself will bring success. I am convinced that many other baits would have achieved similar results to my examples, and the important point is that the capture of those fish came from observing, deciding what problems needed overcoming, and then thinking of the solutions. Of course, it is not always possible to come up with the right answers but, when it does happen, it nearly always means that the easiest part in getting the fish on to the bank becomes the actual fishing itself.

Chub

Kenneth Seaman

I can recognise a keen chub angler instantly now. He moves distantly across the landscape, or sits invisible in some overgrown retreat. Occasionally, I see his rod arch, hear the urgent screech of his reel, but that is all. He does not bother me, nor I him. There is a quick instinctive appreciation of our mutual desire for solitude. Like the fish we seek, we prefer to remain hidden, shying away quickly from intruders.

I learned the need for stealth, concealment and timing a long time ago when, as a boy, I often cycled 15 miles in the evening to fish a small Midlands river. At this magic time swims that had seemed devoid of fish during the day often came suddenly alive with thrusting dark bodies, and the bites were sometimes so powerful that my rod was almost jerked from my hand.

I have learned many other valuable lessons since those early days, and now I seldom catch other species when I am seeking chub, or fail to catch at least one chub, no matter what the conditions are. The principles on which my success is based are easy enough to define: they are a sound understanding of the nature and feeding habits of the chub, an imaginative and versatile use of baits and methods, the ability to fish selectively at those times, and in those conditions and places where I know my chances will be best. Other important tips are to move quietly at all times, to use every scrap of cover that is available

Netting a chub from a difficult overgrown spot in winter. The leaves are off the trees but the chub are still there. A type of swim difficult to fish but it almost always contains chub

The chub taken from the snaggy spot illustrated on page 89

to conceal your approach and preferably to fish upstream rather than down.

When the water is low and clear, fish when the light penetration is low—at dawn or dusk, or even after sunset. During the bright sunlit hours pay special attention to the hiding-places beneath overhangs, weeds, debris, and undercut banks. When the river is in spate, concentrate on the slacker areas at the edges of the fast currents, and on the side of the river that is normally shallow or even entirely devoid of water.

Learn all you can about the nature of each swim so that you know where the chub are most likely to be at the different levels of water. Try always to fish selectively. Direct all your efforts into the task of catching chub. Ignore the lure of the easier success offered by fishing indiscriminately for anything. Learn also to adapt yourself to the world of nature and fish, rather than expecting that they should conform to some rigid preconceived idea that you have formulated.

For all the methods I normally adopt three rods are enough: a 10ft to 11ft rod for legering, hunting, and upstream worming; a 12ft to 13ft rod for float fishing; and a fly-fishing rod and matching double-taper line. A fixed-spool reel, line, floats, a selection of eyed hooks, some split-shot and legerweights, landing net, and a selection of assorted flies and nymphs, complete the tackle requirements. Remember that the line must *always* be matched to the rod and it should be reliable and strong enough to handle any chub you are likely to hook in the swim you are fishing; use only sufficient weight to sink the bait to the required depth, and you will then avoid gross errors that often lead to line breakage and lost fish.

The methods I use to catch chub are fly- and nymph-fishing, hunting, dapping, surface-fishing, drifting or free-lining, upstream worming, live-baiting, spinning, legering, and float fishing.

Four methods of fishing nymph as used by the author: A— hanging under surface film and for emerging nymph if fished through the surface; B—rising nymph; C—swimming nymph. Fish these methods preferably upstream or across. D—shows nymph fished downstream then brought curving up to surface

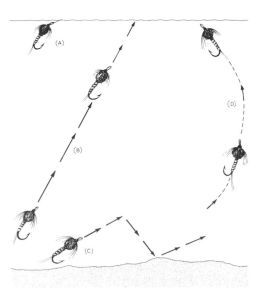

Let us begin in the early season when the water is running low and clear beneath a cloudless summer sky, the weeds are thick on the shallows, the bankside growth is at its most luxuriant and the fly life most prolific. What better time is there to indulge in those two most enjoyable methods—fly- and nymph-fishing?

Equip yourself with a fly-rod, line, a leader tapered to not less than ·006, or 3lb breaking strain, a net, and a selection of nymphs, both weighted and unweighted. Chub will take many nymph patterns, but first try March Brown, any of the Olives, Pheasant Tail, a Corixa (which is not strictly a nymph), or the little Iron Blue.

Alder

Start fishing at dawn when the light is less intense and the chub more likely to be out in open water. Move stealthily upstream, casting and flicking an unweighted nymph up and across, remaining always alert for that tell-tale movement of the leader, or a shimmer of flank that will betray the taking chub. Then tighten quickly and firmly, and bully the chub out of the swim as quickly as possible.

If the chub are not visible, or there are no obvious signs of near-surface feeding activity, try a weighted nymph. Fish it upstream, allow it to sink, and then work it back downstream in a series of little jerks that will imitate the swimming movements of a nymph. Try also imitating the rise of the nymph, bringing it up to the surface by raising the rod and pulling line down through the rings with the left hand. Stay alert for a sudden jolt that will indicate a taking chub.

March Brown

As a variation, try swimming the nymph downstream. Allow it to sink on a slack line; then bring it up to the surface by checking the flow of line. Most takes will occur at this stage. Repeat all these different styles of presenting the nymph, but use two or three wet flies instead. March Brown, Alder, Hawthorn, Silver Butcher, or Peter Ross, are all excellent patterns to try. But do vary your choice from time to time, giving each a fair trial.

Walker's Daddy Long Legs

Next, explore the possibilities offered by the dry fly, and not just the traditional large bushy fly. Chub like these, but they sometimes prefer the smaller flies, and any selection should certainly include, for instance, Cinnamon Sedge, Daddy Long Legs (crane-fly), Damsel Fly, Hawthorn, Alder, Greenwell's Glory, Iron Blue, Wickham's Fancy, Pheasant Tail, March Brown, Stone Fly, Blue Dun, Olive Dun, Coachman, White Moth and, of the very small flies, any imitation Midge pattern such as Black Gnat, Flying Ant, Grey Duster or Green Midge.

If there is a hatch of fly on the water, try to match it, in size if not in type. In the absence of any rise generally use the smaller fly during the day and the larger flies at dusk. Normally, fish the fly upstream, but do not be afraid to cast across the stream, or even downstream, if this can be done without revealing yourself and thus scaring away the chub. Approach and presentation are more important than choice of fly.

Peter Ross

During the full heat of the day, or at any other time when the opportunity occurs, try dapping in those shaded overgrown

Upstreaming a floating crust-bait—an excellent method when the water is clear and low

swims where normal fly-fishing is impossible. Remain out of sight, tie on a hackled fly to the leader, then push the rod slowly through the intervening foliage, and lower the fly carefully down on to the surface. Now give it life and movement, either by lifting and lowering it quickly to imitate the typical egg-laying movement of a fly, or wiggle and gyrate it to imitate a fly struggling to rise from the surface. If a chub rises to take, allow it to suck the fly in and turn down before striking. Once it is hooked manoeuvre it quickly out of the swim, allowing the swim to rest for a while; then try again, or move off to another similar place. One of the big sedge-fly patterns (imitation beetle, grasshopper or crane fly) will often tempt up a chub. If not, try a smaller fly—a Bluebottle, Bee, Greenwell's Glory or perhaps a Wickham's Fancy.

As a variation, try a wet-fly or lure such as a Polystickle, imitation beetle, tadpole, fry, or caddis. Work the lure slowly

Upstream float-legering rig

Link-leger rig used by author. One swivel is used as the stop; the other carries the weights on a short nylon link. A split ring or clip can be used to permit quick change of weights instead of tying nylon link directly to the swivel

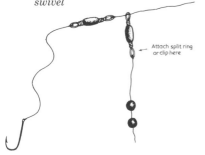

Attach split ring or clip here

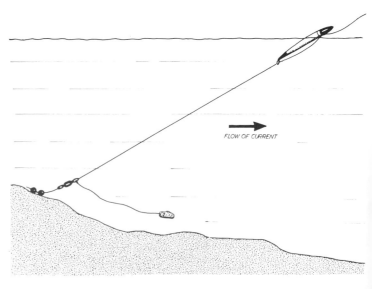

FLOW OF CURRENT

through the swim in an imitative manner, using the legering rod and a line of at least 4lb. Sometimes you can see the chub and actually watch him take the lure. If not, be ready for that sudden jerk that will send your rod tip shuddering over to its limit.

For even more exciting fishing, try dapping a live insect, such as a grasshopper, bluebottle, or beetle, using a size 6 hook, 6lb line, and the legering rod. Present in the same way as you presented the dapping fly.

Another exciting method that I frequently use during the summer is the floating bait. Equip yourself with the legering rod, 6lb line, no 4 hook, and a large piece of crust. Work upstream first, tossing the crust up into all the likely places, but especially into the fast water. Watch carefully for the rise. It will be emphatic and exciting, I can assure you.

Try drifting the crust downstream too, feeding the swim with a few crusts first to encourage the chub to rise. Use a float tackle to fish a chrysalid, live fly, or a small piece of crust downstream on the surface. Evening, when the air is often still and the water tinged with light from the setting sun, is a great time for this style of fishing. Wind makes it difficult. Explore, too, the possibilities of fishing a submerged caster, fly, or small piece of crust, using the float-fishing rod, a small quill float, and a no 12 or no 14 hook.

Another most enjoyable style of fishing that I often use is the upstream worm—deadly in skilled hands at any time, but especially so when the river is falling after a spate. Use the legering rod, 8lb line, no 6 hook, and a big lobworm for bait, and work carefully upstream, tossing the worm up into every known chub haunt. Maintain close contact by reeling in to keep pace with the current, but do not pull on the worm as this will cause it to spin. Use weight only when you have to sink the worm in the fastest and strongest of currents.

When the chub are feeding on minnows—and you may see this happening—what is more logical than to fish a minnow? Use the same tackle, lip-hook the minnow, and fish it upstream in the same way as you fished the worm. Use a float tackle, if you are not confident of detecting the bites, to keep the minnow up above the weeds and to drift it downstream. All of these methods will yield dividends when the chub are feeding.

A natural development of upstream worming is the hunting style, which can be used throughout the season, but is most exciting during the summer when the chub are often visible in the clear water. No ground-bait is required. The style of fishing is essentially that used by primitive man in which stealth, knowledge of the water and habits of its fish are far more important than bait or tackle.

Equip yourself with the legering rod, fixed-spool reel, 6lb to 8lb line, a selection of large hooks and, for bait, a worm, minnow, crayfish, frog, newt, tadpole, mussel, cheese, bread, or dough. Then fish upstream, staying always quiet and concealed, presenting the bait to any visible chub first, but overlooking nowhere that might hold a hungry one. Use weight sparingly,

Chub in typical snaggy undercut bank. A leger rig should generally be used to catch chub in this type of swim

and no float. This is a most exciting style of fishing and you will often see the chub take the bait. Hit him hard, hold on, then bully him quickly out of the swim.

While engaged in this style of fishing you will discover many swims where the pace of the current, weeds, overhangs, and other snags make presentation difficult, if not impossible. Such swims must be fished with a leger tackle which will hold the bait in position. The amount of weight needed varies according to the strength of the current, while the line strength must be such that you can confidently handle any chub you might hook. Use the legering rod, line of at least 6lb, and a link-leger tackle, lowering the bait into the swim rather than casting it. But if casting is necessary, never cast directly into that spot where the chub are lying; rather cast it beyond or above them and allow the current to roll the tackle round and downstream. More chub will be caught then.

When fishing snaggy places like undercuts, weeded swims, and overgrown swims, lower the bait carefully down into the clear spaces, use your strongest tackle, and be prepared for a

Chub lying in hidden position beneath mat of surface debris and weed

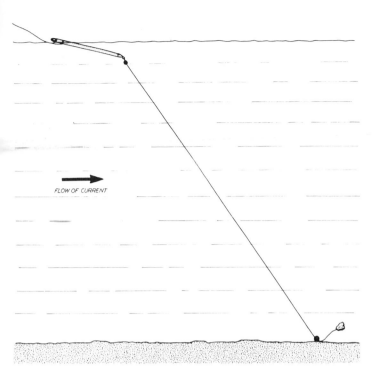

FLOW OF CURRENT

Float tackle for laying-on

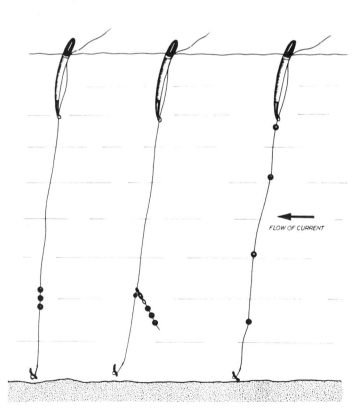

FLOW OF CURRENT

Three tackles for float fishing: (left to right) quick sinking tackle with weights attached directly to the line; the same but with weights attached to swivel; slow sinking rig

stern battle to extract the hooked chub, which will surely break away or ensnare your tackle if it can. With this in mind, choose a position that will allow you to pull the chub away from the snags, preferably fishing upstream so that the current can be used to help you in the struggle.

When legering the fast water downstream, hold the rod higher than you normally do so that you can watch for any unusual movement of the line. Next, explore the possibilities of legering upstream—an extremely useful way of fishing weirs, waterfalls, tunnels and fast-flowing swims. This method usually results in a slack line bite which gives you a little more time in which to strike.

For float fishing—a method that is especially useful for fishing the larger rivers—use the 12ft to 13ft rod, line of at least 3lb, and a selection of floats ranging from small quills that will take one AA shot to really big floats that will take several swan shot. The smallest of floats should be used to fish the slow-moving swims when the water is low; the large ones for fishing the stronger flowing ones and when the river is in spate or running higher than normal.

Fish the slow-moving swims first, using a slow-sinking style, with the depth set so that the bait will just clear bottom at maximum fall. Then try the laying-on and float legering styles, fished either upstream or down, whichever method seems most suitable for the swim being fished. For ground-bait, use the same bait that you would choose for hook-bait, rather than the cloud variety which tends to attract other smaller fish. For baits use bread, cheese, or worms when the water is coloured, and seed-baits or meat-bait if the chub seem wary of the more common baits. Persist if your early efforts do not bring quick success. Chub usually need time to get accustomed to a different sort of bait.

When the lower temperatures of autumn and winter strip the leaves from the trees and denude the water of much of the weed, try drifting a large piece of flake downstream on a floatless line. The method is a bit tricky at first but it can be deadly when the chub are feeding. Drop or lower a large piece of flake into the head of the swim, using just enough weight to sink it, and allow it to drift downstream with the line running freely over your index finger. When you think it has reached that part of the swim where the chub are lying, check the flow of line to bring the flake curling up to the surface. Bites can come at any stage, but most frequently when the check is made.

Later, when snow whitens the banks, chub will still feed. During the day concentrate on the snaggy spots and the undercuts, using either crust or flake on a link-leger tackle; or fish the deeper, slow-moving swims with a float tackle or drifted bait. Concentrate your efforts into the afternoon and early evening period when the light is fading. I have caught chub in conditions so cold that I have had to break the ice and my line has frozen in the rod-rings.

When the spring rains sweep across the fields and the river is running high and coloured, use the same methods but switch to a big lobworm or minnow for bait. The lobworm is unbeatable as bait in these conditions, the minnow or crust more effective when the water falls and clears.

The last few weeks of the season can be the best in the chub angler's calendar. With the coming of the warmer months, when the swims are swept clean of debris by the floods, the chub are eager to feed, and big catches are possible with either bread-flake, crust, paste, minnow or, if you prefer small bait, the chrysalid or caster. I tend to prefer the larger bait though, as the small maggots, casters, or small pieces of bread are likely to attract other smaller fish.

During this halcyon period, I have known days when almost every known chub swim or hiding-place has produced a rod-bending bite. Then I have gone home in the late evening glutted with the excitement of a truly eventful day, when all the hard work I had previously put into observing and learning has been made worthwhile.

When the rivers are unfishable owing to flooding try still waters and canals. Both can hold substantial numbers of chub, some of which reach specimen size. Most of the methods I have described can be adapted to fish such waters, fly- and nymph-fishing being especially successful in still waters. As with river fishing, knowledge of the water, the feeding habits of the chub and an imaginative and versatile use of baits and methods are the key to success.

Lastly, do not let your angling fall into a stereotyped routine without scope for change or invention. Occasionally do something entirely different, something spontaneous that is based on observation and the needs of the moment. Try going to the waterside without any bait and see what you can achieve with the baits you find there; or take only a few maggots or a worm, catch minnows with one of these baits, and then go on to catch chub with the minnows. When you have spent some time unsuccessfully stalking a chub—perhaps because no matter how careful your approach it seems to sense your presence—try waiting for it with your bait lodged on a reed, leaf, overhanging branch, or shelving bank; when the chub appears from its hiding-place, ease or twitch the bait into the water and see what happens. If your approach to a swim fails consistently, try a different one, such as a new position to cast from. If a bait fails to attract the chub you are seeking—probably because it has been hooked on that bait before—try another. A switch to the unusual sometimes brings a dramatic change of fortune.

Finally, never stop looking and learning from experience, for it is the little things, the accumulated store of knowledge gleaned over many seasons fishing in many different conditions of weather and water, that will bring you the kind of consistent success you seek.

12 Dace

Richard Walker

Though the dace is an interesting fish, it does not reach great size. A half-pounder is a big one, and the anglers who have caught dace of a pound or more are very few.

Dace are river fish, seldom found in lakes and ponds, and the biggest specimens are found in the smaller rivers, or the head-waters of larger ones, usually where the water is alkaline and not subject to great variations in flow rates. This is not an invariable rule because there are big dace in some of the Welsh trout rivers but, for the angler seeking large dace, lowland chalk or limestone streams of modest size are the more likely waters in which to find them.

The food of dace includes a large variety of organisms. They eat algal growths such as silkweed, the seeds of various riverside plants from elderberries to grass seeds; fresh water shrimps, a wide variety of insects both aquatic and terrestrial, tiny fishes of their own and other species, small snails and mussels, and worms of all sizes. Consequently the angler does not need a wide variety of baits and among the most useful are red worms, maggots, casters, hemp-seed, elderberries and bread-crust, all readily available. Dace may also be caught by fly-fishing and no extensive selection of patterns is needed. My biggest dace, 1lb 5oz, and two others over 1lb, were caught on a small Black Gnat and this pattern has taken far more dace for me than any other.

Dace feed at all depths of water—for they are less susceptible to low water temperatures than most other coarse fish. Their level in the water is, however, dependent on the temperature

A full length view of a dace

and the colder it is, the more will the dace hug the bottom. Conversely, in warm weather, many of the dace will be feeding close to the surface, on insects that are either hatching or being carried down by the current. However, even in warm weather, dace will come up to the top only when there is something there for them to eat so, generally speaking dace fishing is done near the bottom at all times of the year.

It can be done by float fishing, legering, laying-on or stret-pegging. While the weight of lead or shot and the float, if any, will be chosen to suit the depth and above all the current speed, the line need not be strong for so small a species and 2lb breaking strain is a useful size, with hooks ranging from no 16 to no 12.

Maggots and casters will catch dace at any time of year; seed baits like stewed wheat and hemp are always useful, but specially attractive in late summer and autumn, and so are elderberries. When the river is coloured, and always after much rain, worms are extra-good, and indeed at any time. Perhaps the best worms are the small red Cockspurs that you find in well-rotted mowings or leaves, but the tail of a full-sized lobworm is worth remembering. But the lists of baits on which dace may be caught is well-nigh endless.

Dace are reputed to be fast biters and certainly the smaller ones require very quick striking, specially when you are fly-fishing. In fact, regular fly-fishing for dace of modest size is an excellent way of ensuring that when you turn to trout or grayling fishing with the fly, many fish will be missed by overquick striking reactions! Large dace, however, are much more deliberate and require no great speed of strike by the angler, be he fishing with fly, float or leger tackle. Their bite is not only deliberate but usually emphatic; they are much less inclined to spit out a bait after feeling the resistance of the tackle than other species like roach or bream.

One other characteristic of dace is that they are less influenced by light than other species, and they are willing to feed throughout the twenty-four hours of the day. In my experience, however, sport with dace often falls off at about the same time as any roach that are present begin feeding freely. Whether the dace feed less as the light fails, or whether when roach begin to feed the proportions of the two species to be hooked are reversed, I do not know. It is a fact, however, that one often finds that a few dace seem to regard themselves as members of a roach shoal, and these are usually dace of a size well above average for the water.

Dace may vary considerably in size from one stretch of river to another. The dace in one swim may average from 2oz to 3oz and in another, only a hundred yards away, up to 6oz or 8oz. For this reason, it takes many days of fishing and exploring to assess the potential of a river holding dace.

You should not assume, after catching a great number of small dace from each of three or four spots, that a river holds no large specimens. Even if scale readings show a modest growth rate, there may still be big dace in the river because there is a

Royston Smith of Sedgely Working Men's Club lands a dace

very wide range of growth rate in this species. Many years ago, I investigated the growth rates of dace in the River Cam and found that it averaged less than 1oz per year, but there were exceptional fish that grew at more than twice that rate and I caught dace over a pound there.

I wonder how many small chub have been mistaken for dace, and how many large dace have, sadly, been mistaken for small chub? Every angler is assumed to know the difference, but in case any do not, here it is: the dorsal and anal fins of chub have convex outer edges; those of dace have concave edges. The eye of a dace is half as big again as that of a chub of the same weight; the dace has a much smaller mouth. Dace have buff-olive tail fins; chub have dark tail fins, navy-blue to black. The ventral and anal fins of dace are very pale pink in colour; those of chub are usually red, though chub vary considerably and this is not an infallible diagnostic characteristic. Fortunately, inter-breeding between dace and other fish is extremely rare; a dace-chub hybrid would take an expert ichthyologist to identify.

Extensive ground-baiting for dace is seldom necessary; a few samples of what is to be used for hook-bait usually suffices, thrown in loose a few yards upstream from where the fish are. But when the river runs high and coloured, it helps to enclose some worms in a ball of mud, about the size of a tennis ball, and drop this in the upstream end of your chosen swim.

If you want to catch very large quantities of dace, you may, if you are not squeamish and can do it without upsetting other people, follow the example of Fred J. Taylor and me, when we acquired a dead sheep from a friendly farmer, cut it in half and hung the halves on the branches overhanging the water. Within ten days or so, the swims below were swarming with dace, and these shoals stayed in those swims for the rest of the season, long after the maggots had ceased to fall from the dried-out mutton.

In very fast moving water, where ground-bait thrown in loose may be carried too far downstream before reaching the bottom, a bait-dropper is a most useful device. Many anglers, when legering for dace, use the block-end swim feeder, but for so small a species, the drag of the feeder on a hooked fish removes its already rather limited fighting powers and for that reason the technique does not appeal to me.

Next to fly-fishing, the most entertaining sort of dace fishing is long-trotting; but some of my biggest dace were taken by laying-on, with suitable float tackle, in slacks formed by midstream clumps of rushes or other obstructions which divide the current, allowing very small floats, lightly shotted, to be used. In such small areas of still or slowly moving water, a little loose ground-bait—like maggots, hemp-seed or elderberries—sink very nearly straight down, ensuring that ground-bait and hook-bait are in the same place. This often needs no more than a single BB shot on the tackle to ensure the float to be anchored to the float chosen to carry, but only *just* carry. This shot completes the rig, and it is sensitive to delicate bites. This is important, because with ground-bait concentrated in so small an area, fish may take the hook-bait and move only a little way to the next food particle. If the bite is undetected the bait may be swallowed. To avoid that, the shot is placed only 2in to 3in from the hook, and the angler tightens at the least indication of a bite. I need hardly add that the method is equally effective for roach and often other species as well, such as chub, barbel and grayling.

These then are the usual ways of fishing for dace, but on occasions, less orthodox methods will succeed. There is a fly pattern which does not, in fact, imitate an insect, but a fresh water shrimp. The inclusion of lead foil under the dressing makes it sink readily, and sometimes dace will take it eagerly. It can be fished either on fly or on float tackle; in the latter case, one trots it downstream, checking the float firmly at intervals, which causes the shrimp to swing upwards in the water; it is at

Collyer's Shrimp

Walker's Leaded Shrimp

101

A good catch of dace, taken from the Usk

this point that it is usually taken. The method was devised for grayling, but it also took so many dace that its use has extended far beyond grayling rivers. Size 12 is suitable. Often enough to make the fact worth remembering, dace eat tiny fish fry. When they are doing this, the same method used for the shrimp can be applied to fish a small Polystickle, tied to a no 10 or no 12 long-shank hook. That can also, of course, be used with ordinary fly-fishing tackle.

These, however, are methods for use on comparatively rare occasions; the conventional, well-tried methods of long-trotting, laying-on, light legering, and in winter particularly, stret-pegging, are the ones that catch the most and usually the largest dace.

102

Eels

13

Fred J. Taylor

Most anglers regard eels as pests that take baits intended for worthier species, but in recent years eel fishing has become more popular. The formation of the National Anguilla Club did much to stimulate interest in the behaviour and feeding habits of eels, and nowadays anglers recognise that specialised tackle and approach are needed to catch them. Eel fishing in many rivers and enclosed waters is permitted during the coarse fish close-season and as eels are often very active during April and May they are a worthwhile close-season species. Many restrictions are, however, in force, and these vary from water to water. Anyone contemplating eel fishing during the coarse fish close-season should make enquiries beforehand. Reference is made to eel fishing in the by-laws printed on most rod licences and there should be no confusion. Club secretaries and officials should make it quite clear to their members whether eel fishing is allowed or not.

The eel record was set up in 1978 with a monster of 11lb 2oz from a lake near Ringwood in Hampshire. There are, however, records of other, even larger eels being taken by means other than rod and line and I believe that there is scope here for the record-conscious angler.

Few anglers expect to break records, however, and an eel of 3lb can rightly be regarded as a big fish. It is a powerful adversary and will strain tackle to the utmost before it ends up on the bank. Nor is it beaten once it is landed! A second fight usually ensues before the hook is finally removed.

Small fish or big worms are ideal eel baits and in rivers where there are crayfish a 3in specimen will probably prove even more acceptable. Small fish baits such as loach and bullheads can be found in stony shallows and caught with a small net. Crayfish baits are procured in the same way, but they can also be extracted from their holes in the clay banks—if you have the courage to put your hands in after them. Stale prawns (cooked) are superb eel baits on some southern salmon rivers!

It is often said that eels are lovers of mud but I have never found this to be so. I have found most of my eels in clear water over a stony or gravel bottom. Sometimes they will take a live-bait or one which, though dead, is made to move in the current but, generally speaking, a stationary bait is preferable. I have actually seen an eel take an artificial streamer fly—but I do not suggest fly-fishing is effective. Experienced anglers are

Two nice ones

all agreed, however, that most eels of any size are taken on dead fish or fish portions, and methods have changed very little over the years; nor has tackle.

In the dogdays of summer, when carp are not interested in baits of any kind, the wise angler snatches out a few small rudd or roach baits, puts them on an old carp fishing outfit, tosses them out with the reel bale open, and waits for the run to commence. Not *all* carp waters hold eels; not *all* serious carp

104

anglers would agree with light-hearted eel fishing during the day, but to many of us it serves to while away the hours that would otherwise be wasted.

Some serious eel anglers inject their baits with strong-smelling oils and essences, others ground-bait the area with high-smelling minced fish or offal. Most take the trouble to pierce the small fish bait with a sharp knife in several places, mainly to puncture the swimbladder, but also to allow the natural juices to flow.

Opinions are divided regarding the correct method of mounting a dead bait. The accepted way, back in the 1940s and 1950s, was to thread the reel line through the vent of the bait and out of its mouth. A big single hook (one that rode clear of the bait's head) was then tied to the line and the bait was prevented from slipping by pinching on a large shot where the reel line left the vent. The idea was that the eel could not expel the bait up the

These four eels were caught on dead fish

105

A successful session

line once it had taken it. Nor could it bite through the nylon because of its mouthful of dead fish. I still find this method perfectly adequate today and for daytime, light-hearted eeling, nothing more complicated is necessary.

It takes some time for even a big eel to pouch the bait, and slack line should be allowed once it has been taken. This is easy in the still waters of ponds and lakes, but rather more difficult in a fast stream. Here the line has to be fed out slowly so that the eel, and not the current, takes control.

Despite their unpleasant appearance and their slimy exterior, eels are delicious to eat and are, in fact, more nutritious than fresh salmon, as many Londoners will confirm. I see no point in returning them to the water as I can never get enough to keep my many eel-loving friends supplied. But I believe they deserve a better fate than that of being thrown on the bank to rot.

Serious eel fishing sessions at night require a little more preparation. It's difficult enough to unhook an eel by day; it's virtually impossible to do so by night, and for that reason it is advisable to have a number of mounts made up in readiness. It takes a little time, but it really is worth the effort when the eels are well and truly 'on'. Bait up a dozen or more small, 4in rudd or roach in the manner already described and tie on a swivel where the line leaves the vent. Leave only a few inches of spare line between the swivel and the bait. Pinch on your stop shot if you think fit. Have an open, dry sack ready and a keep net made of fine mesh in the water.

When an eel is hooked and hauled ashore (you simply haul an eel out; you do not attempt to play or net it—so use a substantial line) hold it over the open dry sack, cut the line above the swivel, and tie on another prepared and mounted bait. Transfer the eel to the keep-net where it will be safe. Do *not* keep eels in wet sacks on the bank. You may *think* you have tied the sack tight, but you may well find they've all escaped by morning, and rats are experts at locating and chewing through eel sacks—as many an eel angler has discovered to his cost. If you have no desire to keep the eels, you can, by daylight, either unhook or cut the nylon links and release them. I believe this is a waste for eels are harvest fish and should be cropped by those who like to eat them.

Occasionally it is possible to witness what I can only regard as an eel migration, and the angler who likes eels and is fortunate enough to watch eels passing through a chalkstream run, will have a great deal of fun. I saw such a spectacle once myself on the River Test and caught eels until I ran out of bait.

The method known as 'babbing' is not practised so much these days but a few local experts still reap their annual harvest. Using rod and line, they thread a great gob of worms on to a length of worsted and ball it up into a writhing, wriggling mass which they lower into the quiet near-bank water. The eels are *not* hooked. They take the bab and their teeth become enmeshed long enough for them to be lifted out and shaken into the waiting sack. I have watched this done often enough to be impressed, but it is not eel fishing as I know it.

106

Grayling

14

R.V. Righyni

One of the many good characteristics of the grayling is that it provides excellent sport to both fly and bait during the autumn and winter months when the trout is out of season. And although everyone is not agreed that this species (definitely a member of the salmon family) is truly a prize game-fish, some of the most experienced fishermen are just as enthusiastic about their grayling fishing as going after salmon and trout at the appropriate times.

This is a question about which the individual is advised to gather his own evidence and make up his own mind; but if you find great delight in hooking and playing a beautiful grayling on a dry fly in October, or on a little red worm trotted down the stream in December, you will probably conclude that only ignorance of the joys which the grayling can give must be responsible for the views held by the disparagers.

The most useful and revealing introduction to the grayling, its character and ways, is to see the sport on a suitably good, calm, dry-fly fishing day in October.

In the first place, locating the fish is no problem. Either the

The author casting with a centre-pin reel on the River Eamont

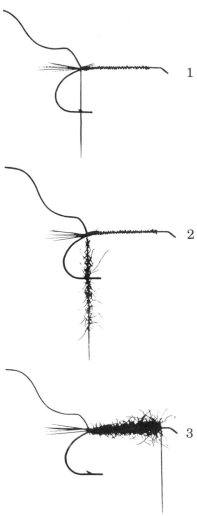

Gold Ribbed Hare's Ear. Materials: working silk—primrose; tails—four longish hairs from hare's ear; body—hare's fur dubbed on to working silk, ear fur nearest bend, longer, darker fur fibres from hare's body nearest eye of hook; body rib—oval gold tinsel or fine flat gold tinsel. (1) Tie in working silk behind hook eye, then wind it in close turns to start of bend. Tie in the four tail fibres (natural points extending approximately 1/8 in beyond bend) and the oval gold tinsel; (2) preferably pick or cut the fur from the ear and, after applying liquid wax sparingly to the working silk, dub the hare's fur (not too thickly) on to the waxed silk; (3) wind on dubbed fur. A second dubbing of fur may be necessary to complete the fly and this should include some of the longer darker hairs. Tie off behind eye

dimples if they are smutting, or the more pronounced but neat bulge when taking a dun, spinner, or perhaps a rising nymph just a fraction before it reaches the surface, will disclose the chosen lie of the fish for the particular circumstances. On rough rain-fed rivers, the rises are most easily seen on the smooth glides at the tails of the pools and the grayling do seem to have a particular liking for that type of flow. But when there is a hatch of fly in progress in the run at the neck of a pool, or in shallow streamy areas, the popply water may then be equally, even more, productive.

The question of the artificials to be used is equally uncomplicated. Only rarely are the grayling very selective about the patterns they will take and usually many of the popular trout and grayling flies will attract their interest equally well. Consequently there is seldom any reason why one cannot make the choice simply on the basis of the ease with which one can keep sight of the artificial on the water, and that is vitally important in practically all dry-fly fishing. Many anglers believe however, that size is very important and have more faith in 18s and 16s than anything bigger.

Next it will be found that grayling are not nearly so easily upset and put down as trout. Ordinarily you can stand in full view of the fish and get offer after offer without moving and perhaps take several grayling from the same place. Often individual fish will rise repeatedly to the same artificial and ultimately get hooked.

Finally, there is the subject of the fight of the grayling. Sometimes when the river is rather low and the water is relatively warm, they may not put up a very good performance, which is understandable for a winter fish. But in normal conditions, a very determined, unique kind of fight can be expected. The struggle is made directly against the restraint of the rod via the line and it is very unusual for a grayling to make a run at a tangent, in trout fashion, or to start thrashing about on the surface. The most characteristic fight of the grayling is to use the hook as a pivot and perform a gyrating motion, holding its great dorsal fin across the flow, putting a strain on the tackle far in excess of the more customary type of pull you get with trout. This can be very exciting indeed and may necessitate giving a lot of line. Then the fish has to be manoeuvred into a position where it cannot exploit the current to such telling advantage. It becomes a battle of wits, and when the fish is finally in the net, you feel you have really earned it.

Now, with this general picture in mind, let's get down to tactics. The equipment, of course, will be just the same as we have been using for the dry fly during the trout season—a light, accurate rod of, say, 8ft 6in, although in carbon it may be of 10ft or so, and a double tapered floating line, preferably no heavier than an AFTM no 5, and a leader of about nine foot tapered down to about 2½lb test.

We will consider the easiest set of circumstances first, when there is a hatch of duns in progress and good rises can be seen repeatedly in exactly the same spots. (Incidentally, when you

A grayling

4

5

have spotted your rise, always remember to note points of reference so that you will know the precise position when you come to cover it with the fly for you can easily be feet out with your judgment if you don't do this.)

The medium olive is very likely to be the fly on the water so a Gold-Ribbed Hare's Ear, Greenwell's Glory, Imperial, or a John Storey are some of the many popular patterns that could be trusted to do well and a size 16 would be the automatic choice of many grayling regulars.

Now that we are ready to start casting, some of the differences between grayling and trout fishing have to be considered. The normal habit of the grayling when feeding on the surface is to lie very close to the bottom, no matter how deep the water is. If the glide where the fish is lying is four feet deep, and we want to give it a chance to intercept the artificial without too much difficulty, we should aim to drift the fly over the lie from a distance of at least two yards upstream. As drag has to be kept down as much as possible, we must work out the best angle at which to drop the line on the water. Usually the easiest way to prevent too much drag is to cast as nearly straight upstream as possible—a course not favoured by most grayling fishers for two reasons. Firstly, the leader precedes the fly while it is within taking range and this is thought to put the fish off. Secondly, the grayling's mouth is rather small and it sucks the fly in more quickly than the trout, with the result that often the snout knocks the nylon and pushes the fly away when it ought to be going into the mouth. So, we will make the cast as squarely across as we dare in view of the problem of drag. Often this will

Gold Ribbed Hare's Ear (4) Wind on the tinsel tightly in open turns to eye and tie off. Remove surplus tinsel, add a whip finish and varnish the whip; (5) using a dubbing needle or similar instrument, pick out a few of the longer hairs at the eye end

work out nicely, but one cast will tell us what we want to know, and, fortunately, if drag does develop, it is unlikely to upset the grayling at all. The drill to follow then is to fish downstream to the grayling. From a position several yards upstream from the lie, we make a square cast which places the artificial three or four yards further across the flow in relation to the lie; then we make a biggish upstream mend that also draws the fly back across the surface to such a point that when we allow everything to drift downstream unchecked, the grayling will be covered fairly accurately by the artificial leading the nylon.

If we are lucky with the state of the light, background, etc, we shall be able to watch the fish rising through the water to intercept the artificial and it is intriguing to see how rapidly it makes contact and turns again to go down to the bottom. Often the rise will be almost vertical, and then the descent will be equally so.

Not infrequently the grayling will appear to ignore the artificial until it is some little distance downstream of the lie, but then, after making a neat turn downstream, it sets off, seemingly quite unhurriedly, catches up with the fly and takes it just as if it had always intended to do. But sometimes there is a rather unusual feature with a take of this kind. Normally, as mentioned above, the contact with the fly is a very rapid, unhesitating action, but when the fish follows the fly downstream, it occasionally examines it carefully at close quarters before taking hold.

In this context, when the grayling are feeding steadily on duns, and a fish takes the artificial, the best policy is to allow it to get its head down again before tightening, and then we shall be almost certain to get a good secure hook-hold in the upper jaw; but if the grayling is hooked in the corner of the mouth, it

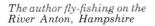

The author fly-fishing on the River Anton, Hampshire

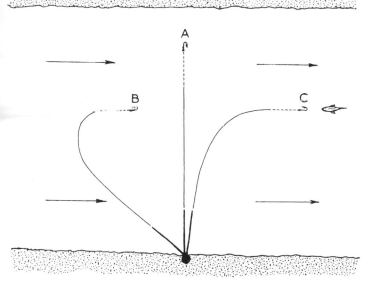

Drifting the dry fly downstream to a grayling: A—position of the fly after the first cast, made square or a little downstream; B—position of the fly after large upstream mend; C—position of the fly approaching the grayling

will probably tear away. And most grayling fishers hate to lose a fish, because often it does appear to put the others down. On a good day, you can hook, play and land several fish from exactly the same stand and the spectacular fight does not lessen the interest of the others in the vicinity, but once you have lost one, it is good policy to find another place without delay.

Good sport, however, does not necessarily depend on there being a noticeable hatch of fly. It is not at all uncommon to see beautiful grayling rising at short intervals up a stretch of river and not be able to spot just what they are taking. The different rods out will probably account for equally nice catches on widely differing dressings of artificials. The Treacle Parkin is a popular standard in the North in cases like this but a Grayling Steel Blue, Yellow Bumble, Green Insect, or any random choice may do equally well. As mentioned earlier, though, it does pay to pick out a pattern that is easily seen on the water against the prevailing tone of the background.

The most testing situation in dry-fly fishing is, as often as not, when the grayling are smutting. Then they may give a relatively meaty-looking dry-fly as good a welcome as on more promising occasions, but don't be too disheartened if everything we try is totally ignored (for a while). It is tempting then to put on the tiniest imaginable artificial, but it is extremely unlikely to be the right answer. And even if the grayling should eventually start to show interest in the minute artificial, they should be tried again with a normal fly before any firm assumptions are made. The chances are that there will have been a change of mood and a size 18 or 16 will then attract the fish.

Although opinions differ, most seasoned grayling fishers consider that when the fish are making these speculative rises to the floating artificial (as opposed to the take of a fish that is

111

Netting a grayling

feeding steadily on duns) the best policy is to tighten as quickly
as possible. If, as an experiment, you do nothing when the bulge
at the fly comes, but just keep your eye on the artificial, you will
see that, at the very most, it only disappears from view for a
fraction of a second—clearly that is the time you would have
had to hook the fish on that particular occasion. So, slack line
must be avoided and every effort must be made to keep direct
contact with the fly in order to minimise delay before the strike
is made.

There are some little dodges which may be useful when the
grayling are smutting. Probably the best of them is to give the
fly periodic little twitches of drag as it drifts down with the flow.
This is well worth trying in any dry-fly situation when the
artificial fails to attract attention from the grayling.

When there are patches of fine ripple on an otherwise smooth
area, all the dimples of smutting grayling will probably be
confined to the undisturbed water. If the artificial is then placed
right on the edge of the ripple, it may be taken quite freely even
though it had failed to do so elsewhere. Another ploy is to allow
the fly to reach a position judged to be vertically above the fish
and then draw it away smoothly at a speed that makes a very
slight furrow.

However, the difficult mood of the grayling when smutting is
not usually a very long lasting affair and happily it is often
followed by a spell of quite keen interest in any reasonably
well-presented artificial.

It is not at all uncommon, specially on the chalkstreams, for

112

response to the dry fly to continue non-stop throughout the day, and, what is particularly gratifying after the summer trouting, there is usually no dead period during the middle of the day. Even so, the evening always seems to come far too soon—no doubt a measure of how keenly the grayling have held your interest. And incidentally, the last little spell before it is too dark to see is often the best time to get an offer from any big specimen you may have marked down.

On breezy days it is often possible to have success with the dry fly in well sheltered spots but, in the absence of trees or high banks, it pays to resort to the wet fly. Now you can no longer say that grayling fishing is easy compared with trouting! The great problem is not attracting the grayling's interest but hooking them successfully, their takes being so rapid. This does not mean to say, though, that the prospects of a good basket of fish are poor: indeed, on average they will be fully as good as with the dry fly. The real crux of the position is that you miss such a high proportion of the offers which come that you don't feel very proud of your efforts. Also, the grayling will not keep on coming up to the wet fly repeatedly as they do to the floater and you have to move steadily down the pool all the time. Hence you need longer stretches of good water to go at if you are to be kept as busy with the wet fly as you can expect to be with the dry.

When duns are hatching, the appropriate wet trout patterns are usually very reliable. Popular favourites include Snipe and Purple, Snipe and Yellow, Orange Partridge and Gold Tinsel, and Rough-Bodied Poult. The Dark Needle is also worth a place on the cast. When no hatch is in progress, many anglers have more faith in the fancy grayling patterns: Red Tag, Grayling Witch, Bradshaw's Fancy, the bumble dressings probably being the best known. But the grayling are probably more fancy-free in this respect than the grayling fishers.

As winter approaches it is customary to use the North Country style leaded grayling flies—just the usual patterns but with a strip of thin lead sheet wrapped round the shank of the hook before the dressing is put on. This makes the flies fish only a few inches deeper but usually that is enough. Even in very cold conditions, something which requires the grayling to rise a little through the water makes them respond, and a non-floating line is recommended only for strong currents.

On chalkstreams where the location of grayling in their winter lies is known precisely, upstream fishing with weighted nymphs can be very successful, as also can the 'grayling lure' type of artificial, looking something like a large, off-white grub. But on rain-fed rivers where one may have to search large areas of suitable water before finding the fish, the traditional style of downstream fishing with the leaded flies is the most practical.

There are some grayling anglers who stick to the fly in one form or another throughout the winter, but some thoroughly enjoy the alternative method of trotting a bait. Traditionally this was practised in the North with little red worms—probably long before it was possible to purchase maggots from easily

113

accessible shops—and there is not the slightest doubt that gilt-tails and brandlings are greatly liked by the grayling in all classes of water. And normally small worms can be relied upon to give as good sport as it is possible to have. But there may be occasions when a sprinkling of maggots will rouse dormant grayling and bring them on to the feed. Also, in a very wide, deep pool where one may hope to catch a big specimen, steady light feeding with maggots may attract the fish to come nicely within reach of the float tackle but, as baiting swims with maggots can also bring the trout on to the feed, many clubs restrict bait-fishing to the use of small worms and feeding of any sort is forbidden. However, once the angler has got used to the practice of trotting the small worm and keeping on the move down the river with only short spells in any one spot, it is unlikely that he will have any regrets about regulations which rule out static fishing with maggots, especially in chilly weather when exercise is welcome.

The modern tackle available is excellent for long trotting: a good match rod of up to about twelve feet, in glass, or perhaps thirteen feet in carbon, can be used all day without fatigue. A very free-running centre-pin reel with a drum of about four inches, or a fixed spool reel should be loaded with fine line. For ordinary waters two to three pounds is the most suitable, but four to five pounds is not too strong for very big rivers where a heavier float can be used and thus prevent the thicker line from imposing any severe restriction on the distance that can be thrown or trotted.

Bob floats of various kinds have always been favoured because of their suitability for use in rough water as well as smooth flows. A very popular model is semi self-cocking with a balsa wood bob and antenna, and a long piano wire stem which acts as a keel and keeps the antenna upright in rough water and visible at very long distances.

Hooks from size 18 to 12 may be used according to the conditions. The leader is adjusted to allow the bait to travel a few inches from the bottom and, in order to reach that depth quickly, one lead shot is placed about 10–12in above the hook, and any others that may be needed are grouped a further 6in higher up.

If the small worm is hooked by the tiniest bit of skin at the back of the head, it wriggles very attractively and also reduces the risk of failing to hook the fish. Normally the grayling sucks in the whole worm at great speed and, on the strike, even the smallest hook pulls away from the worm and gives a good hook-hold in the top jaw.

Watching the grayling-float trot down the current, and expecting a bite at any moment, is considered by many anglers to be the next best thing to drifting the dry fly over a feeding fish. Indeed, some find it to be such a pleasant change that they are tempted to start trotting quite early in the season, long before the dry-fly fishing becomes at all problematical.

Bites are indicated in a variety of ways. In a fast flow the float will usually go straight under without any preliminaries, but in

*Fishing for grayling on the River
Test, Hampshire*

steadier water it may just stop, or even move sideways a little.
When the grayling are well on the feed, a quick strike
gives the best results but, just occasionally, the fish are a little
more hesitant and then it pays to give them fractionally more
time before taking action to set the hook.

The fight of a good grayling at the end of thirty yards or so of
fine line in a strong flow is an experience that no angler should
miss. It is good enough to tempt a large following to face the
harshest winter weather cheerfully and hold the grayling in
great esteem.

Other forms of bait-fishing may also be successful, particularly in special situations. Free-lining, laying-on and stretting, and
static and rolling legering may all give you a better chance of
catching a known big specimen than trotting but, on a seasonal
basis, there can be little doubt that trotting is by far the most
productive method of bait fishing.

No matter which style of fishing appeals to you the most,
however, making the acquaintance of the grayling will almost
certainly prove to be most gratifying.

115

15

Perch

Ken Taylor

The perch is a fish that is widely distributed throughout the British Isles. It is distinctive in appearance, good to eat and interesting to fish for. Due to the incomprehensible vagaries of the Record Fish Committee, the present record stands at 4 ¾ lb, but everyone knows that bigger fish than that have been caught, and that in the most favourable conditions perch may reach weights of 6lb or more.

Perch are catholic in their tastes, feeding on insects, molluscs, crustacea, various kinds of terrestrial and aquatic worms, and also on small fish. The larger they become, the greater is the proportion of small fish in their diet. However, perch never become so big as to refuse a fat worm and most of the big ones I have caught were taken using worms as bait.

As with most species of fish, the most important thing is to find where they are, if you want to catch them. Perch cannot swim nearly as fast as other predatory species like pike and trout, so they tend to hunt in packs surrounding smaller fish which can be grabbed as they try to break out from the encircling perch shoal. Or, where possible, perch lie in ambush among aquatic vegetation that suits their striped camouflage.

In rivers, the perch shoals tend to split up after spawning in the spring, and thereafter are found in ones and twos all along the river, taking advantage of whatever cover and food is available. In the bigger rivers, larger shoals may stay together in such areas as the slacks of weir-pools, loch cuttings and at the

A perch, well displayed (Angling Times)

tails of islands. In large lakes, where there is relatively little cover, larger shoals of perch remain together throughout the year, relying on encircling movements rather than attacking prey fish from ambush.

In the autumn, the dispersed shoals in the small rivers tend to form again, but having formed, they move up and down the river, seldom remaining long in one place. Probably having eaten most of the available food in one swim, the shoal moves to another and it may take a lot of walking and experimental fishing to locate them. The shoals in still waters are equally difficult to locate in summer, though in sustained heatwave conditions they tend to seek deeper water, sometimes as deep as 40ft, which to an angler familiar with the varying depths of the water he is fishing, may give a clue to their whereabouts. In early autumn perch also repair to greater depths, where these are available, in still waters.

In summer, the planktonic crustacea come to the surface after dark, and at first light are followed by small fry. These are then often attacked by perch, and a feeding spell at the surface ensues which may last as little as ten minutes or as long as an hour. This gives the angler a chance to catch some of the perch, using a very small dead-bait, a tiny surface plug, or a fish-imitating fly, fished an inch or two below the surface. If I am fishing at dawn for carp, tench or bream on a lake that I know holds big perch, I often have another rod ready which I can use if some big perch start chasing fry at the surface near me.

On rivers, I usually postpone my perch fishing until October, and long experience has shown that most are caught on dull but fairly warm days when it is hard to say whether what falls from the sky is mist or rain. On such days I can move from likely swim to likely swim, spending about twenty minutes trying each till I find one that holds perch. I look for a good bed of rushes, reeds or sedges adjoining a clean gravel bottom and moderate water flow, and having found such a place, I fish as close to the growth as possible.

This is done by using either a self-cocking float or one with most of the shot as close as possible to the bottom of the float. I

A 2¼lb river perch taken on a sinking plug (E. M. Grant)

Perch being transferred from the boat to the storage cage (Ron Osborn)

117

like the line to come away from the very tip of the float, usually via a piece of cycle-valve rubber, so that if a big fish runs among the rushes I can pull it back without the float catching-up. The purpose of having the bulk of the shot close to the float, is that this makes the float fly ahead of the bait when I cast in such a way that the float hits the rushes and falls close up to them. The baited hook, with perhaps a single BB shot about a foot from it, then swings under the float, close to the rushes where the perch are hiding. The current then moves the tackle down the swim and if perch are there, it seldom takes more than half-a-dozen casts before the bait, usually a worm, is taken. The drawback of this tackle arrangement is that the baited hook sometimes catches the line above the float when you cast, but that simply has to be accepted and when it occurs, you wind in and clear the trouble.

For some unexplained reason, there are days when the perch take only big worms and refuse small ones, and other days when only small worms are accepted. It is necessary to take sufficient worms of both sorts, and to try them in each swim before leaving it. There is no doubt that live-baits, like minnows or gudgeon, are very attractive to perch but when fishing close to rushes as I advise, they very often take the hook round a stem, or attract small pike, so I prefer to stick to worms—I doubt if I have ever failed to catch perch with them when I could have caught some with live fish.

Because of the proximity of rushes or similar growths, it pays to use tackle that is not too fine and I usually use a line of about 4lb to 5lb breaking strain with a no 6 hook for big worms, and a no 10 for small ones. A 6in length of peacock quill suffices as a float; it is easy to see and not very expensive to lose; one must expect to lose both hook and float occasionally when casting close to beds of reeds or rushes.

Still waters present different problems altogether, specially the larger ones. Those who fish trout reservoirs often catch perch, some of them very large, when fishing with big lures on sinking lines either from boats or the deep water near a dam. On many coarse fishing waters where no boats are available, the deep water holding the perch is accessible only by very long casting. On some waters the deeps cannot be reached except by boat.

In the 1950s, numbers of very big perch up to nearly 5lb were caught at Arlesey Lake in south Bedfordshire when it was found that they congregated in water about 40ft deep from September onwards. This deep water involved casting upwards of 70yd from the bank, since boats were neither available nor allowed. 10ft carp rods were used with 6lb monofil lines to throw weights, with a swivel at the narrow end. This swivel allowed any tangles that occurred in casting to come free, either as the tackle sank or when a perch ran off with the bait. This type of lead became known as the Arlesey bomb and is in very wide use nowadays, for all kinds of fishing.

About seventy perch from 3lb up to 4lb 13oz were caught in three seasons at Arlesey, all of them on big worms. No other bait

*Ken Taylor lands a 3lb Ouse
perch* (Richard Walker)

proved successful, though many others were tried. Fish as baits,
alive or dead, caught only eels or pike—no perch. It would,
however, be wrong to suggest that the same would necessarily
apply to other waters.

In those days, before it had been discovered that a large
fly-type lure fished at the right depth would catch big perch, no
such methods were tried, but it seems certain that they are
worth trying. It is not necessary to use fly-fishing equipment; a
fixed-spool reel, a suitable rod, a nylon line of 5lb to 6lb
breaking strain with a feather lure tied to the end, and enough
lead to give adequate casting range added, would probably
prove very effective. Perhaps the most effective lure for perch on
the trout reservoirs has been the Hanningfield lure, which
incorporates the recognition points of a very small perch. It is
dressed on two tandem no 8 hooks, with bodies of white
fluorescent wool ribbed with silver thread, and a wing of white
goat hair with speckled turkey feather fibres over it. The throat
hackle is a tuft of cobalt blue ahead of hot orange, and another
hot orange hackle is wound at the tail and clipped to size. On
one occasion this lure, which is about 2½in long, was fished on a
fast sinking fly-line at Hanningfield, and in a timed hour it

119

Gary Bostock of Peterborough with two drain perch (Angling Times)

accounted for twenty-three perch between 2lb and 3¼lb, plus a 4lb 6oz trout.

Unfortunately, perch are subject to a disease which, when it strikes a water, kills off upwards of 90 per cent of the perch, and recovery takes a long time. During the last quarter-century, many formerly excellent perch waters have been devastated in this way. Consequently the angler seeking big perch must treat accounts of captures in former years with a great deal of reserve. Nobody catches perch of 3lb and 4lb at Arlesey nowadays; nor can I catch perch of 2lb to 3½lb, a dozen at a sitting, from the Great Ouse as I could a few years ago.

It is difficult to predict how fast perch will grow, because the rate varies very much between individuals in the same water. One of the biggest caught at Arlesey had reached 4lb 13oz in between six to seven years; another caught in the same spot a few days later had reached only 3lb 6oz in between seven to eight years.

Generally speaking, the biggest perch usually come from alkaline rivers, and large alkaline lakes of considerable extent and depth, but now and then a big perch, 3lb and sometimes 4lb, is caught in a very small pond where most of the perch caught are around 2oz to 3oz each. I cannot advise you about how to select one perch that has reached good size from among thousands that have not, since even a 2oz perch can and will take the biggest worm you can find. The only hint I can offer is that if you know a pond that holds lots of little perch and has a stream or ditch feeding it, you should watch for the day when, after rain, a mud-stain is spreading from the stream mouth. Fish around the edges of this mud-stain with a fat worm and see what happens. My brother Fred did and caught a perch over 4lb. Not long afterwards, Dick Walker encountered similar conditions, remembered what Fred had done, tried it and caught another 4lb perch—but not, I must add, the same fish.

It is well known that perch, sometimes big ones, are taken accidentally on artificial lures like spoon-baits, plugs, etc, intended for pike. But this is not, in my experience, a very good way of fishing deliberately for perch, simply because pike then become nuisances and the proportion of perch to pike taken is very small indeed. The exception is when you fish a water that holds no pike but some good-sized perch. You can then use fairly light tackle, no wire traces, searching the water with a spoon or plug of modest size, covering much more water than you could with worm-baits in a given time. In coloured water especially, the vibrations of a suitable artificial may attract a perch that would have failed to find a static bait.

In some waters, perch will take dead-baits lying static on the bottom, but mostly this method is frustrated by either pike or

Two perch lie safely netted (Ron Osborn)

eels finding and taking the dead fish before the perch. Again, if it is known that neither eels nor pike are present, this may be a method worth trying.

As countless writers have pointed out, from Isaak Walton onwards, if a perch bites at all, he usually bites boldly, and at modest ranges it is not necessary either to strike very fast or delay the strike very long. An exception was found at Arlesey and some other waters where very long-casting was necessary; if the line ran out, it paid to let 7yd to 8yd go before striking, or many bites would be missed.

I should mention that at ranges of 50yd or more, if you cannot feel the fish after striking at a bite, wind in the slack and strike again, and repeat if necessary. The reason is that with a running lead like an Arlesey bomb, the fish may have run towards you, and for every yard he has run that way, you have to recover two yards before you tighten on him. Many big perch and other fish have been missed when anglers have been fishing at long range and have failed to connect with a biting fish in their first attempt at a strike.

Perch are not among the most powerful fighters in our range of fresh water fish, but they can give some very savage tugs that will reveal any tackle weakness or careless knots. In addition, they have mouths in which hook-holds are not always very secure. Therefore, play them with care and apply no more pressure than is necessary to keep them away from weeds, snags or other obstructions. When landed, do not mix them with other species in a keep-net, because their rough scales and prickly back fin can cause damage. Watch that back fin and also the sharp-edged gill covers when you remove the hook.

We have many species that grow bigger than perch, but when a perch of 3lb or more comes to the surface at the end of your line, I know of no more impressive or exciting sight in all angling, a view that is shared by fishing friends of mine who have taken salmon, carp, barbel, bream, trout and pike in double figures of pounds. One of the earlier angling writers said that if you ever caught a perch over 4lb, you could sell your tackle and commit suicide because you would have nothing left to live for. I wouldn't put it quite as strongly as that, but I do know that any angler who catches even a 3lb perch will never forget it, however long he lives.

Pike 16

Barrie Rickards

For as long as I've been fishing, about a quarter of a century, pike angling has been struggling to lift itself out of the nineteenth century. Not that there weren't men with good piking knowledge in the past—Bickerdyke is a witness to the contrary—but the tackle was cumbersome and the techniques necessarily complicated. There is no earthly reason why we should carry old tackle and techniques like *Fishing Gazette* floats, hauser-like wire traces, and 6ft long billiard-cue rods into the 1980s, for today there is a choice of materials that will replace everything that was bad in the old tackle.

What sort of rod should we be using? Even today you see all sorts and, although there is a case for 8ft rods for some spinning and for 11ft rods for certain specialist techniques, a rod of about 10ft is the best all-purpose length. I do all my spinning, as well as 90 per cent of my piking as a whole, with such a rod. The only open question is whether you need a fast or slow action rod, the fast one having a lot of tip action when you swing it about in the shop, whereas with slow action the rod bends throughout much of its length. An 11ft, fast-taper rod will throw a 2oz bomb and a *small* bait, and will reach up to 70yd by *firing* it with the top third of the rod. This is specialised piking. Normally the slow action ten-footer, capable of throwing 6oz comfortably, and with a slow, spring-like build-up of power during the cast, is the rod you need.

Rods made to these specifications can be bought either as glass blanks or as made-up rods. The two that I like are the 10ft stepped-up carp rods made by Olivers of Knebworth, and the East Anglian Rod Company's Piker 10 which I designed myself on the lines of the Olivers' rod. These rods have a test curve of around $2\frac{1}{4}$lb which means that a pull of $2\frac{1}{4}$lb is needed on the rod tip to put the upper part into a line at right angles to the lower half. Lighter rods, such as a Mark IV designed by Richard Walker will *play* any pike in the country, but they will cast only relatively light weights, say up to 2oz at the most. It is better to opt for one of the $2\frac{1}{4}$lb test curve rods, not only because they cast the weights needed in piking, but because they are nice tools for playing any pike over 4lb to 5lb. Rods with a test curve over $2\frac{1}{4}$lb are too near the poker-like rods of the past.

When it comes to reels, the choice is centre pins, with which I love to fish pike, and multiplier reels for heavy plug and spoon fishing; but a good fixed-spool reel will do all these things, I

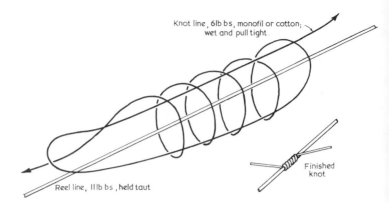

Knot line, 6lb bs, monofil or cotton; wet and pull tight

Finished knot

Reel line, 11lb bs, held taut

A Billy Lane knot

A sliding pike float

uphold, much more efficiently provided it will hold 150yd of 11−15lb breaking strain monofil line. The various Mitchell reels—Intrepids, Ryobi and Shakespeare—all have their good and bad points, but they are all good quality.

Two excellent monofil lines are the Intrepid Superline and Sylcast but there are several others. Plaited lines are popular in some quarters but they are a luxury unless all you do is plug fishing with a multiplier and lures of certain weights. But, if you want a flexible outfit, a number of spools of 11−12lb bs and 15lb bs dark monofil, will cover most eventualities. I usually dye Superline with hot Dylon simply because I don't like its pale colour. I tend to reject most traditional equipment: not because it is not a pleasure to use—it just isn't flexible enough, particularly for newcomers to pike fishing.

The next step is to set up a tackle arrangement suitable for piking. The system I favour, after fishing for pike in many different types of water, is the following: thread the dark 11−12lb bs monofil through the rod rings, then tie a stop-knot, usually called a Billy Lane knot, on the line at roughly the depth you intend fishing. Use 6lb bs monofil or thick cotton for this and tie the knot as shown above. Next slide on a small bead (see left) with a hole just big enough to take a line in the 10−18lb bs category. The stop-knot will stop the bead dropping below the depth you intend fishing while the bead in its turn will stop the 'pilot' float. The float is the third item to put on the line. I normally use a 1¼in diameter round slider, sold as a 'pilot' float, or a longer cigar-shaped slider which I make myself from balsa dowel.

A swan shot is placed on the line to stop the float sliding down over the trace swivel (see left). The position of the shot is important. For dead-baits it can be placed immediately on top of the trace swivel, but for live-baits (the tackle I am setting up is perfect for both) the swan shot needs to be 18in to 2ft above the swivel. I'll explain why below.

The trace is important and it should be wire, no matter what you are told to the contrary. I use 20lb bs sorrel-coloured cable such as Tidemaster. This wire is thinner than the monofil of the same breaking strain and I'd go as low as 12−15lb bs if I could get it. Single-strand wire is only suitable for dead-baiting. All

124

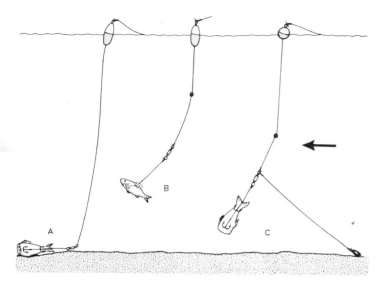

Float-legered dead-bait: when shallowed from position A, with swan shot moved, it produces at B suspended free-swimming live-bait or suspended free-drifting dead-bait. With paternostered link of 6lb bs monofil added it produces, at C, float-pater-nostered live- or dead-bait

my spinning traces and the snap-tackles for both dead- and live-baiting are about 12in long. The first step in making both is the same: pass the wire (about 2in from the end) twice through the swivel eye, lay it along the length of the trace, and then twist the two together. The wire should be supple enough for you to do this fairly easily with the fingers only. Close-twist it for about one inch, then trim off the loose end and finish the job off by coating the join with a little Araldite or Superglue.

For a spinning trace, repeat this process at the other end using a safety-pin style link swivel. For a snap-tackle, slide on to the trace a Ryder Hook (size 6 or 8), wrapping the trace wire once round the shank of the hook before running it out of the small eye near the bends of the hook; then fix a no 6 or 8 treble hook on the end of the trace in the same way as the swivel was fixed at the top end. The business end of this snap-tackle is shown alongside a herring in the plate (right).

A herring dead-bait with snap-tackle

By setting the stop-knot slightly over-depth, a dead-bait can be laid on the bottom as shown in A above. Alternatively the tackle can be shallowed and fished off the bottom with a suspended dead- or live-bait (B above) so that it drifts with the current be it river flow or wind drift on a lake. Thirdly, a paternoster link can be added (C above) by tying an appropriate length of 5–6lb monofil to the trace swivel at one end and an appropriate lead weight at the other. These three different styles, which are effective for piking on a great variety of waters, are accomplished in this way with one basic tackle rig.

Imagine how quickly one can switch from laying-on a dead-bait to paternostering a live-bait! If you wish to spin, simply cut the line above the swan shot, take off the float (it will drop off) but leave on the bead and stop-knot in case you change back again to bait-fishing. The stop-knot is useful for spinning because when it clicks through the top ring it tells you exactly how far the lure is from the bank. These changes are effectively made in seconds, and the rigs are superb for catching pike. The

125

vast bulk of my 600 plus 10lb fish, were caught with them.

These are the main items of tackle but every pike angler carries in addition some ancillary equipment. Umbrellas, chairs and whatever makes for comfort are personal choice but there are some essential pieces. You need a big landing net; any very large, modern, triangular net will do, but I prefer a 30in diameter round frame. This can be made cheaply with a length of ¼in diameter steel rod, cut into three pieces and put together by a wrought-iron worker who will also weld a ⅜in BSF bolt to screw into your landing-net head.

I also carry a rucksack for housing everything else I need such as:

spare tackle for trace making	a variety of floats
a snap-tackle holder in a milk-tin	knife
	barometer
frozen bait	some plugs
various leads	artery forceps
spinners and spoons	spare spools and reels
scissors	binoculars
camera	Salter spring balance
weighing net of lightweight curtain material	soap solution for sinking floating lines
mucilin floatant	an injecting needle for blowing up dead-baits
a spool of paternoster line in 5—6lb bs	silver paper and spare line spools as indicators
PVA or its equivalent	

When to fish for pike is the next question. Summer piking is good sport once you get used to the weed-beds, and spinning is then productive. I rate the various techniques in order of preference as: live-baiting, wobbled on spun baits, artificial baits, static dead-baits. In winter, the order is: live-baits, static dead-baits, wobbled or spun baits, artificial baits. My own favourite method is static dead-baiting, plugs and spoons coming next, but neither of these is as effective as live-baiting.

Particularly in winter, I like to fish from dawn until lunchtime. Pike can feed at any time but on any one water there is a 'feeding pattern' which can be observed by fishing from dawn until dusk, or half days during the early and later periods of the season. As a rule, mid-morning is a good time in summer, in the autumn around dawn, and in winter nearer mid-day. Often a feeding pattern will change quite suddenly after several weeks. Of course, there is always the odd chance of catching a fish at any time, particularly in the first half of the day but successful piking doesn't depend on the odd chance.

For picking up the feeding pattern use two rods, one with live-bait and one with dead-bait, perhaps even casting a spoon around and between the two. Experience has taught me that when the barometer is rising pike feed actively on live-baits, and even lures; and when it is falling they are likely to stop, but will take dead-baits when the barometer reaches the bottom of

(right) Author returning 31½lb pike, caught on a mackerel head in Fenland drain

126

This 29lb 10oz pike was taken on a suspended dead roach

its fall and stays there. There are several other factors to consider—sun, wind, rain, water-colour and water-strength—but these are all relatively unimportant.

First choose a water with pike in it! One winter I spent a couple of days fishing a water without any! The local and national angling press will tell you when they are to be found. But where to fish on a particular water?

There are certain swims likely to hold a pike or two, particularly small pike, such as where a feeder stream runs in, near a gravel bar or close to a thick weed-bed. But most waters have concentrations of pike in quite small areas, not in shoals but gatherings. In Fenland, on Loch Lomond or on a large gravel pit, you may find dozens of pike over 10lb holed up in a 20yd by 30yd area. They may stay there for several years using it as a base *most* of their time. In such hotspots (as I call them) they are not necessarily actively feeding but will respond briefly on most days either to dead- or live-baits. On occasion, all the fish will go on a feeding spree, ranging far and wide, particularly during a high barometric pressure, but as a rule a hotspot can be identified as much by the scarcity of pike elsewhere in the water as by the fish caught in it.

Hotspots can be found by fishing a water in company for several weeks, by talking to the local bailiff or anglers, and by one person trying a day in each swim. It is crucial in piking to identify these feeding patterns and places and it is all part of the sport.

Striking a run with the simple outfit I have described is not difficult; only remember the hooks and float should be small and runs are usually positive. I recommend baits in the 2oz to 6oz range (whether dead or alive) for then a strike can be made immediately the pike is running steadily whether it has

Close-up! (below) *R.V. Righyni fishing for grayling* (J.B. Lloyd)

*Salmon fishing on the Tweed below
Peebles, late autumn* (Arthur
Oglesby) ; (below) *waiting for a
chub to bite* (Kenneth Seaman)

(opposite) *Barrie Rickards is not
apologising for this pike* (Barrie
Rickards)

(above) *Circumventing snags for chub* (Kenneth Seaman); (below) *a perfect setting for chalk stream trout* (Gordon Mackie)

*Richard Walker in his study. Not
all the books in his library are on
angling* (Angling Times)

(above) *Unmistakably – a barbel*
(Frank Guttfield) *and* (below) *an
equally recognisable zander*
(Barrie Rickards)

(opposite) *Not necessarily the
biggest carp caught by Kevin
Clifford* (Kevin Clifford)

(overleaf) *Shore fishing can be
enjoyed in settings often as
beautiful as those of rivers and
lochs* (Leslie Moncrieff)

Graham Marsden lands a bream
(Graham Marsden)

(opposite) *Leslie Moncrieff makes his cast* (Leslie Moncrieff)

*Worm fishing on a flooded River
Spey, Manse Pool, Castle Grant*
(Arthur Oglesby)

(opposite) *This chub is being
carefully placed in the keep-net*
(Frank Guttfield)

*Leslie Moncrieff and friend
satisfied with their catch* (Leslie
Moncrieff)

(opposite) *A Hardy craftsman
checking the alignment* (J.L. Hardy)

Frank Guttfield jr with his roach
(Frank Guttfield)

travelled 3ft or 10ft. Wind up rapidly until you feel the fish, then give one hard, sweeping strike upwards or sideways. Keep the rod very firmly bent into the fish for the first few seconds to give yourself time to assess the coming battle, and this also helps to get an unbalanced fish a little off the bottom.

I always recommend planning where to land the fish before striking. Lay the net down by your netting-hand and sink it in the water before drawing the fish over it. I never play out a fish until it is tired but net it as soon as possible so that I can return it fresh. Let the fish sink deep into the net, bundle the net around it, and lift it well clear of the water on to a soft, grassy piece of bank before unhooking.

Unhooking a pike is a straightforward procedure if you do it like this: get the fish well clear of the net, lay it on its back and then sit *gently* astride it—if you wish covering it first with a soft cloth. With a gloved left hand take hold of the lower jaw and pull; the mouth will open easily and you can use artery forceps in the right hand to free the hooks.

The hooks should be inside the mouth, perhaps in the scissors, but not deep in the back of the throat if you have struck in the manner I have outlined. Occasionally, in spite of your care, the hooks will be in the soft tissue at the top of the throat, and in that case use the forceps through the gill cover. Grip the shank of the hook, reverse it sharply, and it will almost always pop clear quite easily, the hooks being smaller than are normally used. If you have a companion, everything is a little easier as he can hold the line taut until you ask him to slacken off a little.

I have tried to give practical instructions on tackle, and on where, when and how to fish, but there is much more to piking than that. It is the little wrinkles which you will learn with time that count. Above all there is excitement when a battling pike upsets your best-laid plans and calls the tune, and the pleasure of sharing a good day with like-minded companions in wild and beautiful countryside; but these delights are only enjoyed to the full if your tackle and techniques are sound.

A 20¼ lb pike taken on a float-legered sardine

145

17 Roach

Richard Walker

Although its popularity has waned somewhat during the last half-century, the roach remains Britain's most sought-after fish, probably because there are few waters where it is not found. It can live in almost any water that is not too polluted, from a farm pond or canal to great salmon rivers like the Tweed and Wye. Extremely prolific, the size it attains varies considerably from one water to another. Generally speaking, a roach of one pound is a big one, a two-pounder is a monster and anything bigger would have been thought worthy of a glass case in the days when stuffed fish were popular. The only roach ever caught weighing over 4lb was taken in June and was carrying about 12oz of spawn; but a roach of 4lb in good condition remains a possibility. I once caught a roach of 3lb 4oz from the River Beane in Hertfordshire that was very emaciated, but that may well have weighed over 4lb when in its prime; the length was 19in.

The food of roach varies; the smaller specimens are very catholic in their feeding, but as they grow, it would seem that ample supplies of two food items, silk weed and snails, are

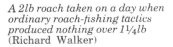

A 2lb roach taken on a day when ordinary roach-fishing tactics produced nothing over 1¼lb (Richard Walker)

needed if the fish are to reach large size.

Because roach are found in such diverse environments, angling methods have to be equally diverse. The equipment and methods that succeed on one water might be quite useless on another. Consequently, one could write a fat book about roach fishing; indeed, there are several already. I shall therefore deal here only with what I think most anglers are most interested in, which is catching the bigger roach.

Clearly, the first step is to discover where big roach are. Because roach populations are susceptible to factors like pollution, predation, disease and over-fishing, it is impossible to provide a list of waters likely to hold big ones. A lake or river that held numbers of two-pounders a year or two ago may hold none today. A water that has not yielded big roach for generations may produce several next year. The would-be catcher of big roach must therefore keep alert for reports and information that may help him to find waters holding the fish he seeks.

Having found a suitable water, there are three things about big roach that have been learned from the combined long experience of many successful roach fishers, that can be of great assistance:

1 Big roach feed most freely from approximately one hour before until one hour after sunset.

2 A bait lying still on the bottom is more successful than one suspended above the bottom or moving with the current.

3 While there are hundreds of different baits that have accounted for big roach, it is rare to find roach anywhere that refuse either bread, in one form or another, or large worms. This means that if no roach are caught on either of these baits, it is unlikely, though not impossible, that a change to any other bait will succeed. Failure is much more likely to be caused by some other factor.

All these things are generalisations; there are no inflexible rules, but if the angler bases his methods on probabilities rather than possibilities, he is much more likely to catch the fish he wants. I have caught many hundreds of roach over 2lb in weight; and the majority, indeed the great majority, were caught on either bread or worms, fished lying still on the bottom, between an hour before and an hour after sunset; and I think it likely that most other successful roach fishers will have had the same experience.

In choosing tackle, we do not have to pay much attention to the fighting powers of roach, which even in the case of large specimens is not very great, nor do roach seem intelligent enough to take much advantage of weeds or snags to escape. We do however have to consider physical factors, of which the most important is distance. A powerful rod may be needed to obtain enough casting range. For example, on the Tring group of reservoirs, it may be necessary to cast from 40yd to 70yd, using a lead weighing as much as an ounce, or a loaded swim feeder of

Gary Hodson fishing for roach on the north bank of the River Nene

147

Jim Clarridge at Swanholme Lakes, Lincoln, swings in a small roach from this fancied swim (Bill Goddard)

similar weight. This will involve a rod with a test-curve rating of at least 1lb with, of course, a suitable fixed-spool reel and a running line of about 5lb breaking strain which is twice as strong as is needed to land a hooked fish but only barely strong enough to withstand the forces involved in the long-casting.

For shorter ranges, a wide choice of suitable rods is available, usually described as 'match rods'. Nearly all are of fibreglass but carbon-fibre will certainly supplant glass for the best roach rods, possibly by the time these words are in print. It allows important savings in weight and reductions in thickness and therefore air-resistance. A rod of from 11ft to 13ft, the usual length for a roach rod, can be tiring to hold and difficult to control in a stiff cross-wind if made of fibreglass, and therefore of large diameter in cross-section.

The roach fisher will, if he wants to cover every sort of water that holds big fish, need at least two rods, one of 10ft to 12ft and able to cast an ounce a long way, and the other from 11ft to 13ft, nice and light, with a top delicate enough to cast light tackle and to smooth out the plunges and jerks of a hooked fish.

For long-casting, a fixed-spool reel is needed, and if this has two or three interchangeable spools loaded with lines of different strengths, let us say 5lb breaking strain, 3½lb bs and 2lb bs, it will serve for every circumstance when large roach may be found.

The popularity of match-angling has encouraged the use of ultra-fine lines, tiny hooks and small baits which, however necessary for the purpose of winning matches, are not needed for catching large roach. Early in this century J. H. R. Bazley and his fishing friends caught hundreds of roach of 2lb and over at Hornsea, on size 6 hooks baited with big lobworms. I have many times caught roach between 2lb and 2lb 14oz by accident when carp fishing with big worms as bait, on hooks as large as no 2. Even when using bread-crust, there is no need to use a smaller hook than a no 12 and I usually choose a no 10. Spade-end hooks are inexpensive and entirely adequate.

Whenever the nature of the water makes it possible, float fishing is preferable to legering. Remember, we have to fish a static bait to catch big roach consistently, and if the current is too fast to allow a float to be anchored, then we shall have to leger; but wherever possible, the float should be used. It is seldom necessary to use an elaborate float or to carry a great variety of types and sizes. On only one river, and in only one swim on that river, have I ever needed a more elaborate float than a simple bird or porcupine quill for fishing in daylight. The exception involved some very big roach that lived in deep slack water on the River Beane; these fish would spit out the bait very quickly if they felt the weight of the shot, so I used a float with a balsa body and a very long, thin antenna, set so that when the single shot was on the bottom only the tip of the antenna showed above the surface. A fish could therefore lift the shot some 8in before feeling the weight.

In rivers, the big roach will usually be found in slack or slow water at the edge of a faster current, and it is necessary to choose a combination of float and shot that, when cast into the faster water, will swing and settle at the edge of the slack area. The buoyancy of the float and the weight of shot needed will vary according to the depth and the speed of the faster water. You don't want the tackle so heavy that it holds bottom in the fast current, or so light that it swings too far into the slack.

In lakes, locating big roach is very difficult. The experience of other anglers can help, as can plumbing depths and discovering areas of bottom that are gravelly or sandy rather than muddy. In summer, bright green silkweed on the bottom attracts big roach, and there you should fish bread-crust baits, which do not sink into the weed; this applies to every kind of water where roach may be found. However, whereas in rivers roach stay in small areas, in lakes they cruise about in shoals, following the same track day after day, as do bream. Unfortunately, they seldom provide similar indications of their whereabouts. Bream conveniently send up bubbles, stir up mud and often roll at the surface. Roach do relatively few of these things, though now and then a fish will break surface and reveal its position. It must be realised however that unless an angler is very lucky indeed, he must expect to do a good deal of investigation and fruitless fishing before he locates shoals of big roach in a large lake or reservoir.

Perhaps the easiest kind of water in which to find big roach is the artificial lake, usually constructed on a large estate in the eighteenth century, through which a small stream runs. Whenever the flow of this stream increases after rain, the roach will usually be found either close to the inflow, or to where the lake narrows at the outflow, or both. In larger rivers, big roach haunt the vicinity of underwater lily leaves, the pale green fragile sort that some anglers call 'cabbage patches'. These leaves are attractive to water snails, which is probably why roach are usually there.

To encourage roach to feed on whatever the angler chooses for bait, ground-bait is useful, but there are two vital points to remember about that. Never put in ground-bait unless you are

Safely in the landing net—a good roach

certain that it is in the right spot and that you can place your hook-bait amongst it. Always err on the side of too little rather than too much ground-bait; roach have small mouths and small stomachs and are very easy to overfeed.

When the bait is bread, all that is necessary for ground-bait is white bread, soaked and mashed up, the water squeezed out and the mash kneaded into balls. The faster and deeper the water, the stiffer the ground-bait should be. On waters where the roach prefer worms, half-a-dozen worms can be cut up and thrown in from time to time. For hook-bait, cubes of crust cut from the bottom and sides of a tin loaf can be used, either cut or damped and pressed between boards under a heavy weight. Alternatively, crumb from a fairly new white loaf can be pinched on the shank of the hook, taking care not to obscure the point. With bread baits, one tightens directly a bite is observed, but with big worms, it is better to wait till the float goes well under or sails away or, when legering, until a foot or more of line has been taken.

Often the presence of other species of fish will decide whether bread or worms are used; small perch, ruffe or eels will, if present in numbers, make fishing with worms virtually useless. While these two baits are usually all that one needs, there are circumstances when the large roach have learned to avoid them through having been caught and released. If this is suspected, there are many other baits that can be tried, such as sweet-corn; cornflake damped until tough and flexible; cubes cut from ox blood poured into a tray and allowed to congeal; cubes cut from cheese, preferably Dutch or Cheddar; pieces of fresh water mussel; cubes of cooked fat bacon; and many more. I must stress that if it is big roach you want to catch, many of the more generally accepted roach baits like maggots, casters, stewed wheat, tares, elderberries and pearl barley, are inferior. They may and often do catch large numbers of small and medium-sized roach, but only rarely do they account for large specimens. For those, they impose a positive handicap, being easily taken by smaller and more agile fish, often before they reach the bottom where the big ones feed.

Some waters, among them the River Kennet and parts of the Hampshire Avon, the Test and certain stretches of the Great Ouse, can be almost infuriating, in that one may start fishing a very promising-looking swim and, within no more than a quarter-of-an-hour, catch a big roach: 'Ah,' one thinks, 'I was right, this is a good roach swim and I am going to make a fine catch of big roach!' Four hours later, the second roach is caught and it weighs 5oz. It seems that here and there, solitary big roach take up abode and few other roach (and they only small) are in the same area. It does not pay to persist in any area after catching a big roach, if no more are forthcoming within half-an-hour. Even on lakes, a travelling shoal will come round again in less time than that.

For static float fishing, or 'laying-on', there is no need to distribute the shot; simply bunch them at the right distance from the hook, and remember that in order to move the float, a

(right) *Eric Anthill who, with Don Bridgewood, took a catch of 150lb of roach in three and a half hours on the River Sneum at Allerup near Esbjerg, Denmark. Running to just over the pound, the fish all fell for maggot* (Don Bridgewood)

fish has to move all the shot. With bread baits, particularly crust, the shot need be only a few inches from the hook, in which case the bite will usually be indicated by the float rising in the water. With worm or other heavier baits, leave about a foot between hook and shot. If the bottom is of soft mud or silkweed, attach the shot to a separate link, as long as you think the mud or silkweed is deep.

For legering at modest ranges, the most useful tackle is the swan shot leger, but at long range the streamlined Arlesey bomb is better. In running water, the best way of detecting bites on leger tackle is by touch: hold the rod between forearm and thigh as you sit comfortably with thighs horizontal, grasping the rod at the reel. In this way you can avoid strain on the wrist. Hold the line delicately between butt ring and reel with the fingers of the other hand and feel for bites. You can, if you like, support the rod in a rest, but unless you hold it and the line, you will miss many bites, the fish feeling the resistance of the rod top and ejecting the bait.

In still waters, however, it is very difficult to hold the rod and keep constantly in touch with the end tackle. It is therefore better, in these conditions, to rely on some kind of butt indicator of which there is a wide choice. Swing tips and other rod top indicators are effective enough in showing bites but unfortunately they reduce casting range very considerably.

Catching roach of modest size may involve a wider range of baits and methods than fishing for the larger specimens. In river fishing, trotting float tackle down the current—using lines as fine as 1½lb or 2lb bs and small hooks from size 16 to 20, baited with maggots, casters or hemp-seed—will produce greater numbers of roach, and probably other species like dace and chub as well, but it will not catch many big roach. In still waters and canals too, this system of very fine tackle used with a sensitive float, small baits, and usually slow sinking baits with the lowest shot a long way from the hook, will yield catches that are large numerically. But this is of interest mainly to the match-angler or the pike fisher who wants small roach for bait.

The angler who wants big roach will do best with good sized baits: worms, bread or perhaps sweet-corn, anchored so that they remain still on the bottom, in the right place and at the right time.

The British Record roach of 4lb 1oz caught from a lake near Nottingham by Richard Jones

Rudd

Ken Taylor

Many anglers would agree that the rudd is the most beautiful of all British fresh water fish. Its shining metallic scales are silver in small specimens, brassy in larger ones. The under-fins and tail are blood-red, though there is a variety in which these fins are golden yellow. The record stands at 4½lb, but a two-pounder is a big rudd, and a three-pounder a monster.

Rudd are sometimes found in slow rivers but the species is primarily a still water one. Roach and rudd can breed together to produce fertile offspring and it seems likely that both species stem from a common ancestor in the evolutionary past, which diverged into two present species, one adapted to river and the other to still water life. Part of this adaptation is to be seen in the mouth; that of the rudd is adapted to surface feeding, whereas that of the roach is clearly better for bottom feeding.

Part of a bag of 31 rudd taken by Ed Foottit on free-lined flake. Average weight between 1lb 11oz and 1lb 12oz; total weight over 50lb. Included in this bag are fish of 2lb and 2lb 2oz (Dr Ed Foottit)

Sean Duffy with two rudd caught on the River Shannon at Lanesboro

This gives the angler the clue to fishing methods, for while rudd will at times pick a bait from the bottom, they feed much more often at or near the surface, specially when water temperature exceeds about 60°F.

In lakes where they are plentiful, shoals of them patrol the edges of beds of reeds, rushes, water lilies or weeds. Often enough they can be seen breaking the surface; if not, they may usually be induced to do so by throwing bread-crust, puffed wheat or other suitable buoyant ground-bait on to the water in such a manner and place that it drifts up against the weeds or reeds where the rudd are thought to be. When the fish are seen accepting these free offerings, float tackle can be used, set very shallow, to present a baited hook in the right area.

Here I must emphasise that, while rudd are bold and positive biters, they are easily frightened and perhaps the most important factor in making a good catch is the avoidance of anything that may alarm the fish. This usually means fishing at long range, specially when fishing from a boat, which on some reed or rush-fringed waters is almost essential. The angler who can approach the haunts of the rudd, moving his boat and lowering his anchor or mooring weight with great stealth, so as to be able to cast 30yd or more downwind to where the fish are, can catch great numbers of fish. The careless fellow who splashes his oars, drops anchor with a rattle of chain and a

154

thump on the bottom, who fishes at 10yd to 15yd, thumps his feet on the bottom of the boat and knocks out his pipe on the gunwale, will have very meagre catches.

Where rudd are accessible from the bank, it is often possible to fish at shorter range, but the necessity of keeping the fish in ignorance of the angler's presence remains. In either case, it pays to exercise restraint and to wait for a few minutes after landing a fish, before making another cast.

When float tackle is used, a rod of 12ft to 13ft, of the kind usually described as a match-rod, will be suitable; the kind that flexes all through is better than the sort where bending is mainly confined to the top 3ft. The more flexible rod casts better and is less likely to break the tackle on the strike or when dealing with a big fish. Fortunately, rudd are not fish of great power, nor are they very tackle-shy, so lines of about 3½lb to 5lb breaking strain can be used. Neither is it necessary to use tiny floats, light shotting or very small hooks; the need to cast around 30yd and to see the float clearly at that distance means a float able to carry a couple of swan shot, with a top that can be easily seen. Because long-casting is so often necessary, choose a fixed-spool reel.

A rudd safely hooked

An alternative is fly-fishing, or at any rate the use of fly-fishing tackle. A rod of about 9ft carrying a no 7 floating fly-line, preferably of a dark colour, will allow a good fly caster to reach rudd at 25yd to 30yd. Rudd will often come freely to a Gold Ribbed Green Nymph, about size 10 or 12, drawn steadily through the water. Early in the season, a no 8 Polystickle will also often catch big rudd; but the fly-fishing equipment can also be used to cast a bunch of four or five maggots on a no 10 hook, with the advantage that there is far less disturbance when the bait arrives among the fish than there would be with float tackle. A catapult can be used to project loose maggots to the fish; bites are indicated by the floating line being drawn across the surface. If difficulty in seeing this is encountered, a little cork ball can be threaded on the fly-line, painted in flourescent orange and about ¼in in diameter; 6ft is long enough for the leader.

Rudd are not hard to please and will take most ordinary baits including worms, maggots, bread-crust and bread-paste. There is no need to seek exotic baits; if you cannot catch rudd with one of the above, either you are not putting your bait where the fish are, or else you have alarmed them in some way, or they are taking cover from predators, usually pike. In waters where pike are numerous, you may find that the rudd keep right in the reeds or water lilies and you have to fish close up against these growths. In that case, use a float with a valve rubber at each end, as I recommend for perch in similar circumstances, with most of the shot right up against the float. Cast to hit the reeds so that the baited hook swings down and under the float.

In these conditions, the rudd usually stay in the reeds till the sun sinks below an angle of about 10° to the surface. After that they come out into more open water. By that time your float may be hard to see; use one with a bright Betalite top if you can

A fine swim for rudd and tench

afford one. Alternatively, you can try fishing a floating fly, using your fly-fishing tackle. A big White Moth or Brown Sedge will attract rudd; cast it out, then draw it slowly across the surface. Rudd like a moving bait, and if you do not have fly-fishing tackle, you can use float tackle and detect bites even when it is too dark to see the float, by drawing the tackle slowly towards you and feeling for the bites, using a bait that does not easily come off the hook, like a worm or a bunch of maggots or, perhaps best of all, a piece of bacon rind boiled to make it soft and flexible. That will cast for fish after fish. But do not be surprised, when you are drawing float tackle across the surface after dark, if either the bait or even the float itself is attacked by a pike or a perch.

In winter, rudd largely abandon their surface or near-surface feeding and move into deeper water, where they are hard to locate. The best chance is when the wind is blowing towards the deeper part of a lake, specially if it comes from anywhere between south and west. Use float tackle if the waves allow it; a float with a long antenna fitted with a fluorescent orange sight bob at the top will remain steady and visible in quite rough water. If you keep the bulk of the shot well down towards the hook and set the tackle for the right depth, the undertow will move the tackle away from you, into the wind. If the depth of water demands it, use a sliding float. Ground-bait need only be thrown in quite close to the bank; if you use a fairly slow sinking mixture like soaked mashed bread and sausage rusk, that friendly undertow, in a good breeze, will take it out into the lake

156

and your tackle will follow it, so that long-casting into the teeth of the wind is not needed.

Not only in winter, but also during sustained heatwave conditions in summer, you may have to fish deep for rudd, though it takes much higher surface temperatures to put them deep than it does for most other fish. However, if they show no sign of surface activity in very hot weather, you may suspect that they have sought the depths and fish accordingly.

Carp fishers will know from experience that after dark in summer, rudd will come in very close to the bank to eat floating bread. To the carp fisher rudd are nuisances, but a scaled-down version of the carp fisher's tactic of margin fishing can be used to catch big rudd with deadly effect. This tactic consists simply in dangling a hook baited with bread-crust on to the suface directly below the rod top, the rod being set in rests. Fish with the wind in your face, preferably over or through marginal rushes, reeds or tall grass. Free offerings of crust are thrown into the water to attract the fish. For carp, the crust on the hook, usually size 2, is as big as a matchbox; for big rudd the hook can be size 8 or 10 and the crust about ½in across. You must allow some slack line or the fish will suck the crust off the hook. You must not be surprised if the large rudd that sucks in your crust turns into a monster tench or carp after you have hooked it. You may even land it, since in this method the fish cannot see the line and you may therefore use a strong one, 6lb or even 8lb breaking strain. Indeed I would advise you to do so whenever you fish for rudd in a water that also holds tench or carp.

There it is then: rudd, even big ones, are not hard to catch provided you take reasonable care not to frighten them, and if you are willing to spend time finding out where they are. The best specimens live in lakes where the water is very clear and there are plenty of reeds, rushes, or water lilies, and many shallow areas. Don't expect to find outsize rudd in waters that are always muddy.

A fine rudd, taken from a Lincolnshire lake

19 Tench

Fred J. Taylor

General behaviour and habitat

Though mainly lovers of still or slow-moving waters, tench turn up in the most remarkable places from time to time. Swift-flowing rivers like the Avon, Test and Stour have occasionally produced them, but they are the exception, not the rule.

They are reputed to be lovers of mud and, in many waters, where there is a choice, the soft-bottomed areas are those most likely to make good tench swims. But tench can also be found over hard sand, gravel and stony bottoms—perhaps because food is acquired there more easily. They appear to be equally at home in bulrush-beds, where the bottom is usually gravel, and in soft weed-beds where there is much routing, delving and water discoloration when they decide to forage.

Tench usually begin to show in late May or early June when they become active again after a winter of so-called hibernation. I do not believe that tench hibernate in the true sense of the word; winter catches, both accidental and intentional, have proved that they do not stop feeding altogether during the winter months. They *do* slow down, however, and in most waters they remain true summer fish. To all intents and purposes, and with few exceptions, tench fishing ceases to be worthwhile after the first frosts have appeared.

The fish themselves are often at their peak of activity and feeding enthusiastically by the end of May—at which time we must stand by and watch in frustration until our season opens on 16 June. Experiences with Irish tench, which enjoy no close season, suggest that the biggest bags and the biggest specimens are likely to be taken well before our own season opens.

There are years when our tench have already spawned by 16 June and, though somewhat thinner, are back in good fighting trim. Other years, they remain full of spawn well into July—which accounts for many of the exceptionally heavy early-season tench reported. Just once in a while, a general spawning exodus takes place on 16 June itself and immediately puts paid to expectations of big fish or big catches that day, for then tench simply will not be tempted.

They vary in size and behaviour from water to water. As with other species, some waters hold enormous fish, others hold good quality fish, and there are some where two-pounders are rare and the average less than half that weight. These last-

Frank Clarke with a fine pair of
tench from the River Lee Crown
Fishery

mentioned waters offer ideal spawning facilities, little predation and insufficient food to sustain their populations. Not
surprisingly these are the easiest of tench to catch.

If we divide the tench waters of this country into two basic
categories, those with soft mud bottoms and those with hard
gravel bottoms (there are many in-betweens, of course), it is
easier to discuss the accepted feeding behaviour of the fish.
Generally speaking, the tench in traditional soft-bottomed lakes
dig for their food which is, in the main, small, often minute
forms of larvae, molluscs, leeches and such like. Those in
hard-bottomed gravel pits and reservoirs tend to pick up their
food more easily, and snails, small mussels, caddis grubs
(complete with house) and many other larger items of food
provide the bulk of their diet. When tench feed, bubbles come to
the surface but they are smaller, more widespread and certainly
more pronounced when the feeding is taking place in or over
thick mud. In the main tench are bottom feeders. Traditionally
they are expected to feed at dawn and dusk, and they are said to
prefer big baits such as lobworms or paste lying hard on the
bottom.

There is much to be said for this simple and relaxed style of
fishing. Tench are not lovers of strong light, and it is reasonable

155 tench, totalling 600lb, netted in the bottom lake and about to be liberated in the top lake, Burton Constable (Roy Shaw)

Chas Severn of Stonebridge Park, North London, landing a tench (Ron Osborn)

to expect a big bait to be taken boldly during the early morning hours before they retire to the shade of the weed-beds, lily-pads or rush-beds as the sun grows higher.

Any angler who, having cleared a swim of weed, has baited it thoroughly with proprietary ground-bait and bread, will sooner or later have his hook-bait taken in traditional fashion. Many anglers ask for no more than that. For them tench fishing is a *slow* sport: the bait is cast and left to lie in one place until it is taken boldly and decisively. But it's a lovely style of fishing that epitomises the layman's idea of how coarse fish anglers *always* behave! Not all tench feed on the bottom, however, and not all tench stop feeding during the day.

They will feed in some waters at night more than by day but if swimming and boating are going on, night-time offers the best chances. I have known tench feed enthusiastically for several days and nights on end during a spell of settled but overcast weather when the small and well-baited swim was so stirred up that little or no light could penetrate.

In these circumstances, the intense activity of a shoal of fish tends to keep the ground-bait well stirred up and it is not unusual then for tench to take moving baits well off the bottom. It makes sense then to present the hook-bait in the same manner either on a long link leger which will rise and fall in the swim or on a self-cocking float which allows the bait to sink under its own weight. On days when this fierce activity is taking place in the swim, there is also a case for allowing the breeze to take charge of the float and drag the bait (and one small bottom shot) slowly across the baited area, but this is *not* a method to be practised in a strong wind.

Early morning sessions in very hot weather are usually short-lived and I have often watched tench swim over a patch of ground-bait with no inclination to feed and retire to hide their heads under lily leaves or take shelter in the marginal rushes.

Some, however, move into deeper water and continue to feed throughout the day. One assumes that at the bottom in 12ft of water tench are more comfortable owing to the temperature and filtered light. Tench do like warm water but, unlike carp, they seldom feed with any real enthusiasm in a warm surface layer.

Where the shelter of marginal reed or rush-beds attracts them, tench will often feed throughout the day for there is natural food in and around the rush stems and these can often be seen shuddering violently as tench browse there. I believe that their bodies dislodge food from the stems and that this accounts for their being persuaded to take a slowly sinking hook-bait.

It is not always easy to fish in or very close to marginal rushes or reeds but a hook-bait, sinking slowly very close to the reed stems will often be taken with no preliminaries. As likely as not the tench will swim back into the thicket with it and the chances of lost fish are fairly high, but a powerful rod that will allow the fish to be 'pushed' out can help. And, of course, if the margin is approached by boat, the fish can be *pulled* into open water. This is then the more sensible approach. Using a zoomer

A tench: just landed

float (or a makeshift zoomer), margin fishing for tench can be exciting and productive.

In old-established waters, where the bottom is of very deep silt or mud, a type of feeding occurs which has, in the past, been referred to as 'preoccupied feeding'. That is to say the tench are diligently seeking very small items of natural food to such an extent that anglers' baits like lobworms, paste, or crust cubes, are completely ignored. This often accounts for the occasional complete lack of bites despite the intense activity in the swim.

Tench are not usually regarded as surface feeders, but here and there they have mingled with rudd and carp and learned to take floating crust-baits—a possibility not to be overlooked either by day or night.

Tactics, tackle and baits

Having learned a little about what to expect from tench, and bearing in mind that their behaviour *does* differ from water to water, let us consider ways and means of catching them.

I've always believed that you get as much out of tench fishing as you're prepared to put into it and the first essential is to find a water holding good tench in fair numbers. There are not many of them but are there if you look hard enough. Most of them are heavily weeded and the swims will have to be cleared before they can be exploited. This means hard work with drags and a great deal of preparation towards the end of the close season.

A throwing drag can be fashioned from two garden rake heads wired back to back or from a strip of Dexion. At a pinch even a loaded strip of wood with long nails will serve. A larger and much more efficient drag can be made out of angle iron with welded spikes. This, like the smaller versions, should have rigid arms to ensure that it comes back broadside-on to the weed and not lengthwise. It follows that the basic shape of a good drag should be triangular.

The large model can be used with double rope and see-sawed across the area until it is completely weed free. It is a drastic operation, but almost guarantees success.

The very fact that the weed has been removed will have some effect upon the tench for they will almost certainly investigate shortly afterwards. Then they can be held by regular pre-baiting and the few remaining whisps of weed missed by the drag will eventually disappear as the tench move in and begin working. The ground-bait can consist of bread and meal mixtures, lobworms in earth, brandlings in compost, loose feed like sweet-corn, soaked maize, stewed wheat, maggots, or almost anything else that's edible. Diced boiled potatoes and baked beans are other forms but really there's no end to it, but it's worth remembering that if you pre-bait with very large quantities of small baits you may create a state of preoccupied feeding that spoils your chances.

For instance, heavy pre-baiting with gallons of loose maggots can result in your having to make the very delicate presentation of a single maggot hook-bait. Early in the season that is

The conditions for catching tench on this damp August day were obviously favourable

unlikely, for big baits will be taken from ground-baited swims and, as these can be presented on substantial tackle, there seems to me to be little point in making life more difficult than it need be!

One good way of baiting a tench swim is to place about a dozen stale loaves into a large mesh net or sack, weight it with half-a-dozen bricks or heavy rocks and lower it into the swim. Mark it with a cork for removal, and watch how the bread disappears.

Ox blood, always an old favourite ground-bait additive of mine and of many before me, should be collected from the abattoir a few days in advance, allowed to 'gel' and then mixed in with a good ration of simple soaked bread and bran. Sometimes it acts like magic, sometimes not, but I'd rather fish with it than without it.

Pre-baiting and ground-baiting on the day serve either to attract tench into the swim or to make them interested in a particular bait, but you can ground-bait heavily with bread and then catch tench after tench on lobworms, although bread or crust is the only effective hook-bait in a bread-baited swim. The

163

truth is that the decision to be, or not to be, consistent is one of the finer points you have to find out for yourself.

The numbers of hook-baits that have been successfully used for tench could not all be listed here. Some have stood the test of time while others have been so unusual that they have had only novelty value. I feel well equipped to go tench fishing with a loaf of bread and a tin of worms but for a serious session I take a selection.

'Big baits for big fish' does not strictly apply to tench, for a two-pounder can take a big one just as easily as a six-pounder, but big baits in a baited swim *do* tend to encourage tench and not small roach or rudd. It is only by watching them feed regularly that you can decide what to use. Observation has taught me that baits are inside tench mouths much more often than is generally realised.

Ignoring a large bait completely, a tench is liable to suck in a small one and spit it out at once. With a traditional tench fishing tackle in use, such a bite would not be noticed and so the 'lift method' was further developed to deal with that kind of registration. It is an old method, used in the past mainly for roach, but it can work with tench.

The tackle consists of a length of peacock quill attached to the line at the bottom end only by means of a wide, tight-fitting band. The hook is tied directly to the reel line and one large shot is pinched about 2in above it. The tackle is set slightly deeper than the water and all is drawn taut until the float cocks. Usually the float is better overloaded; that is to say it should sink under the weight of the shot and only float when the shot is on the bottom, thereby ensuring that shot and bait are always on the bottom (buoyant crust rises up slightly, of course, but is to all intents and purposes being fished on the bottom).

At this stage you must set the rod in rests and wait for the bite. It will be noticed by a lift of the float which will eventually keel over and lie flat on the surface. Then it is essential to strike while the float is still 'lifting', but the strike should be made directly from the rest. Pick up the rod and strike in one movement. Any attempt to hold the rod in readiness causes the float to keel over and upsets the delicate setting. I regard the 'lift method' as the best for general tench fishing and use it for baits both large and small with appropriate adjustments to the distance between the shot and bait.

Today's modern antenna floats, some with sight bulbs attached, are perhaps an improvement on traditional lift floats and though their shotting is more critical, the bites appear to be more leisurely. It is possible to fish tench at long range with monstrous slider floats, but I believe the simple leger rig is just as effective.

Large baits are normal, but today's feeder-link type attachments make legering with maggots reasonably simple. The feeder is loaded with loose maggots and the hook baited with one or more, as the situation dictates. There can be no real guarantee that each cast will put the feeder in the same spot, but it must be close to the hook-bait. You must keep an eye on the feeder which should be refilled regularly if it is to be successful.

Leger and float rods are really matters for individuals to decide for themselves. I have a preference for a 12ft soft-actioned but fairly powerful fibreglass trotting rod for float fishing, and I have an ultra-light 9ft leger rod that is a joy to use. It has power when handling a big fish, but it casts a light soft bait sweetly.

All anglers would not agree, but I think it is fair to say that almost any rod will serve as a tench rod provided it is long enough and powerful enough to handle lines up to 6lb breaking strain and to set a no 6 hook past the barb. Such a rod is not too hard on smaller fish, it can be used with lines down to 3lb breaking strain, and can cast a light float tackle accurately to a swim that is not too far away.

A standard-sized fixed-spool reel loaded to within $\frac{1}{16}$in of the lip of the spool with 6lb breaking strain line serves for most weedy or snaggy tench swims, but remember that very few floats are capable of coping with lines of that strength. A spare spool filled to the same capacity with 3lb breaking strain line will suit almost any open swim. Tie hooks directly to the reel line for maximum strength, keep hooks sharp at all times, use a large landing-net and, if you want to photograph your catch, keep it in a large, soft, knotless mesh keep-net.

If you don't want your tench, it is as well to return them to the swim at once. It does not deter the others and I have known of occasions when one has been caught and released several times from the same swim.

20 Zander

Barrie Rickards

The nature of the beast! Small fish taken on a legered dead rudd

Zander fishing is made out to be a complicated business by many anglers, but in reality it is simple enough. In fact, only one difficult decision has to be made: fish for zander with tackle specially chosen, or fish with pike tackle and take the zander as they come? At least, this is what applies in the Fens where most of the good zander fishing is found. The decision is difficult only in that the outfit I recommend for basic piking, namely 11lb to 12lb breaking strain line and 2¼lb test-curve rods, is a bit heavy on zander because they are only average fighters. On the other hand if one steps down to lines in the 6lb to 9lb range, ideal for playing zander, quite a few good pike could be lost in the course of a season—which seems a pity.

My own thinking on the matter is fairly straightforward since anglers, least of all myself, do not fish for zander for their fighting qualities, and since 11lb bs lines do not in any way detract from results, I normally fish with refined pike tackle. If I fished more often in still waters such as Woburn and Claydon Lakes or those near Cambridge, I would probably use lines about 8lb bs for then I'd get a better fight out of the zander and I wouldn't hook as many pike as on the Fenland rivers and drains. Whatever line you choose, I recommend the basic paternoster rig that I outlined in my chapter on pike, perhaps coupled with a leger outfit, using either small dead- or live-baits. But I will return to the detail later.

Zander are now found in England in fifteen counties* but in most of them there are relatively few. The Fens are the exception: there they are abundant and grow big, whatever the size of the lake, in at least nineteen major watercourses, such as the Relief Channel, Cut Off Channel, the Great Ouse, the River Delph, and the Old Bedford River. They are also to be found in smaller drains and rivers and the enterprising angler will get good sport if he searches away from recognised areas like the Relief Channel. Naturally, different waters may require a different approach.

The simple free-lined or legered dead-bait (opposite right) is the simplest to use for zander, as was the practice on Woburn and Claydon and to some extent, more recently, on the Fenland waters. Although free-lining is possible on many of the drains in

* Kent, Surrey, Berkshire, Essex, Hertfordshire, Suffolk, Worcestershire, Buckinghamshire, Bedfordshire, Cambridge and the Isle of Ely, Norfolk, Lincolnshire, Warwickshire, Staffordshire, and Yorkshire.

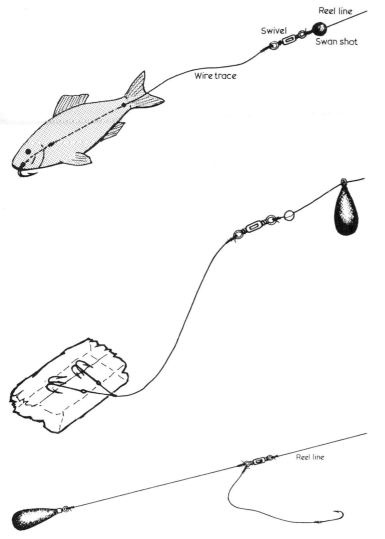

Basic free-lined dead-baiting with no 2 hook and threaded wire trace. Bait can be scored to increase smell or air-injected to lift it off the bottom. A free-lined live-bait would be lip-hooked.

Legered dead-bait using strip of fish (cut away in fig to show position of hooks underneath, set in fish skin)

Fixed lead paternoster rig for use with small baits and leads

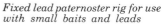

the Fens, the Great Ouse itself (and the bigger drains in winter) usually need a lead up to 1oz in weight to hold bottom.

When the water flows strong and coloured (incidentally one of the best times for zander) leads up to 2oz may be needed. On these occasions the tackle can be arranged as a fixed paternoster (above), or as a running paternoster (page 168) which I prefer. There are occasions when you want to fish at ranges of 60yd or so and then the running paternoster with a big lead is excellent. The only problem is that the strike may set up a fair drag through the lead if the zander has run off at an awkward angle and, before you can wind up tight to strike, the fish feels the weight as it begins to bump across the bottom and lets go of the bait. But, of course, there's not really a lot to be done, for free-lining in any case allows the bait to sweep round to the edge in no time at all. The hazard of dropped baits however, can be

167

Running paternoster for use with heavy leads at long range

minimised by using very small stuff, such as strips of fish, and two very small trebles (certainly no bigger than size 8), the strike being made more or less immediately. Then the zander gives a positive run so it is usually easy to distinguish between that and a current drag pulling the line off the spool. As you can imagine, fishing under these circumstances can be tricky, but you must persist in spite of the rubbish that collects on the line because the zander feed well.

In clear water conditions, zander give less positive runs and tend to feed during the night (though not as commonly as is widely supposed) and at dawn and dusk. All the evidence favours an hour before dawn to one hour after dawn as being the best period of all, and this even when the water is coloured. What I like to do then is to fish the paternostered live-bait. Baits in the 1oz to 4oz bracket are good for general zander fishing but I am certain that lively baits in the 4oz category are more likely to produce the bigger zander. Hooks should be size 6, 8 or 10 trebles in the snap-tackle arrangement in my chapter on pike. Wire is needed for big zander, not just in case you may hook a pike. Incidentally, how does an angler know he's been bitten off by a pike (the usual assumption)? After all, zander are also caught with hooks to nylon in their mouths.

A close-up of a zander showing the array of teeth and the 'wall-eye' appearance

The takes at dawn are usually quite positive on float tackle but there are then fewer very fast runs than you get in coloured water conditions. With the tackle I have described it is possible to strike, indeed it is sensible to strike, as soon as the zander is

running positively. Ignore tentative bobs of the float, but not the kind of bite that holds it steadily just under the surface—hit it. I once did that and broke the British Record!

The fight of a zander, as a rule, need not worry anyone. Netting and handling should be done in much the same way as for pike, except that the zander's jaw is a little more powerful than the pike's of the same weight, and the unhooking system I outlined in the pike chapter is even more pertinent. It can be very difficult to insert a masked gag into a zander's mouth for it is smaller than the pike's, compared weight for weight, and the small hooks I mentioned are a great advantage in that they slip unnoticed into the fish's mouth along with the bait. Use large hooks and a zander will remove the bait. Small hooks take a better hook-hold and are easier to remove.

Zander have a reputation for being rather weak on the bank and in keep-nets. It is true that they are less robust than pike, but not all that much. My 12lb 5oz British Record was transported thirty miles in wet grass, kept overnight in a bath, weighed by the official of the British Record Committee, taken back to the Relief Channel in a tank and, when it returned to the water, it swam off very powerfully indeed. My first British Record was twenty-six hours in a keep-net without suffering the slightest damage. If it is unhooked and returned to the water quickly there should be no trouble at all.

Although I have emphasised the approach and techniques rather than the baits used, baits *are* important. For example, don't use sea baits such as sprats and herrings. I've caught quite a few zander on sea fish baits but, as a rule, they are very poor. For live-baits, dace, roach, bream, bleak, gudgeon and rudd are all excellent; and for dead-baits any of these either whole, in halves, or in strips are also good. Many modern zander fanatics are using eel portions as dead-baits with great success, and they are a good solid casting weight so that free-lining can be practised more often. Preserved baits are less effective than frozen ones but the difference is nothing like so marked as that between sea fish baits and fresh water fish baits. Finally, artificial lures: these may well become effective but at the moment they are not particularly good except on certain days. I've caught zander on spinners, spoons, and plugs, as well as on plummets and Arlesey bombs! But you could spin a whole winter for zander and not see one, although why this should be so is a bit of a mystery. There are many imponderables in zander fishing and this is part of its attraction. There are plenty of waters to discover, plenty of new techniques to try out and a lot of good fish to come before interest will wane.

Part Three
Sea Angling

21 Safety at Sea

Jack Smith

Human beings were not designed to live on or in the hostile environment of the sea. Nevertheless a breed of seamen has evolved who have, for centuries, wrested a living from it and one of their skills is the ability to survive.

In recent years their ranks have been joined by men from the land who have made the sea their playground. Some of these newcomers develop into first-class amateur seamen, some rub along with just enough basic ideas and luck to survive, while a few run out of luck or act with such incredible lunacy that they finish up as food for the crabs. It follows that all boat anglers would do well to acquire a seaman's instincts. You are up against the same hazards.

The first consideration is a boat. It must be seaworthy and if you don't know what that means, seek the advice of someone who does. The boat will be a lot safer if it has adequate built-in buoyancy tanks to support itself, and the crew, when full of water. A poor alternative is attaching slabs of polystyrene firmly to the undersides of thwarts, side-benches and decks. It is amazing how difficult it is to spot a small boat in a choppy sea so its colour makes a tremendous difference. Avoid dark colours, especially greens and blues. White shows up well in a calm sea and in clear night conditions, but in a rough sea or a mist, bright orange is the best and the same goes for your oilskins as well.

The engine is the other major item. First and foremost, it must be reliable and again, if you don't know anything about engines, seek help. In choosing one, you must strike a balance between an engine with enough power to get you out of trouble and one that is so heavy that your boat is in danger of filling at the stern. If it is an outboard, see that it is securely fastened to the transom, either by recesses for the clamps, or, better still, by a bolt-on bracket. Always carry sufficient tools and spares in a watertight box for simple adjustments or repairs that can be done afloat.

Finally, don't stint on fuel; you may need enough of the stuff to save your life as well as get to the fishing grounds, or even to tow some unfortunate home. It follows that it is always safer to fish in company which is precisely what professional fishermen often do. In case you are faced with spending a night at sea, owing to engine failure for instance, always, even in midsummer, take adequate warm and weather-proof clothing with you. Exposure cases do not occur only in winter in this country.

Not so far at the back of your mind you should remember that the sea can look like this (Glénans Sea Centre)

The next requirement is an anchor, not only for fishing in reasonable weather, but big enough, if need arises, to hold you clear of a rocky shore in a gale until help arrives. Always stow the anchor and its cable neatly, without coils trailing all over the bottom of the boat for someone to step in when the anchor goes down; and in the same context, keep the bottom clear of any other dangerous traps such as boat-hooks, gaffs, fish-hooks and wet fish.

Remember to check that you have enough cable out to allow for a rising tide; and remember too that some synthetic ropes float, which means that at slack water your cable may coil itself round the propeller. I use plaited terylene for my anchor cable; it is expensive but easy on the hands, doesn't float, and stows neatly without kinking. Always retrieve the anchor over the bow roller and never amidships. If the anchor becomes fouled, especially in a strong tide, a small boat can turn broadside, and the pressure applied to the cable amidships is quite capable of tilting the boat to an angle where the gunwale goes under water. A power winch is particularly dangerous if used like this. It is always sound practice to carry a spare cable and anchor.

There is a miscellany of other gear which is optional. If your boat, though motorised, is capable of being rowed, take oars. If it cannot be rowed, consider carrying a small auxiliary outboard which will at least give you a couple of knots. If you reject both these suggestions, then think about what you *are* going to do in the event of engine failure. If you rely entirely on oars, carry a spare one and secure the rowlocks with lanyards.

Other essentials include a compass (for use in fog) and some means of signalling for help. The standard equipment is two packets of flares. They are not cheap and have a short shelf life but they save lives. I don't carry them myself, pinning my faith on a very powerful signalling torch which is completely watertight and visible for miles even in bright sunlight. It can

173

be used over and over again, and I am not limited to three or six flares which may not be seen. But flares or lamp, you must take something.

Other distress signals are ship-to-shore radios, but obviously only in large boats, and there are two signals in the International Code which are feasible in a small boat: one is an article of clothing (usually a shirt) tied by the arms to an oar; the other is given by slowly raising and lowering your outstretched arms. Any mariner or coastguard will recognise these signals and organise help.

An absolute 'must' is life-jackets for everyone on board, but the rules for wearing them are not easy to lay down. I believe in wearing them at all times when afloat, even if you are a good swimmer, and some people do. However, many more don't and I must admit that on a clear hot summer day with a sea like glass, in a large well-found boat, it does seem an unnecessary precaution. If you can't face wearing them all the time, then I suggest that you at least don them at the slightest sign of danger and, when not wearing them, keep them to hand to grab in an unexpected emergency be it fire or collision with some menace just below the surface. I am not being fanciful; such things do happen and that is why some people wear their life-jackets all the time, so think hard before you leave yours off. If it helps you to think harder, there are two incidents in which I have been involved on the Dover lifeboat, both cases of three men fishing from a small boat in suicidal conditions. One in a Force 8 gale, the other at night, without lights, in a shipping lane. We found each of these boats barely afloat, supported by a little air trapped in the bows, but we didn't find any of the men;

174

what we did find in each of these tragedies were three beautiful new life-jackets, still in their polythene wrappers, securely stowed under the foredeck.

There are three pieces of equipment which must be carried on a large boat but which the small boat-owner may consider to be more trouble than they are worth (if they are ever needed, though, they *will* be worth the trouble): a fire-extinguisher, a simple first-aid kit, and a radar reflector which may save you from being run down in fog or darkness and could be the means of finding you if a search is instigated.

That completes your equipment, but before you actually launch, consider one more point. Don't overload your boat. Decide on the maximum number of people that it can safely hold and stick to that number, and insist that no anglers in small boats fish standing up.

When you are ready to go to sea, always launch bow first as you are less likely to swamp the boat or finish up aground, broadside-on to the breaking waves, as you try to turn round. Consider whether the wind and current are likely to carry you sideways on to a groyne. If so, get further away to give yourself more sea room.

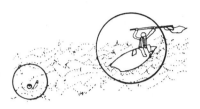

A hull can be seen, a swimmer cannot

The biggest anxiety is returning to a beach when a high sea has got up, forming big rollers, compounded perhaps with a high tide and a steeply sloping beach that prevents the boat grounding firmly while you get out. That is a problem. If there is no other better landing place and you daren't hold off until the tide recedes a little, there is only one thing for it: drive the boat full tilt, straight for the beach, and get out as fast as you can. Don't worry about damaging the boat or the engine, worry about damaging yourself. It will help tremendously if the first man out takes a bow rope with him and pulls like mad while the others pile out, they in turn helping him to heave.

If your boat does end up broadside-on to the beach in big waves, never stand close to it on the landward side: it can easily be flung on top of you before you can leap clear.

The best course is to avoid such conditions; you have the choice when you go out but not when you return. With weather forecasts, opinions of the locals and your own observations, you can make an intelligent assessment of the weather and when in doubt, don't go! If the weather deteriorates, come in. If you are not sure, still come in. Occasionally you are going to lose some good fishing days which turn out to be perfect after all, but that is not so bad as bereaving family and friends.

Good maxims are: don't go out in fog and come back if fog develops; an offshore wind means a calm sea inshore, but remember you have to battle your way home against it if it strengthens; an onshore wind will help you home but makes for bad conditions for landing if it increases; knowledge of local tidal currents is essential; avoid coming home against a strong tide if you can; if you are working out of a harbour, find out about the snags at the entrance and the harbour-master's signals; inquire if there are any hidden dangers in the vicinity. Remember too that if you fish along a coast for a long distance

175

past cliffs or rocks and the weather turns nasty you have the extra risk of coming back, possibly against wind and tide, and not being able to run straight ashore.

Always consider other people's safety as well as your own. Don't upset smaller craft with your wash; when night fishing make sure your navigation lights are in order; keep clear of sailing boats and any boats you are overtaking; when meeting another boat head-on, pass port to port, that is, keep him on your left side as you face forward; watch out for swimmers, especially when close to the beach, and bear in mind that any mishap may result in a heavy claim for damages against you; include third-party coverage in your boat insurance.

When you reach the fishing ground, as soon as you have anchored take bearings on the shore with your compass in case fog comes down. Keep an eye on something ashore to check whether you are drifting or not. Don't anchor in a shipping lane and don't tie up to a navigational buoy.

If you have misjudged the shipping situation and a vessel appears to be heading for you, take action in good time. Always assume that he has not seen you and, if he doesn't alter course, don't delay in getting up your anchor and moving out of his way. He doesn't have to hit you to drown you, for his wash will do that. In emergency, cut the anchor cable or better still, have it permanently buoyed, ready for ditching and subsequent retrieval.

If the worst happens and you are all in the water, then keep together, you make a much better visual target. Get rid of your boots and waders but keep your clothes on to trap a warm layer of water round your body. Don't waste energy unnecessarily by swimming or thrashing about. If the boat is still afloat, though half-sunk or capsized, hold on to it or at least stay with it. Finally, tell someone ashore that you are going fishing so that the alarm can be raised if you fail to return.

A novice may feel that the whole business is too dodgy and that there are too many things to do and remember, but this is not so. If you have any common sense at all you will find that abiding by most of the precautions will soon become second nature and you should enjoy many years of safe fishing. Never forget though that anyone who thinks that the principal reason for going to sea in a boat is to catch fish, is mistaken. The fundamental purpose of your boat is to protect *you* from a hostile environment.

(right) *A mullet being brought safely into shallow water by Leslie Moncrieff on the west coast of Ireland*

Bass and Mullet

22

Des Brennan

Bass and mullet are inshore species often found sharing the same ground. Handsome and silvery, they can easily be mistaken for each other although there are pronounced differences in their appearance and behaviour. The bass is an active, efficient predator that forages on the tide in search of food. The adults tend to be solitary although they can be present in numbers off a beach or in a particular area, and, when small fry are plentiful in summer, they may combine to harry the shoals of brit and sand-eel. Immature bass, or 'schoolies', are gregarious and swim in schools or small shoals. So do mullet. The school may be anything from two or three fish to several thousand strong and it is rare to see a solitary mullet. As its food is plentiful, the mullet's behaviour is indolent, sometimes playful, in contrast to the restless, purposeful swimming of bass.

The bass (*Dicentrarchus labrax*) is a southern European species nearing the northern limit of its temperature range on British coasts, where they are plentiful along the south coasts but thin out further northwards. Small pockets are found as far north as the Causeway coast in Northern Ireland and Luce Bay in Scotland, but generally speaking they have become scarce north of Anglesey in Wales and the mouth of the River Boyne in Ireland and are no longer a practical angling objective.

In our latitudes, they are a long-lived, slow-growing and late-maturing species. The females outnumber the males by about two to one in the spawning stock, grow bigger and live longer. Few males over 5lb in weight are taken and really big bass are almost certain to be female. The females mature later, at ages ranging from 5–8 years (minimum fork length 14in) as against 4–7 years (minimum fork length 12½in) for males.

A mullet that appears to be insecure but—

178

The following random samples will give some idea of the slow growth and longevity of the species:

Length	Weight	Age
9.1in	6oz	3 years plus
11.1in	11½oz	5 years plus
16.9in	1lb 15¾oz	7 years plus
19.9in	3lb 8oz	11 years plus
20.6in	4lb 8oz	13 years plus

Specimen bass (over 10lb) may be 20 years old or more.

Bass are fractional spawners with only a portion of the females' eggs being ripe and ready to be shed at any one time. Spawning happens in areas with strong tides or currents from April to mid-June but, in the far south, it may be as early as March. Successful spawning and survival of the fry is very dependent on the season and only finer than average years are good brood ones. As the species is on the northern limits of its temperature range, it is not numerically strong on our coasts and the stock of adult bass is the product of the accumulated spawning of a great many years—perhaps fifteen or more. Contrast this with a species such as haddock: their exploitable stock may be the product of as few as two or three brood years. Tagging experiments have shown that, although some individual bass may make long migrations, the bulk are essentially local, and when stocks are fished out in an area they are not replenished from other parts of the coast.

Bass are in fact, very vulnerable to over-exploitation and the effects of commercial fishing or intensive angling have already

—it is safely landed

179

been felt in many localities. Bass are in urgent need of conservation and fishing for them, commercial and amateur, should be restricted.

The Common or Thick Lipped Grey Mullet (*Chelon labrosus (Risso)*) is much more widely distributed than the bass. It is found in the Mediterranean and on the Atlantic coast from the Canaries to Norway. The Thin Lipped Grey Mullet (*Liza ramada (Risso)*) is less widely distributed and on British coasts seems to be largely confined to the south, particularly Devon, Cornwall and the Channel Islands. It has only been recorded once on the Irish coast. The Golden Grey Mullet (*Liza auratus (Risso)*) is rarer still but it has been taken off Devon and Cornwall.

The mullet is even slower growing than the bass, lives longer and matures later. Investigations in 1969 by Kennedy and Fitzmaurice in Ireland have shown mature males aged 9 years and 10 years (fork lengths 15in and 14in respectively) while other males of 10 and 11 years (fork lengths 13½in and 14½in) were immature. The smallest gravid females examined were fish measuring 16in and 16½in fork lengths and aged 11 years and 12 years respectively. Our mullet are believed to spawn offshore in deep water in the late spring or early summer. Unlike female bass which spawn annually, only a portion of the mullet do so in any one year.

The first essential in successful bass angling is to be able to locate the fish. They will be found foraging along beaches, in estuaries, over rocky shoals and in tideways. Shore fishing is the most popular form and you must learn to 'read' the different types of beaches. The two main types are lee beaches and storm beaches. The former are normally shallow and sheltered, rarely if ever subjected to heavy surf. They are the most difficult to fish for food is plentiful and there is nothing to attract fish into a particular area, so locating bass there is difficult.

Storm beaches are easier to fish. The ceaseless action of surf makes them unstable and food organisms are not as varied or spread as widely over the bottom. The action of the waves concentrates the food into a narrow band or feeding zone running through the surf parallel to the beach. Naturally bass will be concentrated into it and, once located, the angler has greatly enhanced his chances of meeting fish. On steep beaches, where there is a good depth of water and the waves break close to the shore, casting your bait behind the third breaker out will usually place you among the fish. On shallow Atlantic storm beaches where the surf may break a hundred yards or more from the shore, the feeding zone is more difficult to find. However you will notice an area or 'water table' where the depth remains fairly constant despite the ebb and flow of the surf, and that is where the fish are to be found. Normally it is no more than 60yd to 80yd out and there is a real danger of casting your bait beyond the fish. Proper surf-casting tackle is required for this kind of fishing, eg an 11ft or 12ft fibreglass rod, a multiplier or saltwater type fixed-spool reel, 14—15lb bs monofilament line and grip leads, preferably of the breakaway type. Terminal

(right) Five substantial bass caught by Leslie Moncrieff

180

tackle should be kept simple and a two-hook paternoster or a single-hook running leger is quite adequate. The most effective baits are soft or peeler crab, lugworm, ragworm, squid, clam, razor-fish and fish baits. So, when beach fishing for bass, avoid overcasting. There are times, particularly in calm conditions, when long casts are necessary to reach fish but more often than not bass are close in, even at times well-nigh under your feet. Always hold your rod for you can then detect bites that would not register on a rod left in a rest and you will hook fish that would be otherwise missed if the rod were left unmanned. Don't shift around too much either. Bass forage along the length of a beach on the tide and if you have picked a likely spot the bass will eventually come to you and you might miss them altogether if you move.

Areas of rough ground where scars of rock are split by pools and sandy patches, strewn with weed-covered rocks and stones, can be very productive ground for bass. This type of ground, which anglers will quarter in search of soft or peeler crab for bait but would not dream of fishing for fear of losing tackle, produces bigger-than-average bass for the intrepid angler; but it is difficult to fish and occasional loss of tackle must be accepted. This can be minimised though by keeping the terminal tackle simple—a single-hook paternoster or running leger, and by using some 'rotten bottom' on the sinker. This will break if it is badly snagged but the trace can be recovered. Nuts, bolts or old sparking plugs can be used as sinkers and no one need be afraid of losing them! Ordinary surf-casting tackle is suitable but a fast-retrieve reel keeps you clear of the rough when recovering, and many anglers prefer to use large fixed-spool reels instead of multipliers.

Where deep gullies fissure the rock, float-fishing is an enjoyable and effective way of taking bass. Live prawn is a really killing bait in such conditions and the float should be allowed to wander, searching each gully thoroughly. As bass come in very close, stay out of sight. You may not see them but they can see you. Spinning with artificial lures is another successful method which is equally efficient in the channels of estuaries where bass run up on the tide.

As in beach-fishing, pick places where the bass must come to you. At low water they will be in the lower part of the estuary or outside the bar waiting for the flood tide to push back up channel. As the tide fills, the bass will penetrate farther and farther up and the angler must move from one vantage point to the other as the fish run through. The situation is reversed on the ebb as the fish fall back to the sea again. The best fishing is while there is still a defined channel, for when the tide covers the flats, the fish spread out and are not so easy to cover. Bottom fishing with bait is equally as good in the channel. Your bait can be trundled along the bottom with advantage, so long as it is not swept aside too quickly by a powerful current.

In some conditions, bass may shoal offshore regularly in July and August, but elsewhere shoaling may be spasmodic for special reasons. Spinning with artificial lures such as Tobys,

German Spratts and Rubber Eels is the most effective way but care must be taken not to motor over, or too close to, a shoal or the fish may be put down. In tideways, over reefs and in channels where bass lie in ambush, trolling will take its quota but it does not give as much sport as spinning.

Mullet are much easier to locate as they are frequently visible. The difficulty is to get an enticing bait. Their natural food is microscopic—diatoms, some burrowing amphipods, tiny snails and suchlike which are widespread almost everywhere, so the angler cannot hope to present these as bait; he must either coax them on to something he can use, or go where they have already acquired a taste for other, less natural, food.

Fortunately such places are not too hard to find. In fishing harbours, where trawlers gut their catch, mullet become accustomed to feeding on scraps of fish and offal. Indeed, in popular angling centres, where inedible species, such as shark, skate and dogfish are dumped back into the sea by thoughtless anglers, mullet will feed on the decomposing carcasses. Such mullet are catchable, indeed relatively easy, prey. Sewer outfalls are other likely places, as a lot of edible trash is mixed up in the discharge. Mullet have been taken on a great variety of baits at such places, like peas, ham fat, bacon rinds, cheese, maggots, bread, to name but a few. The outfalls from fish or food-processing plants or any spot where soft, edible refuse is regularly available, also hold out likely prospects.

In such venues, the mullet are conditioned to feeding on bait which the angler can use and the ground-baiting has already

This mullet does not appear to have given the angler much trouble!

been done for you. All that is necessary is to introduce the bait in a suitable manner and then there is every likelihood of catching fish; even if this conditioning has been done it may still be occasionally necessary to ground-bait to bring the mullet on the feed. Harbours or holiday resorts are the places where scraps of bread or even whole sandwiches may find their way into the water and the hotels and restaurants may habitually dump their kitchen refuse in the sea. Mullet will feed freely in such places on bread or pieces of fish, although the angler may still have to encourage them.

Mullet are restless creatures, seldom remaining for long in one spot so, if they are to be held in an area, they must be given a choice of spots and be able to swim around from one to another. Otherwise they will disappear. Pick by observing places where the mullet linger for a reasonable time on the tide. Ground-bait the bottom with little balls of bread, anchored fish carcasses or fish mash in three or four places which are within your casting range. When you are surface ground-baiting with floating bread you lose control over its dispersal. Wind, tide or current may take it away and there is nothing more disheartening than watching mullet walloping floating bread beyond casting range unless it is seeing your ground-bait being mopped up by gulls, swans or ducks before the mullet can get to it!

With preconditioned mullet, ground-baiting should soon bring them on the feed but they are unpredictable creatures and one can never be sure of how long it will take or indeed for how long they will respond. They may start within minutes or studiously ignore your offerings for hours before suddenly feeding for a short period. Wild mullet, however, in natural surroundings away from urban areas are not so easy. They are more wary and must grow accustomed to seeing your ground-bait before accepting it as food. It may take as much as a week's patient ground-baiting on every tide before you even consider introducing a hook-bait. Cover is again important. While urban mullet are used to people and activity, wild mullet are very easily frightened and care is essential.

In many ways, mullet are more a coarse angler's species than a sea angler's and coarse fishing tackle is ideal when fishing for them. They are exceptionally strong and stubborn fighters but their soft mouths require delicate handling. There is no need to fish heavier than 5lb bs line and anything lighter is difficult to handle in the inevitable sea breeze. A single-hook paternoster is suitable where fish are feeding on the bottom in deep water or under the rod tip—along a pier or harbour wall. Otherwise float tackle is generally used. Always fish a tight line as mullet take and reject a bait very quickly and one must be very alert and be able to tighten firmly on the fish.

Shore Fishing for Beginners

23

Michael Prichard ARPS

The best way to start sea angling is to fish from the shore. Almost as many species can be caught without the expense of charter-boat fees and having to find your sea legs while you are learning the rudiments of tackle make-up and casting. Beginners, all too often, get smitten with the idea of fishing, rush to the nearest tackle shop for a rod and reel, rarely stopping long enough to ask themselves what they are going to fish for and where!

Tackle needn't be complicated or expensive for the needs of a shore fisherman are relatively simple; but, before buying anything, seek good advice. Probably the best way is to find a friendly sea angler who is prepared to take out a novice and explain the kind of fishing the coastline offers.

There are four main types of shore-line fishing, each with its rod/reel combination, although not exclusively so; some species require special tackle but experience will show what is required.

Type of shore	Type of fishing	Rod	Reel
Steep angled beach of shingle or mixed make-up	General species that could vary from a few oz weight to 50lb or more	11—12ft casting weights of 4—6oz	Either a fixed-spool or multi-plying reel
Shallow (usually west-facing sandy beach)	Fish up to 10lb with the occasional larger specimen	10—12ft casting 2—5oz	Either a fixed-spool or small multiplier
Estuary (can be either fast or slow-running outflow from the river)	All 4 rods would have a use when fishing this environment	Both casting rods and lighter tackle	Both types of sea angler's reels (alter nylon line strength)
Rock platforms or man-made situations (harbour walls and piers)	Two basic kinds of species (large, such as conger eels; and small, such as wrasse, pollack and mullet)	8ft spinning rod and a 10ft float rod with the heavier casting rod for big fish	as above

A fixed-spool reel with 'knock-on' bale arm and fully skirted spool. These reels can be used left- or right-handed

A beach fisher's multiplying reel showing correct loading of nylon on the spool

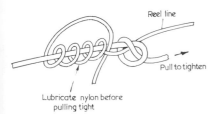

Reel line

Pull to tighten

Lubricate nylon before pulling tight

The casting leader knot for joining reel line to shock leader. A perfect knot for joining lines of different diameters

The newcomer doesn't need all these four rods at once because they are only needed for fishing on all coasts. A couple of initial outings, with advice, will show which of them is right for you, possibly with an extra rod for summer holidays and a change in tactics. The heavy casting rod is needed for winter and when heavy seas put immense strains on rod and lines, whereas fishing in a shallow bay or deep estuary (spinning and float-fishing) requires tackle not unlike that used by fresh water anglers.

Two kinds of reel are used on the shore: the fixed-spool and the multiplier. Both work equally well and the choice is purely personal. The fixed-spool is simpler. A bent wire bale arm is opened to make the cast and it lets the line run freely off the face of a stationary spool or bobbin. Then the bale arm is closed to hold the line which can then be retrieved by winding the reel-handle to wrap the bale arm line back on to the spool. All fixed-spool reels have a slipping drag mechanism that allows line to be pulled off the spool, at a fixed drag, before the breaking strain of the line is reached. The drag is adjusted before fishing begins (above left).

The fixed-spool reel is usually used for spinning and float fishing as it is perfect for casting light weights with little effort and it is perfect for handling the lighter breaking strains of nylon used with light fishing tackle. The multiplying reel, so-called because each turn of the handle produces at least two or more turns of the spool, is more popular with bait-casting anglers. The reel has a spool, usually made of plastic or other lightweight material, that revolves during the cast at right angles to the rod, letting line run off the spool as it turns. Obviously, as the spool turns at high speed, some degree of expertise is required in controlling the spool, so some practice is needed before the new angler has the competence and confidence to take his gear to the waterside (left).

Nylon line is loaded on to either reel according to the kind of rod and style of fishing that is being undertaken. Usually the pattern is:

Beach casting
Heavy rods with 5—6oz leads—18lb nylon with a casting leader of 45lb bs.

Spinning
10—15lb nylon with a nylon or supple wire leader of 12—20lb breaking strain where fish with sharp teeth can be expected.

Float fishing
10—15lb nylon reel line direct to terminal rig with occasional use of weaker weight traces when fishing over rough ground.

Light casting
2—4oz leads, 12—15lb nylon with a casting leader of 20—30lb bs.

The casting leader, used on beach casting reels that throw weights between 2—6oz, is a length of heavier gauge nylon that will take the initial strain of the cast and prevent the line from breaking. It also guards against the lead breaking off should the cast be a bad one. Join the leader to the reel line with a leader knot (below left). Spinning and float fishing call for a gently swinging cast that doesn't put too great a stress on nylon or knots so the end of the reel line needs no strengthening. What is necessary is that knots are always perfectly tied and so preserve the full breaking strain that the manufacturer builds into the line. The Tucked Half-Blood knot and Overhand loop (right) are all that the newcomer needs to learn for simple rig making.

Now, with the line loaded on to the reel, casting practice can begin. Choose a lengthy field, away from houses and people, for a weight that flies off a broken line travels a long way and is a dangerous weapon! The easiest and best cast to adopt is the 'Lay Back' system, devised by Leslie Moncrieff many years ago (*vide* chapter 27). It is a perfect technique for the beginner and the cast will propel a sinker far enough out over the waves to satisfy most anglers and fishing conditions. Keep casting until you master the mechanics of controlling rod and reel and then, and only then, it is time to go to the seashore.

The part of the fishing line that has hooks, lead weights and bait is called a trace or terminal rig. There are two basic forms. The paternoster, where the lead is at the end of the rig below the hooks; and the leger, where the lead sinker is fixed, and slides freely, on the reel line (below). These rigs have different uses. The paternoster presents a tethered bait on to the sea-bed where

Tucked Half-Blood knot

Overhand loop

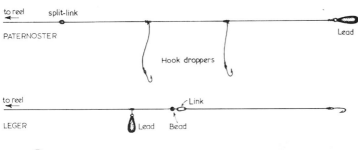

Paternoster and leger rig set-up. Note position of leads

Casting weights: (left to right) *a slab-sided bomb, a plain casting bomb and a pear lead with fixed grip wires*

The breakaway casting lead: (above) *grip wires in the fixed position;* (below) *the wires relaxed from the holding position, which allows the terminal rig to be retrieved with little strain placed on fine line or rod*

a feeding fish may feel the weight of the sinker as it pulls at the bait. Many species, such as cod, whiting and flatfish are not put off when they feel resistance as they pull at the bait. But some fish, notably the tope and occasionally the bass, like to pick up a bait and run off some distance with it before swallowing the offering without feeling any pressure, however slight. A leger rig is the one that allows a taking fish to do that because the lead slides on the line and the fish can pull away freely.

There are various kinds of lead weight for, apart from having the weight to take the bait out to waiting fish, sinkers have to perform other tasks. They hold the bottom effectively in strong currents. Their shape is important (page 187) both aerodynamically to reduce drag as it passes through the air and to cause minimum resistance to the flow of the water. Some currents will be too strong for a particular weight but a heavier weight will affect the casting capability of rod and angler. This is where the grip lead comes in: its shape is similar but it has wire spikes that grip into sand or shingle to give a better hold on the ground. The trouble, though, with grip leads of the standard variety is that they put a great strain on the rod when the end tackle has to be retrieved; but the 'breakaway' lead overcomes this problem (left) with its swivelling grip wires that release from the in-use position when a strong tug is applied. Retrieval is simple as the wires fold back creating little resistance on the sea-bed.

Shore anglers come to have their personal preferences for particular patterns of hook. There are thousands to choose from but only four are necessary (page 190). Fine wire, long-shanked hooks are recommended for the smaller species, flatfish in particular, where a rag or lugworm can be threaded over the metal of the hook. (Catching fish becomes more likely if the bait presentation is near perfect!)

A good-quality, forged, round-bend hook with a needle-sharp point and fine cut barb is the mainstay. Used in sizes 4–6/0, this type is good for most occasions, but the predatory species (tope, dogfish and the smaller skates and rays) put a great strain on tackle. Their tough jaws are immensely powerful and a stronger hook is needed to withstand the stress of the fight. But not all of the shore-caught species are huge and the successful baits are often tiny fragments of fish or worms too small to cover a conventional sea hook, whereas float fishing for mullet, wrasse and rock pollack is a delicate operation that demands fresh water style hooks, similar to the carp angler's, in sizes 2 to 8.

Three basic shore rigs will cope with most of the new angler's fishing. All use the two simple knots illustrated on page 187 but the paternoster incorporates a blood loop (opposite top right), a simple way to form a dropper or hook link. Two hooks on a paternoster are enough. Leger and float rigs have only one hook as more would tend to tangle during the cast. Join the trace to the reel line or casting leader using a strong spring link. I never use swivels these days when beach casting as there is always the possibility of a bad cast straining the metal connections. But use a swivel for spinning or float fishing for, as there is little

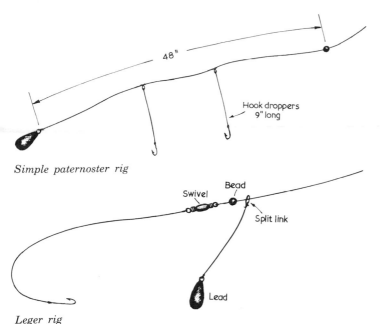

Simple paternoster rig

Hook droppers 9" long

48"

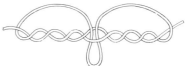

Blood loop

Leger rig

Swivel   Bead

Split link

Lead

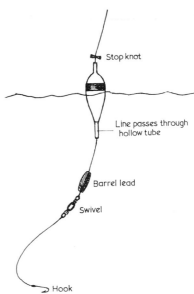

Stop knot

Line passes through hollow tube

Barrel lead

Swivel

Hook

Float rig

stress in casting, the fish swim in all directions and can twist and turn on the trace putting tangles into the nylon.

Nylon is the best trace material except when sharp-toothed or rough-skinned species are being fished. Then the trace is made up from fine, cable-laid wire, either nylon covered or plain. The joins to hook or line-connecting link are made by crimping the wire with metal ferrules. This is easily done but remember to tuck in the loose end which ensures that the wire will not pull free (right).

The float rig is the only tackle system that fishes off the bottom, therefore the float must be fixed so that the bait is suspended at the right depth. The water may be only a few or many feet deep so the float must be fished as a slider. This is achieved by having the line running down through the float to the rig. The depth is adjusted by tying a stop knot on the reel line (top left, page 190). This knot will pass back through the rod rings when the tackle is brought in for re-baiting. A small piece of rubber band can be easily clove-hitched into the rig after the depth has been gauged. Some fish, like the pollack, swim in mid-water whereas ballan wrasse will need the bait near the sea-bed. Mackerel and garfish feed near the surface so a bait can be set just under the float.

Bites on a float-fished rig are fairly easy to detect for the float bobs then slides under the waves and a swift sweep back over the shoulder with the rod will set the hook and the fight is on. But fishing a bait on the bottom with paternoster or leger rig is a different story. The only visible indication of a bite is a sharp nodding movement of the rod tip when the rod is set up in a rest. Anglers who hold the rod in their hands will feel a jerking sensation transmitted through the line to their hands. Re-actions should be immediate with beginners, but as experience

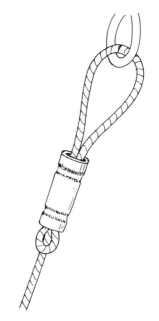

Use of crimped ferrules for a wire trace

189

Stop knot passes easily through rod rings but not through float tube

Stop knot for float fishing: the rubber band stop knot is clove hitched on to the reel line

Hook patterns for the shore fisherman: (left to right) *long shank, fine wire hook for flatfish on worm baits; bronze forged general purpose hook for all species; mustad 'Seamaster' hook for the really big fish; straight-shank carp hook for the float fisher*

A cheap rod rest made from three 5ft battens lashed together with twine to form a tripod

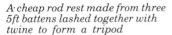

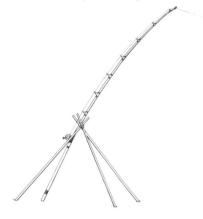

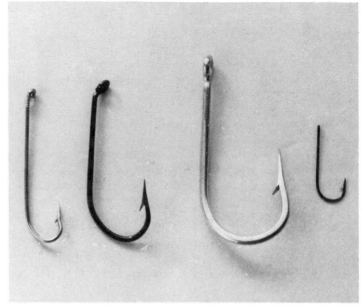

is gained of the various types of fish and their bites, the angler will work out his own timing reaction to a particular form of bite. The tope, for example, takes his time before moving off with a bait, so the reel is left out of gear after the cast is made. Of course the ratchet is set so that there is a noise when the fish moves away. The fish must be given time to make a first run with the bait. Then the run will stop, the reel is put immediately into gear and a vigorous strike made as the second run begins.

Striking a flounder bite is quite different. The fish will pull at a legered bait for quite a time before it succeeds in getting the worm into its very small mouth and a shrewd guess has to be made when to strike. Winter cod are greedy shoal fish that grab at the bait producing a number of solid thumps on the rod tip. A hard strike will usually hook a fish—it's all a question of experience, and good timing will only come with regular practice and attention to the rod.

A rest allows the rod tip to be held above the wave pattern, clear of interference that can be misread as gentle bites from small fish. A simple one can be easily made by lashing three 1in diameter dowels together (left).

Now that you have new bits and pieces of tackle, take a few score lugworm and a few spare leads and hooks, and be off to the coast; but buy a tackle box for the gear because it deserves protection, and the rust and corrosion wreaked by sand and salt water are the enemies of all fishermen's gear. Rinse the reel under the tap when you get home, with an occasional oiling to the maker's instructions. Finally, give a thought to your own safety when fishing. Watch out for the rogue wave that can sweep you off the rocks, and don't wade out on a steep beach in case there is a strong undertow.

190

Wreck Fishing and Drifting for Turbot

24

Ernie Passmore
and John Trust

Off our coastline there are many wrecks, just how many would be impossible to guess, and the majority are to be found along the shipping lanes. Where these lanes come close to land, in an area like Brixham, Devon, wreck fishing can be a very rewarding form of sea angling.

Even quite small wrecks can be the homes of large colonies of fish, and soon become a refuge for small fish where they can shelter from the run of the tide. Larger fish also come to inhabit a structure that offers a plentiful supply of food. Trawlers normally give wrecks a wide berth and fish can grow to a great size; there must be many fish that are larger than the current rod-caught records living in comparative safety in this way.

Our boat uses Decca navigational equipment, essential to pin-point the location of a wreck (often out of sight of land although that can be well within the thirty miles limit in poor visibility) and then we turn on the echo sounder to get its precise position and size. We then drop a weighted dan-buoy alongside the wreck to indicate tide speed and direction. This enables the boat to be anchored in a position where the anglers can fish their baits into the area where the fish are. If the tide is too strong for effective anchoring, we drift the boat across the wreck using artificial lures, pirks and baited hooks.

When conger fishing, the position of the angler's boat in relation to a wreck is specially important. The sophisticated Decca navigational equipment carried by many commercial fishermen will pin-point the wreck without fail, and a marker-buoy denotes its position. From now on the skill and knowledge of the boatman and his use of the echo-sounder is vital in getting the angler's bait into the tide scour, which is a trough formed around certain parts of the hull, and the natural home of the conger. This scour is somewhat similar to the depression formed around the base of a rock left by the receding tide on a sandy beach. As tide is never constant during the ebb or flow, the art of regulating and maintaining the boat's position to allow the angler's bait to fish the precise area constantly is of paramount importance. The difficulty is often aggravated by a strong cross-wind swinging the boat out of position.

Many species of fish are to be found on wrecks. The conger-eel is probably the most popular for all the very large ones have been caught off wreck marks. Although over the years we must have caught more large conger than any other boat, our largest

191

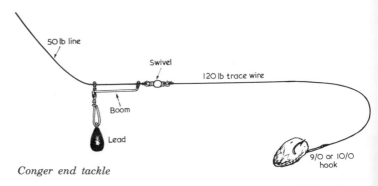

Conger end tackle

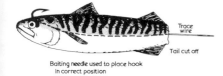

Baiting needle used to place hook
in correct position

Hook placed in mouth of bait and
out through top of head

Mackerel bait

(right) *A superb catch of conger*
eels from a West Country wreck.
These fish are probably the
hardest test of men and tackle in
sea angling (Michael Prichard)

was 96lb and we are sure that much larger fish have been hooked and broken free. The tackle we recommend for conger is a good strong rod in the 50lb class, a good quality multiplying reel with a large line capacity, such as the Tatler 4 or Senator 6, and nylon monofil line of about 50lb strength. It is generally better to use monofil line, because braided lines are twisted by the tide and make detection of a bite more difficult. Furthermore, these lines fray readily when in contact with the rusting superstructure. Lead weights of between 1lb and 2lb are needed to keep the bait on the bottom, and the trace should be of very strong wire or heavy-duty commercial nylon (above). The hook should be large enough to take a big bait. When fishing in 30 fathoms of water, a conger bite gives a jerky pull on the line and when it is felt the angler should give the fish a short time to swallow the bait before tightening his line. It is best not to strike; just lower the rod tip, winding in the reel at the same time, then lift the rod and start to pump the fish off the bottom. In this way a conger can be raised a good distance before it fully realises what is happening. The clutch on the reel must be set to let line be taken in if the fish starts to fight its way back to the bottom. A large conger will make several dives in this way and can easily break a line if the clutch has been set too tight. It is much better from every point of view if the fish can be played out before reaching the surface.

A conger that is full of fight on the surface can be very difficult to gaff and get on board. A whole mackerel or half a very large mackerel is a good bait (left), but many anglers prefer to use a whole pouting or red bream. These baits should be put on the hook with the barbed point protruding from the head of the bait. Conger always take the head part of a bait first, and with a large bait you have to make sure that the part with the hook in it goes into its mouth first. Hands and feet must be kept clear of the conger's powerful mouth for it can inflict a serious bite.

When a wreck is fished for the first time or after being neglected for a year or so, ling will predominate. The further west you go down Channel, the more ling are to be found. They can grow to a much larger size there than off reef marks, and we are certain that even larger fish than the record 57lb 2oz are to be caught. Ling do not have the fighting ability of a conger, as their swim bladder becomes extended due to pressure changes as they are drawn to the surface, and are mainly caught with

192

Gaffing a large conger eel aboard is a tough business but Ernie Passmore on Our Unity *makes it look fairly easy* (Michael Prichard)

the tackle we have described and on pirks and artificial lures.

The cod we catch on wrecks are mostly large, about 25lb on average. They are taken near the bottom usually on conger tackle; but the record cod, on our boat in 1972, weighed 53lb and was taken on a set of three Rubber Eel lures, worked sink and draw as the boat drifted across the wreck. Pollack and coalfish can also be plentiful. They are best fished for when there is a run of tide, for slack water seems to put them off the feed and moving water makes an artificial lure look more natural. Lighter tackle is best for getting the utmost enjoyment from catching cod; 20lb class gear and a light, reliable multiplying reel are what you want.

The terminal tackle is a boom with a trace line attached to it

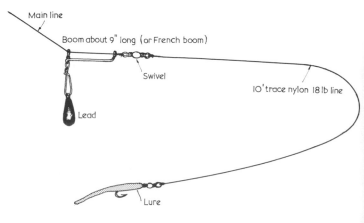

Main line

Boom about 9" long (or French boom)

Swivel

10' trace nylon 18 lb line

Lead

Lure

Pollack tackle

Leslie Moncrieff with two good turbot that came from a bank alongside a wreck out in Torbay (Michael Prichard)

by a swivel. This trace should be about 10ft long and has to be lowered carefully down through the water to prevent it becoming entangled with the main line (below left). A plastic sand-eel is attached at the end of the trace, and the tackle is lowered to the sea bed and then slowly retrieved. The speed of retrieve should be varied, as the fish are sometimes attracted by a fast movement of the lure while at other times a slow winding of the reel seems to work better. Bites can come at any depth, for the fish are usually either above or at the side of the wreck, and they will sometimes follow the lure some distance before being hooked. The secret of this kind of fishing is to keep on winding up the line, even if you feel a bite. When a fish takes your lure there will be a strong pull and the fish will then turn and dive and, as with the conger, your clutch must be set to allow line to be taken off. The fish will perform a series of runs before playing itself out and the angler can wind in as it tires.

Coalfish are becoming scarce. They are found in the same areas as pollack, but sometimes higher in the water. They can be stronger fighters because their bodies are more streamlined but you play them the same way. When the tide is very slack and the pollack and coalfish are not feeding, there are usually bream to be caught. Red and black bream are both very good sport and fish of 4lb or 5lb are not uncommon. They are usually fished for on a three-hook paternoster with small hooks baited with strips of squid or mackerel. The bait should be firmly threaded-on for if part of it is left trailing the fish rip it off all too easily. Bream bites are unmistakable: a jerky powerful tug,

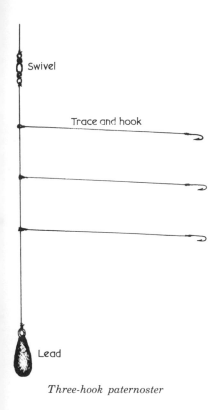

Swivel

Trace and hook

Lead

Three-hook paternoster

It is not all conger fishing over deepwater wrecks. This superb ling was hooked above the rigging and superstructure of a sunken vessel (Michael Prichard)

followed by a strong jig-jag motion of varying speed. A net is needed to boat these fish as their mouths are very hard and the hook falls out once the line goes slack.

When wrecks are far offshore, weather conditions and tide are prime considerations when a day's fishing is planned. The angler may have to accept spending more time in getting to and from the wreck than on fishing. Take plenty of spare equipment: tackle is all too easily jammed in the wreck and wire traces will also be lost, or badly kinked. Many anglers detach their traces from a fish when it is landed, putting on a fresh one each time. The old ones are easily retrieved later. Efficient and warm wet-weather clothing is essential and you will find a butt-pad, in which the rod butt can be placed when playing a heavy fish, is a godsend.

Large pirks can be very effective when a boat is drifting over a wreck. These can be used either with or without bait on the hook for cod, ling and pollack. They are best fished 'sink and draw', the pirk being allowed to drop nearly to the bottom and then jerked swiftly to mid-water. The three-hook paternoster with rubber eels (left) is usually deadly bait when the tide is running. It is made up from heavy-duty commercial nylon of 100lb to 200lb breaking strain with a lead weight of about 1½lb. This tackle is lowered to the sea-bed and swiftly retrieved in the same way as a pirk. Heavy line is needed because it is quite possible to hook three fish at a time. Only the top fish can be played through the rod and, if all three are heavy, the strain on the trace is tremendous.

Apart from the species that are expected around wrecks, there are others nearby. One of them is the angler fish, a predator that lurks on the sea-bed, attracting unsuspecting fish into its jaws by waving a lure which juts out from the front of its head just above its large mouth. This fish grows to a very large size and will take a big bait if it happens to pass nearby. The British rod-caught record is 82lb 12oz.

A far more popular capture is the turbot. Our boat has accounted for some really fine specimens, many of them caught near to, but not in the centre of, wrecks. As the tide runs across a wreck it moulds the soft sand or mud, forming depressions, scouring out gulleys and building banks of sand on the lee side. Turbot lie on the sides of the banks, facing the tide, and swim out to take a fish if it approaches. The best chance of catching a turbot will come when the anglers' lines are passing just beyond the wreck. The tackle is the same as the conger one, but if it is baited with a side fillet of mackerel instead of the whole fish, the odds are improved. When weather conditions or tides are not right for wreck fishing we take our boat drifting for turbot. They arrive off the South Devon coast and go for banks of shell for feeding and spawning. One famous mark for these fish is the Skerries Bank off Dartmouth, but it is becoming less productive and only an occasional very good fish is taken.

We have already mentioned that turbot like to feed when lying on the side of a bank facing the tide, and the tackle we use to attract them to feed has a trace of about 50lb breaking strain,

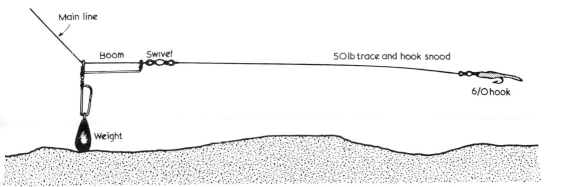

Main line

Boom Swivel 50lb trace and hook snood

6/O hook

Weight

Turbot end tackle

to allow for a fish of 20lb or even 30lb, and for the weight of the boat as it drifts. The trace should be about 6ft long, attached to the main line by a swivel and clements boom with enough lead to keep the boom securely on the bottom (above). As the boat drifts across the banks, the lead should bounce along the bottom, and the trace will then float a foot or so above it. The bait is still a fillet of mackerel, hooked at the narrow end to give the bait a good action, fluttering in the tide. Some anglers also attach a spoon flasher about 6in above the bait. Turbot have large mouths and it is advisable to use a hook of about size no 6. It is important to remember a hooked turbot will lie back in tide, imposing considerable strain on the hook snood, and the see-saw action of their sharp teeth could soon part monofilament of less than 50lb breaking strain.

A bite on this kind of tackle is a very heavy pull; the rod tip bends right over. It is most important to keep the strain constant on a turbot once it is hooked, for excessive pumping can tear the hook from its mouth, and a too-slow retrieve or stopping winding allows the fish (a very strong swimmer) to swim forward and eject the hook. A large net is needed to bring the turbot on board, and it should be ready in the water for the catch to be slipped over it, with great care, before the fish starts to thrash on the surface of the water, endangering the trace.

25

Shore Fishing Techniques and Baits

Alan K. Yates

Shore fishing techniques

The first step for the sea angler is to find feeding fish. Too many anglers turn up at any beach, jump out of the car and fish the first vacant spot they come upon. Catching nothing, they are rather like a golfer without a hole to knock his ball into and they go home disillusioned. With a little thought and planning the angler can improve his chances of contacting fish, maybe not on every trip, but more often than not. There is no substitute for experience so on every successful trip the type of fish caught, state of tide and bait and tackle used should be noted.

In general, most areas fish better when the tide is high and the movement of the water is at its strongest. To understand the reasons for this one has only to look at an aquarium where any movement of the water produces instant activity among the fish

The pleasures of shore fishing: this catch of small turbot and plaice taken at Keen Bay, west coast of Ireland, seems to have satisfied the anglers

Turn off the air pump and they lie dormant on the bottom. The sea is the same; the tide causes fish to move and to feed and when a strong tide is flowing that is the time to choose. The height of the tide, which is the difference between high and low water, also has its effect. The bigger spring tides, being stronger, often produce increased activity among the fish as they move inshore away from the strongest flow.

Fish stick to rigid feeding patterns linked with tidal movement and move to different areas of the beach according to the state of the tide, so the angler has a wide range of productive spots throughout. Shoal fish in particular stick to a set pattern when feeding and you can set the clock by the time they arrive. This dispenses with marathon sessions, for a couple of hours spent at the right periods can produce more than marathon stints at the wrong time.

Of the many different species of fish encountered by the beach angler, all but a few are best caught with leger tackle fished hard on the sea-bed; the exceptions are the middle-water species such as mackerel, pollack, coalfish, and sometimes bass which can all be caught on spinning gear. The pier angler, however, can adopt other methods to good purpose. Bait fished down the pier wall or beside piles, suspended under the rod tip or under a float, can, especially during the summer months, work well for fish such as pollack, mullet, scad, garfish and mackerel. Fishing a bait on the bottom, though, is the most productive method from both beach and pier for most of the year.

The only decision the angler has to take is whether to fish for one species, usually a large fish, or to fish for anything that comes along. The former usually entails fishing with one hook and a large bait, and success can be slow so the majority prefer the latter method which, with several small hooks and small baits, will get constant responses from the smaller species as well as giving you a good chance of contacting a larger fish. The saying 'big bait, big fish' is a myth; big fish will readily accept a small bait, often preferring it because, unless they are ravenous, they are more likely to go for a titbit.

However, casting a terminal rig with three small baited hooks out to sea, although it is the best way of catching something for the bag, is not all there is to shore fishing. If there is a shortage of inshore fish in an area, or if they are not feeding, this method is less effective; but there are several steps that can be taken to sort out the odd fish or induce feeding. A variety of baits is the first to try, and I shall deal with this later. Next, ring the changes with the terminal rig or lead. A lighter lead can produce movement of the bait, finer line may also mean that the bait will behave more naturally. Moving the bait is often successful, specially in strong tides. Release the reel spool at short intervals allowing the lead and line to trundle down tide or retrieve line in the same way. Vary the distance cast, for the fish may be feeding between the angler and his tackle. Alternatively they may be further away from the shore, so reduce the terminal rig to one hook or reduce the bait size so that distance is gained. The most successful method of angling

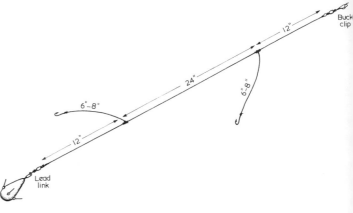

Two-hook mono paternoster

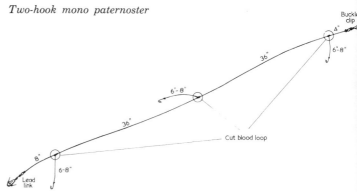

Three-hook mono paternoster

Cut blood loop

when fish are playing hard-to-get is to move at intervals a few yards along the beach or to cast in different directions from the same position, provided you are not encroaching on other anglers.

Although fishing in tide produces better catches, it poses a few problems for the angler: tackle is swept along with the tide by its force on the line, and not just on the terminal rig and lead as many anglers believe.

When anglers are crowded together on the beach or pier, havoc can be created as lines cross and become tangled. The answer, although simple, is not just the use of an efficient grapnel lead; anglers should space themselves along the pier or beach in strict order of casting ability—a solution that is only practicable among friends. Otherwise rods and lines will have to be passed over and under neighbouring rods and lines so that crossed lines are uncrossed before they are dragged too far by the tide. This must be done immediately after casting. Movement of a grapnel lead is reduced in the strongest tides by bending the grapnel wires correctly and by the use of a lighter, smaller diameter line which will put up less resistance; but when lighter lines are used, you will need a shock leader as you do for distance casting.

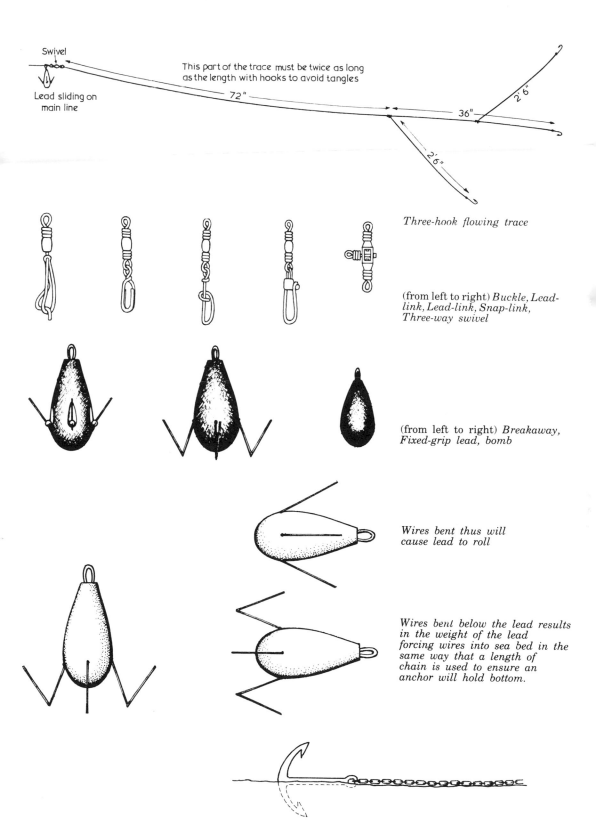

Swivel

Lead sliding on
main line

This part of the trace must be twice as long
as the length with hooks to avoid tangles

72"

36"

2'6"

2'6"

Three-hook flowing trace

(from left to right) *Buckle, Lead-
link, Lead-link, Snap-link,
Three-way swivel*

(from left to right) *Breakaway,
Fixed-grip lead, bomb*

*Wires bent thus will
cause lead to roll*

*Wires bent below the lead results
in the weight of the lead
forcing wires into sea bed in the
same way that a length of
chain is used to ensure an
anchor will hold bottom.*

201

Baits

Bait is of the first importance in shore angling and, despite the common belief that sea fish eat only lugworm, there is a lot to be said for a variety of baits unobtainable from the tackle shop.

Lugworm

Lugworm is the most successful shore bait throughout the year but only because it is used by the majority of anglers. There are many types of lugworm but basically they fall into two categories: blow or soft lug, and the larger black lugworm. Both are comparatively easy to dig or buy. One species of blow lug can be found on any sandy beach and can be dug from its U-shaped burrow by trench digging. It is extremely bloody when punctured, which is an added attraction for fish, and it can be fished either singly or in bunches.

The black lugworm is more localised and found lower down the tide line, preferring a mixture of mud and sand for its habitat. Normally they can only be dug out one at a time, often as much as 3ft down. Whereas the blow lug can be dug with a fork, the black lug is best sought with a small, narrow spade. The black lugworm is also full of blood and juices, but if these are squeezed out of the worm the skin is found to be tougher and more resistant to attacks of the shore crab, and the worms can be kept fresh for longer periods with the juices removed. The

202

size of lugworm used for bait is relevant. Generally large lugworm are needed in the winter for cod and suchlike and the smaller lugworm in summer. Anglers really waste money if they buy the large lug that are sold in the shops in summer when they are plentiful on the beaches.

Ragworm

The three most common species of ragworm are the harbour, the white, and the king varieties. Of the three, the white ragworm is the favourite specially with match-anglers as it is a deadly bait when shore fishing is highly competitive. Fish will often be tempted by it when all other baits fail, its only disadvantage being its attractiveness to crabs, who remove it quickly, and to the smaller species of fish. White ragworm is best kept alive in fresh sea water where it keeps for two to three weeks. It is also easy to keep in an aquarium with a pump and airstone.

King ragworm, as its name implies, is the largest of the family. Fully grown, it is too big to use for all but the biggest species. Small ones are, however, a useful bait for many species, specially flatfish such as flounders. Ragworm is best used where it can be dug locally. The third type, the harbour or red ragworm is small and delicate and can be dug in most muddy harbours or creeks. Being rather fragile it is most suitable when forceful casting is not necessary. An excellent bait for flatfish, pollack and, in some areas, mullet, all three species of ragworm can be dug with a fork, the best areas to dig being where sand, shingle and mud mix, or on mussel beds or areas of sand covered by large numbers of tube worms.

Crabs

The three most common species of crab, the common shore crab, the edible crab, and the velvet-backed swimming crab, provide the angler with the ultimate in bait when they are replacing their outer shells by growing a new one underneath. They are then called 'peelers' and are an excellent bait for all species of fish—the body of the crab is used for the larger species, and the peeled legs for the smaller ones. Peeler crab is specially useful as it is rarely eaten by other crabs and it will stay intact on the hook longer than most baits. It can also be kept alive for several weeks, even during the hottest weather, as an ever-ready bait supply. Soft crab, which is the peeler crab that has already shed its old shell, is also excellent, but because the new shell quickly becomes hard, it is better suited to the bigger species of fish, such as bass.

Peeler or soft crabs can be found during the summer alongside groynes, under rocks or amongst seaweed in most parts of the country, but during winter only in the southernmost parts of Britain which are touched by the Gulf Stream. When collecting peelers, the angler will find that he will have an assortment of crabs in various stages of peeling. Crabs that are only just starting to peel are hard, and are therefore of little immediate value as bait so they are best kept for a week or so. Peeler crabs are at their deadliest when their backs are just about to lift off and are best fished on short-shanked hooks, tied on with a small length of elastic cotton.

Hard-backed crabs are found in the stomachs of many fish but seldom bring any success as bait except for wrasse when they are excellent.

Other shellfish

Most shellfish are a good bait in their own locality, and after a gale, when rough seas gouge them from the sand, they can be easily picked up at the high-tide mark. At other times they can be dug from the sand. Species such as razor-fish, butter-fish, queen cockles and caper clams are found at the lower end of the low-tide mark, especially at exceptionally low water. Slipper limpets and cockles are found anywhere between the high- and low-tide mark, and mussels and rock clams are found over rocky ground. Clam can be dug from clay or chalk rocks with a small pick or fork and are usually found alongside rockworm which are rather similar in appearance to the harbour ragworm but much tougher.

The baits I have mentioned are only a few of the many but they have taken every species of fish, each in its own area. Lugworm for example is excellent for bass in the Solent area but useless on the Kent Coast. No hard and fast rules can be applied to the whole of the country, with the possible exception of peeler crab which seems to serve everywhere.

The mounting of bait on the hook is as important as the hook itself, not so much from the point of view of the bait looking alive and natural in the eyes of the angler, but for ensuring that the bait will not impede the efficient operation of the hook. Bait should be mounted on a hook equal to its size and should not mask the hook point. Fish feed on many sea creatures and, as it is not unnatural for fish to accept maimed, crushed or disabled food, a tidy-looking bait is not important. Indeed, a crushed or scrunched-up bait releases attractive juices and smells into the water that fish will detect. That is why bait should be changed regularly when blood and juices have been washed away.

(right) *Alan Yates took this 3½lb plaice also at the Princess Parade, Hythe* (Ron Tatt)

All England beach competition, Hythe. Now held annually, as many as 1700 anglers take part over a 7½ mile stretch of the foreshore. It is run in aid of local charities and cancer research. Leslie Moncrieff was the first winner in the early 1960s (Folkestone Herald)

26

Dinghy Fishing

Ron Edwards

More and more anglers are buying fibreglass dinghies with trailers to become independent of expensive charter-boats but it is unwise, indeed impossible, to fish offshore marks in them. The compensation is the independence and greater sport to be had from fishing in small craft. The type of dinghy depends largely on what you can afford, but under no circumstances should you contemplate going to sea for a day's fishing in anything under 12ft in length—even a boat of this size is suitable only for two anglers. In the interests of safety, it is unwise to overload any craft—even a boat of 15ft is big enough for only three anglers.

Small boats with cabins should be avoided as the extra weight above the gunwales adds to instability. They may look very nice in the boatyard but they have disadvantages on the water. Fibreglass hulls are so light that they draw very little water, and when the wind blows across or against the current the sides of the cabin act like a sail and swing the boat to and fro on the anchor warp. Even a boat with a small windscreen does not lay so true in the tide as a plain open hull, and to get the best sport, the boat should lay true to the run of current so that feeding fish are drawn towards the baited terminal tackle. Cabins also complicate anchor work at the bow (never done amidships), and when you are motoring to the fishing area they impede visibility unless you stand up; there is also the danger of being caught off balance and falling on one side, possibly causing a capsize. It is better to give up the comfort of a cabin in the interests of safety.

It is indisputable that in shallow waters (shallow being depths of not more than 8 fathoms) better sport is to be had fishing in dinghies than in larger craft, usually a charter.

There are several theories as to why this is but I believe that the hull of a large boat 'spooks' the fish. A wreck on the sea-bed will cause a disturbance on the surface known as a 'boil' as the tide rushes over it; similarly, (but in reverse) the hull of a large boat that draws some 5ft disturbs the water below, and the stronger the tide the greater the disturbance, but this will only reach the sea-bed in shallow water. Over 10 fathoms the disturbance is negligible on the bottom, and doesn't disturb the fish. It follows that dinghies, drawing only 6in to 9in, cause virtually no turbulence and the fish are not alarmed.

Equipment should include flares, tool-kit for the outboard motor, spare spark plugs and shearpins, all stowed in a plastic bucket with a tight-fitting lid otherwise they will get wet.

Always have a compass in case fog comes down suddenly and visibility is reduced to a few yards. An adequate anchor is most important; a fisherman's loose stock type of at least 9lb for boats up to 15ft, with a warp of at least 25 fathoms attached, is about right. If the cable is too short, it will keep jerking the anchor out of the sea-bed and the boat will drift. Oars and rowlocks are essential as alternative propulsion if the outboard motor fails. Each member of the party must have a life-jacket, and there should be a good plastic bucket for baling even if the boat is fitted with a hand-pump. Lastly—and importantly—take a plastic container for the catch.

Most seaside towns have some form of slipway for launching small craft. This is easy if the sea is calm, but if the sea is running high, the dinghy may ship water as the surf breaks over the transom before the boat is launched. It is much better to take it off the trailer and launch it bow first, for this minimises the risk of taking water aboard. One member of the crew should be ready on the oars, to pull clear of the surf once you are afloat, and get out beyond the broken water while the engine is being started.

When you reach the fishing grounds, avoid anchoring close to other boats even if one of them is catching fish; it is unlikely you will score by being close, as the fish are being drawn to bait which is already on the bottom. Also fish that have been hooked have a habit of regurgitating food they have just consumed, which is carried downstream by the current; this acts as

Launch your dinghy bow first to avoid shipping water

207

Large fenders make excellent rollers for beaching a boat

ground-bait to draw even more fish into the area of the boat that is already catching.

It is better, therefore, to go where you can anchor clear of other boats and draw your own stock of fish around you. Because of restricted space dinghy rods should be shorter than those used in charter boats—6ft is an ideal length. A rod of this size, propped up against the gunwale, extends far enough to register the smallest of bites and is short enough for the end tackle to be reached without the danger of standing up. Longer rods become unwieldy when perhaps three anglers are fishing in a 15ft dinghy, and there is the risk of flying hooks becoming embedded in someone's face or clothing.

It is good practice to prop the rod on the gunwale rather than hold it, unless the fish are feeding really fast. The rise and fall of small boats imparts a natural movement to the terminal tackle on the sea-bed—a technique unsuited to large boats because, as well as rising and falling, they tend to roll, giving a much faster action and a higher lift which does not give a good movement to the bait. Another technique pioneered by the East Coast anglers many years ago, termed 'up-tide fishing', has now become popular and profitable. This means casting the terminal tackle as far uptide from the boat as possible. Spiked leads are used to stop the tackle being dragged back by the tide towards the boat. Line is tightened on the reel until the rod tip is bowed over. When the fish takes the bait, the lead hold is released making the rod tip straighten and indicating the bite. With this method, striking is usually unnecessary as the fish has generally hooked itself by the drag of the spiked lead. This method, although working well in bigger boats, is rarely successful in dinghies unless the tide is running fast in shallow water.

When you are fighting a large fish the temptation to stand up to get better control is great but it must be resisted at all costs; a sudden lurch of the boat may throw the angler to the side where his partner is sitting and the weight of two people on one side can cause a capsize. By the same token, once the fish is on the surface ready for gaffing, the captor should slide across the seat to the side opposite to where the fish will come aboard, while his partner uses the gaff or net to land the catch. If you have to stand up to land the fish, at least steady yourself by gripping the gunwale or the engine with your free hand.

Always keep your weather-eye open and at the first sign of deterioration be prepared to up-anchor and get back to shore. It is far better to err on the side of caution and get home in comfort than to suffer a rough ride. If there is a beam-on sea (waves coming at right angles to your course), the crew should sit towards the weather side to help counter the effect of the waves. It is worth getting wet to minimise the risk of taking water over the side and capsizing!

If you have to land on an open beach in heavy surf, consider laying off and awaiting assistance rather than trying to beach immediately, for it only takes one wave to half-fill the boat and make it unmanageable. Remember every gallon of water taken aboard weighs approximately 10lb, and on an open beach it is often impossible to bale the water out fast enough to defeat the breaking waves. With some help on the shore, the boat can be hauled up before it takes much water. It is common sense to take reasonable precautions. If you do, small craft provide excellent sport at minimal risk.

Settled down for a good day

27   Long-Distance Casting

Leslie Moncrieff

Correct casting is the most important of shore angling techniques. Obviously distance is of no great account when you are fishing from a pier or rocks, but when the bait has to be presented to fish lying well offshore in deep water beyond the surf, the ability to cast far out is vital. Only anglers of modest skill would disagree—to disguise their own shortcomings.

Standards are all too low round the coasts because so many people still practise the popular 'Overhead' style. This old-fashioned method handed down from father to son, is the worst possible action for achieving maximum distance, but it is still the most widely practised. The angler stands upright with the rod parallel to the ground at shoulder height. The subsequent action of rod and body to the point of lead release is stunted and short, thereby restricting distance. It also creates line overrun problems, when using a multiplier reel.

Up until at least 1960, there was wellnigh total lack of information on the mechanics of casting, and bad habits, such as the persistent use of the 'Overhead' cast, are still difficult to break; yet, under correct instruction, a mere four hours is all that is required to master the correct 'Lay Back' style and reach distances of over 140yd.

As an engineer, I realised in 1958 the mechanical shortcomings of the 'Overhead' cast, and I decided to develop and demonstrate my 'Lay Back' method. With it, increased distances improved catches dramatically, especially for the winter cod on the beach at Dungeness. Today the advantage of distance is beginning to be properly appreciated. Even new casting methods recently introduced are based on the theory that the angler must face, and then extend himself away from, the direction of the cast. Since the early 1960s I have demonstrated to angling clubs all over the country that long distances can be achieved, simply by employing the 'Lay Back' style with its smooth, effortless action whereby technique replaces force.

Fish can normally be found where the environment is suitable for breeding or feeding. Under stormy conditions when the sea becomes highly coloured as mud and sand become partially suspended, violent wave action will scour out from the sea-bed various forms of marine life such as worms, shell fish and crustacea. When this food is washed inshore fish will follow feeding greedily. Under these conditions, the angler must not overcast the fish but confine his baits within the feeding area;

but intense storms are infrequent. In smooth, clear seas, food is soon devoured and the fish return to their natural environment which is not, as many assume, beyond the efficient caster's reach but only a little further out where they feed on crabs, shrimps, prawns and small immature fish.

By casting twice the distance of your neighbour you are covering double his area, much of it fertile ground, unfished and beyond the low-water mark, where bait has not been stripped by the commercial diggers. The value of long casts is specially evident in big competitions, with some 500 anglers, when only a minority can achieve distance; these few are enabled to fish in quieter waters to which, according to some serious anglers, the vibration effect of the barrage of weights nearer inshore positively drives the fish.

The results of club competitions prove it is these proficient casters who achieve greatest success. Nevertheless, some anglers are so anxious to get their bait into the water that they will not devote a few hours a month to practise a correct style that will permanently enhance their catch. Distances of 130yd and more are not difficult, if you don't handicap yourself by using a poor casting action. It is a truism in many fields of sport, that the man who reaches maximum performance makes it all look effortless and simple.

Next comes the function of the fishing-rod, the angler's tool. Mechanically it is a combination of a lever and spring, the large and rigid butt section acting as lever. As it tapers towards the tip and diameter decreases, so flexibility increases to form the spring. During a cast, the spring of a rod is compressed by the inertia of a casting weight suspended from the tip, aided by the forward thrust of the caster's hands, using the stiff butt as a lever. The more power and speed introduced into the movement the greater the compression of the rod, with a corresponding urge to return to its original state.

One factor is common to all casters, good or bad: the lead must always be released at approximately the same moment—when the rod becomes fully compressed on passing the right shoulder. Here precise acceleration and timing are essential to produce fast tip speed—the main factor for maximum distance. The time factor is vitally important. It can be appreciated that the greater the rod and body action employed to complete a cast, the more prolonged the build-up period will be; the proficient caster takes full advantage of this extra time gained by guiding and accelerating the lead to the point of release all the more smoothly.

The importance of time is well illustrated in three styles of casting: the stunted 'Overhead' style, which, with its restricted rod and body action before the lead release, gives only limited time to build smoothly, and consequently distances are poor—between 60yd and 80yd. Next the 'Lay Back' style: here the rod is held lower, at waist level, with the body extending away from the direction of the cast, but moving right forward into the follow-through after the lead has been released. This long-flowing mechanical action appreciably increases the time taken to make the cast, and the range improves accordingly—up to 160yd.

A third cast, the 'South African' style, used mainly in tournament events, could be termed dramatic rather than practical. The weight, with a line drop of 10ft or more, is placed on the ground as far away as possible behind the caster's back (see photos A and B right). The up-rod arm is fully extended, the rod tip pointing in the direction of the weight. The butt hand is placed close to the chin, the line taut from reel to weight. During the cast the weight is dragged up from the ground, the rod tip moving through three-quarters of a circle. Unlike the 'Lay Back' style, the left hand is higher and exerts power with a strong controlled pull against the punching strength of the right hand. This forceful sweeping rod, body and weight movement increases the time taken to complete the cast, and consequently distances of over 200yd can be achieved. As rods between 14ft to 16ft in length are commonly used, great care must be taken if other anglers are near you.

These three examples demonstrate how increased mechanical action improves distances but while this is important in tournaments, for obvious reasons it is unsuitable for normal

212

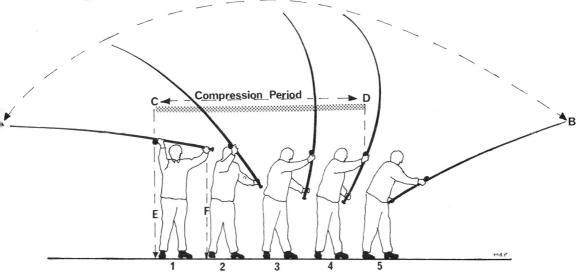

Fig 1 'Overhead' style (line drawings by Michael Prichard)

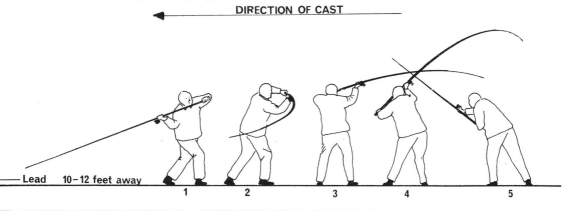

Fig 2 'South African' style (line drawings by Michael Prichard, photographs by Leslie Moncrieff)

fishing. I am not interested in casting for casting's sake, but only in additional distance leading to increased catches. The advantages of the 'Lay Back' style with its limited lead swing prior to the cast is that it is a sensible and practical action that can be used safely in the company of other anglers on crowded beaches.

It is difficult to teach casting if only because the action is so quick it is not easy to follow. As it is important to understand the mechanics of it, let me turn back to the principles. A long jumper has to have a run-up to the take-off to gather power and impetus and the same principle applies to casting. In the 'Overhead' diagram (Fig 1) the caster is trying for maximum distance from a standing start. With both hands held high at E and F and the reel close to the right side, the arc AB of the rod action is stunted, and still more so if maximum power is exerted in this restricted movement. Snatch will be unavoidable, sending the spool rotating unnecessarily fast, throwing off an excess of line which cannot be picked up by the speed of the lead; and overruns are inevitable when multiplier reels are used. The caster has two alternatives: reduce power compatible with smoothness or thumb the spool, but both are useless for good distance.

Compare this method now with the 'Lay Back' style (Fig 3). Here the hand positions E and F are roughly 2ft lower at waist level, extending at least 3ft further away from the direction of the cast. This stance increases the length of the rod and AB. The extra movement expressed in time can now be used (like the introductory action in the long jump I have already mentioned) to gather power more smoothly, accelerating to a whip-like flick, thus avoiding line overruns.

Compare also the important rod compression period CD between both casting styles. It is obvious increased power comes from the extended action of the 'Lay Back'. Again, with the rod starting from a low position E and F, the caster's hands are moving up and forward—mechanically sound if the weight is to be thrown high.

There is a very old maxim that during the cast one should push with the right hand and pull with the left. In the 'Overhead' illustration you will notice that the caster is holding the rod parallel to the ground above shoulder height. Even if the theory were correct, it is obvious that the amount of travel supplied by the right hand push is negligible; and if the pull of the left hand is roughly as strong, then both hands will counteract each other's power, as a pivot point between both hands is established. It must follow that the left hand, with its limited movement, must restrain power; while the right hand, travelling further, should apply power.

It is generally assumed, quite wrongly, that hands and arms are responsible for power but, like the boxer's punch, the main force of the cast comes from the body and shoulder thrusting forward, as the right leg stiffens to act as a brace to this movement.

Correct body and rod movements are clearly demonstrated by

Fig 3 'Lay Back' style (line drawings by Michael Prichard, photographs by Leslie Moncrieff)

using an imaginary clock-face (Fig 3, plates). A line is marked on the ground in the direction of the cast, the seaward end being 12 o'clock, the shore end 6 o'clock. The right foot should be placed on this line at 5 o'clock, the left foot approximately 10in behind. Being out of line, the feet allow body and shoulder to turn unhindered quickly forwards, ready to impose power. This stance enables the caster to maintain balance on completing the cast and during the follow-through (Fig 3/5). Both feet should be comfortably apart. The right arm, with thumb pressing on the spool of the reel, should now be extended, as the right knee bends. The caster must lean back from the direction of the cast, standing slightly crouched and quite relaxed. The full body-weight is now taken on the right leg, while the left simply maintains balance on the ball of the foot. All attention is now concentrated on the rod tip. The left hand should be at thigh level, approximately 10in away from the body—an important point because it governs the angle of the rod during its forward movement which must be approximately 45°. If the left hand is closer, the tendency is for a '12 o'clock' cast to end with the rod butt in the groin instead of on the left side of the body. The rod must be held in a firm but relaxed grip with the left thumb along the rod butt to add purchase power. Avoid a set, rigid pose by relaxing for a few seconds before going into action.

Fig 3/1 shows the action beginning, the left hand moving up and forward to shoulder height to achieve the biggest possible rod arc. It is important at this stage that the rod is kept well away from the body, and not tucked in close. The right and left arms are then between the fully extended and fully closed positions. The body moves forward as the right leg is straightening and the right foot lining up with the left foot at 2 o'clock. The body-weight is now transferred to the slightly bent left leg. To this point the action has been smooth and flowing, introducing the initial compression into the spring of the rod tip. Never use full power at this initial stage, the object being to start slowly and work up power progressively.

Figs 3/3 and 3/4 show the most important movement. As the action progresses, the body must swivel at the hips, to line up in the direction of the left foot at 2 o'clock. Notice how the shoulder and body are now poised ready. The right arm straightens against the forward body and shoulder movement, thrusting outwards against the braced straight right leg, ending with a whip-like flick, the rod butt sweeping to the left side. I have already stressed how the left hand is working all the time only as a tether to the power of the right hand. If it were used as a pulling force there would be overruns with a multiplier reel. Although these movements have been described one by one for the sake of clarity, the whole sequence must of course flow in one fast, unbroken movement. Fig 3/5 illustrates the natural follow-through movement, the essential conclusion to a smooth cast.

It is advisable, when you are learning this new style, to keep the weight stationary and suspended about 33in from the rod tip. The right-hand position is shown in the line drawing. When you are proficient however, greater distances can be reached by introducing other movements before casting. For instance, on reasonably level ground the rod tip can be lowered to within 6in of the ground. You will notice in Photo 1 of the 'Lay Back' style, I have deliberately shown the right hand lower than in the first line drawing to illustrate this off-the-ground technique.

The casting lead, now with a drop of 4ft, should be on the ground at right angles to the rod tip. The caster now completes the action as described above in a fast, unbroken movement, turning quickly to face the sea.

Another method, the simple 'Pendulum' cast, is particularly useful on a steeply shelving beach. First adopt the position in Fig 3/1 but with the lead suspended approximately 48in from the rod tip. With a small rocking movement of the body and rod, the lead is allowed to swing upward in a pendulum motion to some 15in to the right of the caster's right hand. As the lead slows and stops some 6in below the reel, the caster then executes the 'Lay Back' action. Perfect timing is vital to ensure that the power stroke begins when the weight is stationary. These additional movements should not be confused with tournament styles where exaggerated lead movements are liable to menace nearby anglers. They are both thoroughly practical fishing styles, when casts in excess of 140yd with a single-baited hook are needed.

Part Four
The Specialists

Match-Fishing

Clive Smith and
Ken Giles

Match-fishing seems to have originated about a hundred years ago, when there were few accessible big-fish waters and travel was not easy. In those days, for the less fortunate ones in poor fishing areas, this sport was some compensation and it created new interest in local waters. The Englishman's love of gambling was no doubt another reason why it developed.

In England there are two forms of match-fishing: club fishing, which is pursued by the new-comer to the sport, and open match-fishing for all comers. At club level, the angler will be competing against thirty or forty of his fellow members, on more or less equal terms, for prize money up to £20 or £30. The open circuit scene is of an entirely different standard and the contestants compete for prizes approaching £5,000. After three or four years, the top open-class angler may qualify to represent his country—in the five-strong international team.

The Anglers' National Championship, commonly known as the 'All-England', ensures that these experts will have visited every part of the country and practised the methods suited to the different waters. Slow moving Fenland waters require the competitor to be proficient in the art of catching bream with float and leger. He will have had to master the windy conditions that can make float fishing very difficult. The Midlands will have seen the same competitor exercising his skills as a float angler on running water, with much emphasis on stick float fishing and, recently, on the waggler. The swim feeder is another very popular method in this region and that is easier to master. The Midlands is similar to the South West where running water also dominates and the same methods prove successful. The northern region of the country, and the North West in particular, is totally different. There canal fishing is the most popular type of fishing and this part of the country has produced most of our top anglers in this field. Many Northerners will tell you, with devilish pride, that their region demands fishing for bites and not fish! What we think they are trying to tell us, with their North Country mock modesty, is that the North Country angler is a tenacious competitor to beat. The standard of fishing in terms of weights is probably inferior in these parts but we have fished some good waters there in match conditions.

You willl have gathered that we consider the country is split up into four regions. It is no coincidence that the club angler for

instance, and now in the days of expensive petrol, even the 'open' angler, tend to keep to their localities. Perhaps the truly great all-round anglers of the 1950s and 1960s are gone forever. In those days, with fewer fixtures and cheaper travel, they had to (and did) cover the country and were able to master a wide range of regional techniques. Today anglers are as skilful as ever but usually only on their home ground.

We will start with the Fens because, if match-fishing owes its popularity to sensationalism, it was in the 1950s when the big bream catches were so eagerly exploited there by the new angling journals of the day. That was before the days of the popular swing tip and spring tip rods when all the damage was done with enormous floats that became known as zoomers. These could be cast 30yd or 40yd to the far banks of rivers such as the Welland and Witham, and even further on pieces of water such as the Great Ouse Relief Channel. These floats could be anything up to 14in or 16in in length with a body at the base. They were ideal for sinking the line from the rod tip to float, thus protecting it from troublesome winds.

This type of set-up is far less common now that the swing and spring tip have been introduced but, in favourable weather conditions, it can still be used with killing effectiveness. One cogent reason for adopting it is when the fish, specially in the early part of the season, are feeding off the bottom intercepting the bait on the way down and leger tactics don't answer.

A 3lb reel line is required for this method as the point where the float is connected to the line takes some punishment. The hook lengths can be of 1lb or 1½lb depending on the productivity of the swim and the size of the fish. Hook sizes are dictated by

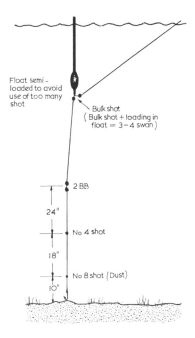

Float semi-loaded to avoid use of too many shot

Bulk shot
(Bulk shot + loading in float = 3–4 swan)

2 BB

24"

No 4 shot

18"

No 8 shot (Dust)

10"

221

Clive Smith gives some thought to the job before casting

the bait. For maggot (or as it is better known in 'bream country', gozzer) or caster, a size 18 or 20 can be employed. Another popular bait, specially in the latter part of the season, is the worm, for which a size 14 hook is a good choice. This size can also be used for bread, that good early season bait. This set-up is shown on page 221.

Ground-bait is essential for this long-distance fishing to carry a sample bait to the fish. In slow to still waters we find brown ground-bait superior to others, but it should be mixed so that it breaks on impact—no mean feat. In fact, good ground-baiting needs practice, and here are a few hints. Always put the water in the bowl first and then add the ground-bait. This ensures a good mix. Adding water last can leave the corners of the bowl dry thus making the mix inconsistent. Always try to mix ground-bait at least twenty minutes before use as the mix gets tighter as it dries. This is very important at the start of a contest for something like twenty to thirty per cent of the whole day's quantity will be used in the opening minutes. Another tip worth remembering is to wet your hands before moulding a large ball, especially when the ground-bait is to be thrown in by hand. This stops the ground-bait sticking and breaking up prematurely. Never mix more than one active hour's supply; casters can be

222

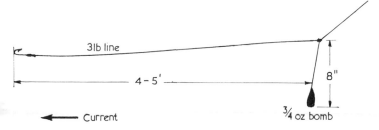

3lb line

4 - 5'

8"

Current

¾ oz bomb

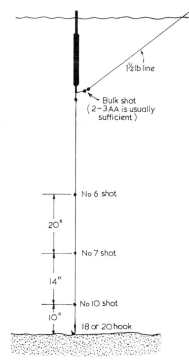

1½ lb line

Bulk shot
(2–3 AA is usually
sufficient)

No 6 shot

20"

No 7 shot

14"

No 10 shot

10"

18 or 20 hook

added at the same time but when more active baits, such as squats, pinkies and maggots are being used, add them to each ball just before throwing. If they are added initially to your hour's supply they will find their way to the bottom of the bowl, leaving the angler with no sample feed to start with, a surplus towards the end of his mix, and the whole bait will disintegrate too soon. Four to six pounds is usually sufficient for a five hour match. A 13ft rod is best in this context and an open-face reel is slightly preferable because of the distances being cast.

The majority of matches in the last few years have been dominated by swing tip and leger tactics. A 9ft to 10ft rod is the best size preferably with 3lb line, and hook sizes similar to those used for float fishing. An open-faced reel again is our choice. The terminal tackle set-up is shown above. The bite indicator itself is our choice but, as mentioned before, the swing tip is the most popular, but the spring tip more and more. The quiver tip on these slow waters is less favoured than in other regions owing to the tautness it creates. One obvious hint for legering is to employ enough lead to fish with ease. A ¾oz bomb is a popular choice. Experience has shown that the rod should be set up at an angle of about 45° to the bank. Where there is movement of water the angler should place himself facing upstream. The line should enter the water as directly as possible from the end of the rod. This minimises disturbance from the wind which can be mistaken for bites.

For bream fishing there are no prizes for being 'fast on the draw' and bites should be allowed to develop gradually followed by a full sweep. This full sweep is all that is required—not a sharp, fast strike. For hooking the bream patience is a virtue and a couple of extra minutes spent playing the fish is justified. A 24in landing net is essential.

Roach also have their moments of glory on Fenland waters, specially in late autumn and winter. For them a 12ft or 13ft tip-action rod is required, and a close-face reel carrying a 1½lb line with a 3aaa inserted waggler is effective in most swims. The set-up can be seen top right. This method is best suited to loose feeding; casters and hemp are good baits when pursuing a winning weight of roach with a dark red caster on the hook, and a size 18 or 20 hook to a pound bottom is ideal. Fish 1½ to 2 rods from the bank, feeding six or eight casters and a few grains of hemp every cast. Bronze maggots also bring success and these are fished in the same way. Pole fishing seems to be ideally suited to these kinds of waters and on a points national it is very

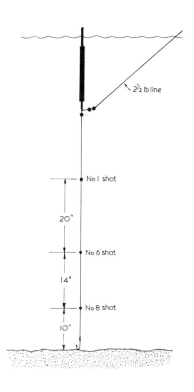

2½ lb line

No 1 shot

20"

No 6 shot

14"

No 8 shot

10"

often used, but in terms of winning matches it seems unenterprising in all but the most adverse conditions.

The Midlands is an area we know well and the float is used by winners there more than anywhere else. The stick float and the waggler win ninety per cent of the matches but it is hard for the inexperienced angler to decide which to adopt. The waggler is a first-class early-to-mid-season method when fish have a tendency to feed at various levels. It is also good for chub fishing as this particular fish loves to leave the bottom in pursuit of food. On smaller rivers, such as the Warwickshire Avon, the far bank is accessible and in areas where over-hanging willows grace the pegs these usually make first-class waggler pegs. The set-up for the waggler can be seen on page 223, below right. Seven times out of ten loose feeding casters or maggots will produce the goods although some anglers have a knack with ground-bait.

First the angler casts, then places the rod in its rest and catapults a pouch of casters or maggots if he is loose feeding, or a ball of ground-bait. This is done after every cast with loose feed and, with ground-bait, every fourth cast.

A 2½lb reel line with a 1lb or 1½lb hook length is ideal for chub, roach and dace; the species and their proportions dictate the hook size. For smaller varieties a 20 to 1lb is ideal, and for larger chub in snaggy swims (and barbel), we recommend a 14

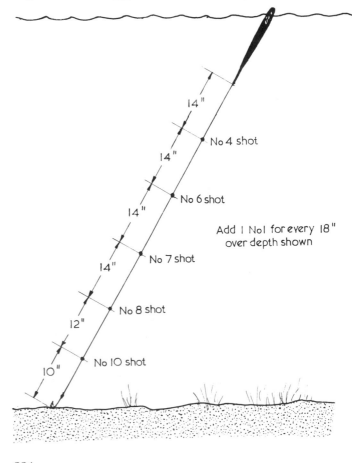

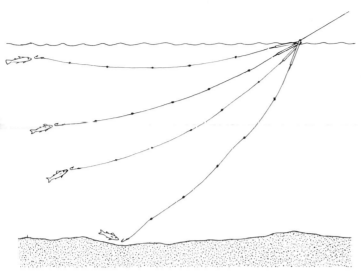

to 2½lb hook with a 12ft or 13ft tip action rod and a close-face reel. A standing position is usually the right one and a bait apron is essential.

The stick float is used in this region more than any other. It was devised for fishing the Trent in the 1950s because it helps you to take fish close in on the drop—a technique that was useful in the conditions of those days. The shotting pattern for indicating bites at all levels is *shown left*. The stick float itself is made of two types of wood: the top third is buoyant balsa and the lower two-thirds hard cane—barely buoyant. This is an unusual sort of float but there is no other that indicates bites so effectively. Most floats settle—specially in still water—in a vertical position lowering themselves in the water as each shot registers, whereas the stick float assumes a low profile immediately after the horizontal position and is capable of settling in a position to register bites very quickly. This can be seen clearly above.

The dimensions of the ideal stick float are shown right. Referring to the figure on page 224, you will note the very sensitive shotting pattern that has proved successful for taking fish on the drop. This formation is also ideal for easing along undulating river beds. A slight retarding of the float will raise the terminal tackle—important when fishing this type of swim. As the line from float to hook must be lightly shotted, the extra weight of heavy hard cane assists casting; although this tackle is never fished as far out as other set-ups. This method can be used all the season but it is most effective in the winter when a slow-moving bait is more acceptable to the fish. A 1½lb reel line is usually right, except for barbel on waters such as the Severn where greater breaking strains are required. One final tip: when using this tackle centre your fishing over a small area, say up to 3yd of swim, and remember that the stick float easily loses its effectiveness if fished at too long a range because the weight of line behind tips it towards the horizontal.

The swim feeder has been used to great effect in the Midlands,

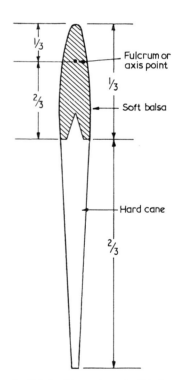

A stick float is made up in thirds: the soft balsa section is one-third of the length and the hard wood two-thirds. The diameter at the widest point never exceeds ¼in and the total length is between 6in and 8in depending on shotting capacities

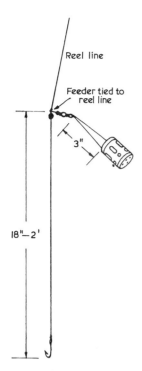

Reel line

Feeder tied to reel line

3"

18"–2'

Feeder is in fixed position. This facilitates refilling as it can be easily caught. A swivel feeder tends to slide up

no doubt because barbel and chub are plentiful. We do not favour it but its effectiveness is undeniable and therefore it must be considered whenever it is likely to produce winning weights. Barbel are probably the easiest fish to catch in this way. Later on in the season they may become suspicious, but they have no fear on 16 June when they are suicidal. In faster moving water lead must be added to the feeder to secure it in mid-stream, so a line of up to 6lb or 7lb is required. Anything lighter would break, but in slower waters where no additional lead is needed a line of 3lb will serve. The set-up of the feeder for chub and barbel can be seen left. The rig shows a set-up which, with minor alterations to the depth, can be used for most of the popular still water baits. When small fish are sought with pinkies or squatts, 3–4in of line on the canal bed is ideal, and for larger fish, using casters or maggots, as much as 18in. There are two reasons for using the longer tail for larger fish: it is much harder for them to spot a line lying on the canal bed than when it is vertical. Secondly, although these waters are still, they do move and a length of line on the bottom holds the bait still for some time—essential in the pursuit of quality fish.

With the small baits a size 20-22 hook with a ¾lb to 1lb breaking strain is right but with casters or maggots size 18-20 with 1lb breaking strain is better.

Bread-punch fishing can be practised with this rig, a size 20 hook being set some 3–4in off the canal bed. The reel line should always be 1½lb breaking strain.

Feeding is more important on canals than in any other kind of fishing as mistakes cannot be rectified. The water is shallow with no current to remove surplus feed so ground-bait is used sparingly (if at all) and loose feed kept to a minimum. Ground-bait is generally used for the small fish especially with squatts, 1lb being enough for a four-hour session. It is fed in small dabs (5p size) every five or six minutes, six sample baits at a time.

Ground-bait is always used with bread-punch. All canal

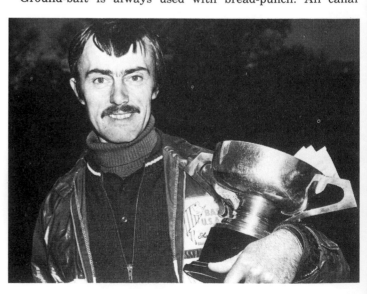

Ken Giles with the Avon Rose Bowl—not his first trophy

226

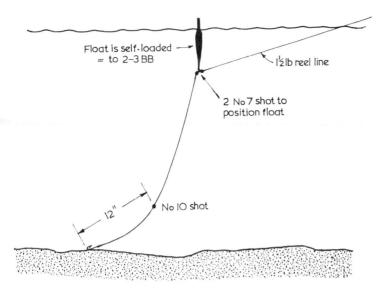

Float is self-loaded → = to 2-3 BB

1½lb reel line

2 No 7 shot to position float

No 10 shot

12"

versions are very fine indeed, but in the case of bread-punch fishing, a few crumbs are added as sample baits. The feeding pattern is more regular—every two to three minutes, as fish are being enticed to feed off the bottom. With casters or maggots, six to eight every ten to fifteen minutes is about right but the rate is adjusted to suit the response.

An open-ended feeder is what you want for bream who go for ground-bait. A 3lb line again is the choice, but note from the set-up for the open-ended feeder that the tail is considerably longer. For bream we prefer an open-ended feeder which was designed for ground-bait and the bream shows a definite liking for cereal feed offered in this way. The bream is not a ferocious eater and therefore more likely to be wary of the cumbersome feeder. You should have rods of varying strength for feeder fishing; for instance, for barbel and chub in faster water a very substantial rod is needed for casting weights of up to 4oz, and bear in mind that a barbel of 4lb or 5lb hooked in fast water is not easily subdued. There is no call for a quiver tip: the weight of the feeder would break it and anyway this type of indicator is unnecessary as bites are very clearly seen with movements of up to 1ft on the original rod top. But chub (and on occasion bream too) demand a more sophisticated approach and a visual indicator is needed on a softer rod.

As conditions in the West Country are similar to those in the Midlands, the same methods are equally successful in both regions.

The northern sector of the country, on the other hand, relies on its still waters thanks to its industrial concentrations. For years the dumping of industrial waste in its rivers was commonplace. Now, in happier times and with more sophisticated means of disposing of waste coupled with vigilant angling authorities, things are improving rapidly, with the emphasis justifiably on the more easily cleansed still waters. And not

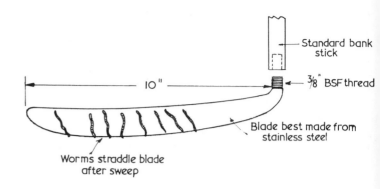

Standard bank stick

$\frac{3}{8}$" BSF thread

10"

Blade best made from stainless steel

Worms straddle blade after sweep

much further north there are the well stocked waters of the Lake District. But it is the still waters, specially the canals, that have really come to life and the North Countryman is once again able to fish the waters on which he made his name.

In the hard school of northern fishing, they soon learn the difference between a 1lb hook length and one of 8oz in their search for the elusive match-winning fish, as well as the benefits of small hooks. In other parts of the country, the average hook size for match-winning is an 18 or a 16, but on northern waters a 20 or 22 is the average. A tackle set-up for a North Country canal can be seen on page 227. It is the rig for using maggots or casters set to be fished well on the bottom—something like 3—4in with the smaller baits such as pinkies or gozzers, and up to 18in when the caster is the choice. Whereas a size 22 is right for maggots, a 20 is better with a caster. Bread-punch, another popular canal bait, can also be used with this type of tackle, usually fished 2in or 3in clear of the bottom. Ground-bait on canals, generally of a fine grain, is used minimally. With bread-punch use the same grade of ground-bait but add a few larger crumbs to simulate the hook bait. With casters, six or eight fed at intervals of ten minutes are all that is required.

One of the few advantages of the industrial North is its deadly canal bait, so deadly in fact that it was banned in most matches, but no longer—the bloodworm. Although fish may be sparingly spread in the North West, the bloodworm is abundant in these industrially polluted waters and it tempts the fish in the hardest conditions so successfully that it was banned for some years but it is now widely accepted and commonly used in matches. The larvae of the gnat are found in semi-polluted still water nestling on the silty bottoms with only their heads showing. The bait is collected with a blade (see above) and, with an underwater scything action, the blade is skimmed along the bed of the pool. The worms conveniently fold themselves over the blade and are then stripped off into a waiting vessel. These are the hook-baits. A smaller version of the bloodworm, fondly known to the angler as the 'joker', is the larva of the midge. It is gathered in exactly the same way but, unlike the bloodworm, it is found in semi-polluted moving water. Ground-bait is essential for depositing the 'jokers' on the bottom. It is made up of finely riddled soil (mole hills are ideal) with peat added to give the right texture. Its make-up is different and it is also fed quite differently from normal ground-baiting: whereas 'little and often' is correct with other methods, with bloodworm a false bed is laid immediately the starting whistle sounds—something like seventy per cent of the supply in the first five minutes and you top up when the catch rate drops off.

This bait seems to be more productive when used on the near side of the canal. The pole has become the accepted tool for the job, very often fished at lengths of around 6ft. A typical bloodworm set-up can be seen right. A special hook with a long shank is convenient for hooking these very soft baits. Use fine soil mixed with peat in equal proportions for jokers, because if it is fed on its own it simply floats and is of no use at all. It is also fed differently in another respect: whereas 'little and often' normally does not frighten the fish, the bloodworm is introduced heavily at the start of a match. The theory behind this is that it creates a false layer on the canal like a bed of jokers in their natural surroundings. It is topped up periodically throughout the match. One of the advantages of this bait is that it can be fed in thousands without offering any real substance, for when it is taken it just disintegrates into a red liquid and the fish remain hungry.

These are some general guidelines to match-fishing in its accepted strongholds, but whatever methods are adopted only the angler who can modify them according to the weather, the time of year, or the caprices of the fish will succeed. Only dedication and practice, not words, will help him to win.

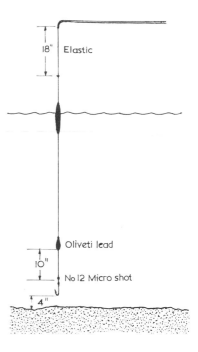

18" Elastic

Oliveti lead

10"

No 12 Micro shot

4"

29 ModernTackle Design

J. L. Hardy

Final inspection of fly reels

The main changes in fishing tackle during the past few years have centred on new materials rather than design. These new materials have been adopted and adapted by fishing tackle manufacturers around the world to further the success and enjoyment of anglers.

The most exciting discovery in fishing tackle for many years has been carbon-fibre, but there has been much misunderstanding over it. Developed at the Royal Aircraft Establishment at Farnborough, carbon-fibre was adopted by American rod and blank manufacturers who called it graphite. There were some failures at first—as with many new materials research and testing had not been thorough before it was marketed. One or two leading rod manufacturers suffered severe losses through breakage, particularly at the jointing. Breakage also took place along the rod as the fibres lie predominantly up its length. Some manufacturers overcame this problem by greatly increasing the wall thickness which also helped enormously to maintain straightness in the blank tips. Carbon blanks can be perfectly straight immediately after manufacture but become bent a few days later, a very costly item for the makers either to absorb or pass on in the cost price. By increasing their thickness, blanks were much easier to make and there were then fewer rejections, but this was at the expense of lightness—defeating one of the main assets of carbon.

The sleeve design of jointing was used in all the early carbon rods, a follow-on from certain blank makers who had specialised for years in fibreglass. The sleeve is often made from fibreglass to limit costs. This type of connection is ugly but practicable. A much neater job is accomplished with spigots such as those used on the better glass-fibre rods, but using carbon in place of the special glass spigot material.

The advantages of carbon over built-cane and fibreglass lie in its lightness and stiffness. Carbon is not stronger than glass and rods made of it will break just as easily if caught in a car door, for instance, or misused. Lightness is an obvious advantage and makes for added sensitivity, the stiffness helping to achieve greater distance and control for a given amount of power. The slimness reduces wind resistance and allows much thinner handles on the larger rods than can be made from glass-fibre blanks. The added sensitivity not only helps in feeling a take but also, by allowing the tug of the line or lure to be felt more

230

precisely, improves the timing of the cast. This particularly helps the tyro fly-fisher to perfect his casting much more quickly than with cane or fibreglass rods because of the better line control. The spin caster finds he has less height in his casting, achieving greater distance and accuracy for the same effort. Distance casting is increased further by immediate dampening of the rod tip at the completion of the cast. The virtual elimination of vibration from the rod tip reduces distance-robbing waves in the line.

Good quality carbon rods suffer much less from fatigue than built-cane or fibreglass. But to be good fishing tools the design must utilise all the advantages of carbon. Some manufacturers claim that their carbon rods are 100 per cent carbon but this statement can be misleading. What they really mean is that the fibre content of the *blank* is 100 per cent carbon. The remaining volume of the blank is made up of the resins required to hold the carbon-fibre filaments tight and form the bond once it is cooked. A precise amount of resin must be used. Other manufacturers use a very fine scrim of glass cloth to hold the carbon-fibres in place during the manufacturing stage. This scrim can also help in the tuning of the blank and is allowed for in the design.

Checking bamboo sections after machining

High and low modulus are other claims bandied about by manufacturers in their advertising. High modulus in a material means it resists bending or deflection more than one of low modulus. The carbon-fibre used in fishing rods is about four times the modulus of the fibre used in glass rods, and three times higher than built-cane. Carbon-fibre can be made with a much higher modulus than that used in rods, and of course it is possible to make fibre of a much lower modulus. As far as the angler is concerned, there is very little difference in the modulus of the carbon used by manufacturers. But there is a difference in the proportion of carbon-fibre in a rod to the proportion of other fibres, such as glass. Generally speaking, reputable companies use high percentages of carbon, though others are inclined to mislead the customer—'you get what you pay for' applies when buying these rods.

Machining bamboo to form the hexagon of built cane

New rod designs are coming on to the market using 'S Glass'. 'S Glass' is of a higher modulus than the normal fibreglass used for fishing rods. Being about 25 per cent stiffer it is possible to design rods using 'S Glass' which are approximately 20 per cent lighter than normal fibreglass rods. Rods made from 'S Glass' fall somewhere between normal fibreglass rods and those made entirely from carbon. Competing with 'S Glass' are various mixtures of carbon and fibreglass and, as more mixtures of materials are used in the production of rod blanks the choice will become increasingly difficult for anglers.

The reduced diameter and sensitivity of carbon are of great advantage in the design of match fishing rods. This is also true for big-game boat rods, where the reduced diameters and slimmer handles enable women to participate much more comfortably than was previously possible. This advantage was discovered nearly a hundred years ago when large 18ft to 22ft salmon fly-rods started to be made from built-cane instead of

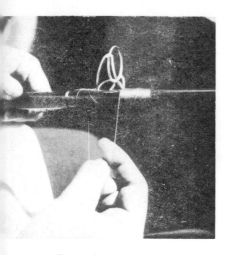

Tying the butt ring

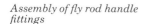
Assembly of fly rod handle fittings

greenheart, so that for the first time ladies were able to enjoy the sport of salmon fly-fishing.

The design for reinforcing the joints on both glass and carbon-fibre rods has developed from extra tyings of nylon to extra carbon being rolled into both glass and carbon blanks at both sides of the joint. Sometimes strands of boron are used but only on the upper spigot.

The design and development of fishing reels calls for complete understanding of fishing equipment plus a mechanical and engineering background. The best reels, whether fly, bait-casting or spinning, are precision-engineered using the most modern materials only where they are an improvement on the old. Fly-reels now have exposed flanges for finger control when playing fish. Carbon-fibre fly-reels are being marketed, but they are no lighter than magnesium. For years companies have tried to market plastic reels for the fly-fisherman without success. The fly-fisherman is generally unenthusiastic about plastic, although it has its uses if the correct make is used. Spinning reels are now either closed-face or open-face. Closed-face reels prevent tangles but reduce casting distance. The open-face reel is now available with skirted or unskirted spools. Skirting saves the line being trapped behind the spool but adds bulk and weight. Skirted spool reels have been reintroduced after nearly twenty-five years and are being strongly promoted. There are relatively few new models of the conventional type being produced. At the American Fishing Tackle Manufacturers Show in 1977, 53·9 per cent of the reels being shown were skirted spool.

The method of keeping a reel in place on a rod handle has not changed much over the years. The main difficulty is that there is still no recognised universal standard for the reel foot or the reel fitting on the rod; even the reels and rods coming from the same manufacturer do not always fit together. A few years ago the major manufacturers held a meeting in Zurich to thrash out this problem. The situation however has not improved very much, except that the Japanese copies of British and Scandinavian reels fit rods made in these countries, and parts of the Japanese reels are completely interchangeable with British and Scandinavian. Why the big companies of Japan have to copy can be explained only by the lack of new ideas in their design departments.

In the 1930s silk was the main raw material used for both fly-and spinning-lines. It was not until around 1958 that vinyl-coated fly-lines began to be accepted. A silk fly-line turns over much better because it is made from a tapered core. A vinyl-coated line is made from a level core and tapered dressing which tends to make a heavy point particularly with floating lines. Today few fly-fishermen would put up with the trouble of drying, greasing and taking special care with silk lines. Neither would they tolerate having to soak silkworm gut leaders overnight before a day's fishing. Nylon leaders have now made the old cast-damper obsolete.

The latest advances in fly-lines have centred round increasing

232

specific gravity to make them sink at various speeds. What is badly needed is some method of measuring the sinking rate of the present sinking fly-lines so that the angler, when he buys one, can have some idea of its sinking speed. The majority of line manufacturers at the present time are against this designation, primarily because they see no profit in it. But surely before long, one of them will take a lead in helping anglers with a problem which is becoming as confused as the line weight problem was prior to the AFTMA standard—which incidentally was brought into this country against great opposition not only from the fishing tackle trade but also the angling public. What a mess fly-fishing would be today if that introduction had not been made!

The use of colours is a relatively recent innovation in fly-lines. Fluorescent colours for sea trout fishing at night are an obvious advantage and it is surprising that it has taken so long for this idea to be brought on to the market.

Finishing rod tying

Silk spinning lines, vacuum dressed, beautifully soft and supple, began to be replaced by gut-substitute in the middle of the 1930s. Silk lines had too much cling, and made the casting of light baits impossible unless much lead was used. Gut-substitute was imported from Japan and was stocked in 100yd and 40yd lengths on wooden spools. The best gut-substitute was specially treated in 'Subdugut' which removed the springiness from the gut making it pliable. To prevent the knot drawing or slipping (a major problem with gut-substitute) a piece of soft copper wire was laid alongside one of the strands of the gut-substitute and tied in with the knot.

Nylon monofilament came into general use following the 1939-45 war and was perhaps the most significant improvement of all for angling in general. It completely revolutionised all types of angling and improved catches of fish the world over. It is ironic though that nylon has also increased the amount of salmon caught at sea, to the detriment of game angling. Nylon was found to exert very heavy cushion pressures which resulted in broken drum plates on reels. In all patterns of reels on which nylon monofilament was likely to be used designs were altered to give resistance to this pressure. The result in many cases was an increase in the drum weight which had a bad effect on the spinning of the drum on centre pin reels.

Final papering of turned rod handle

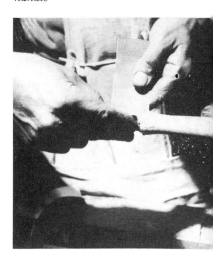

The early nylon monofilaments were not made from a nylon specifically designed for fishing. In consequence, lines often broke. Memory, or the fact that the line tended to remain in coils and did not cast perfectly, was also a problem. Later, nylon was designed specifically for angling, eliminating many of the original problems—but it will always remain a compromise. Soft monofil casts best but has less resistance to abrasion. Hard monofilament is good at resisting abrasion and gives good knot-strength but does not cast as well. The aim is to try to combine as many good features as possible into the line.

Towards the end of the last century, the full open bridge ring was invented. At that time it was considered a great improvement in design over the snake ring which was universally used on fly-rods. Being much stronger, the full open bridge ring prevented the possibility of the line cutting the ring tyings. They were made of steel in a solid piece, properly hardened, tempered and chrome plated. Today full open bridge and snake are still the popular rings on fly-rods. The butt and end rings have ranged from Agate to Agatipe (a hard glass centre much cheaper than real Agate) to ceramics (which were certainly hard but also very rough and wore the line badly) and to tungsten carbide, and brass which was hard chromed. The latest of the ceramic materials used for rod rings is aluminium oxide. One hundred per cent aluminium oxide is probably the hardest, most homogeneous material and gives the best finish—so important to prevent line wear and reduce friction. Shock rings are incorporated in the design of the best ceramic rings to prevent the ceramic itself cracking should it be knocked.

Lightweight single-legged rings are being used extensively on fly-rods and match-rod tips and butts. Whether this type of ring will remain a favourite remains to be seen. Single-leg rings for spinning rods were introduced twenty years ago and are hardly seen today. The advantage of these lay in their allowing the rod to bend better, but this was offset by the rings being easily damaged, knocked off the true, or becoming loose in the single tying.

Lures and baits have increased in quality, but unfortunately not in the mounts used for salmon fishing in the United Kingdom. Soft plastic lures come and go with great frequency. Baits and lures are very much a fashion trade and a real headache for stockists as the variety is legion, and becoming more so year by year.

Every year major tackle manufacturers receive inventions and ideas on improvements through the post from anglers and even non-anglers. Many of these inventions have already been patented or had patents applied for before being submitted to the manufacturers, and each inventor considers his invention to be the ultimate for a particular branch of angling. Many have spent large sums of money in developing prototypes and in patent fees, not to mention legal fees. Inventors seem to rush straight to the legal profession and become involved with solicitors before even finding out if such a product is at all viable and marketable. If the inventor did his research more thorough-ly he would find that in many cases his gadget had been invented years ago and had simply dropped out of use for one reason or another. Many of the 'new-shape' spoons today, for instance, are copies of yesterday's spoons just dressed up in different colours and packaging.

Centre line rods were produced in South Africa in the early 1960s for surf casting tournaments. With these rods the line goes up the centre, which has internal rings fitted. Nevertheless they recently reappeared in the United Kingdom and the United States as something completely new. Certainly improvements have been made but the basic idea has not changed. The trouble with new ideas is that they are too radical for the majority of anglers and fishing tackle dealers to swallow in one large gulp. The amount of promotion and advertising required to convince the public that the new product outdates his old one immediately puts the price sky high, so defeating the new product launch on the grounds of price alone.

A few years ago when reservoir fishing started to increase, an idea was developed to help anglers learn how to cast double-haul quickly and easily. This idea necessitated the removal of the last 6in of the rod handle, with the reel attached by the left hand if right-handed casting—much in the way of today's extension handle. The reel had to be carefully balanced with exactly the right amount of line and backing. Certainly double-haul casting was made much easier to learn, but the extra cost of having the reel correctly balanced and buying the rod and reel as a unit defeated the project, although it was initially taken up by several manufacturers and in each case subsequently dropped.

A surf casting rod was designed some years ago to beat all surf casting rods. It was about 8ft long with the reel spool on the tip of the rod, a drive shaft down the centre, inside the glass blank, and a handle on the butt. In fact it resembled a fixed-spool reel cut in half with each half mounted at either end of the rod and connected by a long drive shaft. A great deal of money was spent on tooling, patenting and even buying the blanks before approaching a manufacturer to make and market the product. Needless to say, it never reached the market.

A devon minnow was invented that had the hooks held into the body of the shell by a spring. This was so that the devon could be fished through weed-beds without becoming hooked up. When a fish took the devon the hooks automatically sprang out into position and hooked the fish. This was the spinner's answer to the keel fly.

All these products and many more must be examined carefully by manufacturers just in case there may be something which will be marketable and viable for a reasonable period of time. The difficult part of design and development in angling is to project the trend into the future. It takes at least a year to perfect and field-test a new product and to tool up before going into production. If three products in five are a success, the design department has done well.

Richard Walker and Jim Hardy in the tackle firm's warehouse for glass blanks (Leslie Moncrieff)

30

Catching Big Fish

Tim Goode

Although mystique has been stripped away from trout fishing it still enshrouds specimen hunting, or the catching of big fish, and the general impression is that it is not for the normal club-coach angler. This is not so and the history of this specialist form of angling and the guidelines set down by its founding fathers will put the beginner on the way to his goal.

The first revolution in specimen hunting took place between 1946 and 1952, when enthusiastic research by a select band of experts produced a catalyst which culminated in September 1952 in the capture of a 44lb carp that still holds the British Record.

Before World War II, the capture of a big fish was regarded as a matter of good fortune. The possibility of narrowing the margin of luck was hardly considered and, if it was, disregarded. The concept of a man directing his angling towards the capture of 'glass-case-sized' fish would have been greeted with laughter.

What changed these views was Richard Walker's reaction to reading the accounts of big fish captured in 'BB's' *Fisherman's Bedside Book*: 'Why—we've caught fish as big as some of these.' An alliance was born between Walker and Peter Thomas—the 'Hitchin School' of carp fishing—and Denys Watkins Pitchford, who produced a few years later the classic *Confessions of a Carp Fisher* which sparked off a welter of thought and literature about the pursuit of carp and led to the formation of the Carp Catchers Club. Then Maurice Ingham, an angler with access to Woldale in Lincolnshire (where a then vast 17lb carp was caught in 1907) came into the picture through the 1951 *Daily Mirror* Angling Contest for clubs, based on the capture of a series of big fish. It was expected that clubs with the best mixed waters, like Christchurch on the Avon, would annihilate a small club in a comparatively obscure angling area of the South Midlands such as Hitchin. But Hitchin won by the vast margin of 464 points to 98. Planned specimen hunting had enjoyed its first public success.

Already, in October 1951, Bob Richards had taken the first of the massive carp from a small Welsh Border lake which entered angling history as Redmire Pool, but 1952 was the real year of the carp. Two CCC members, Peter Thomas and Maurice Ingham, had taken fish over the Buckley record and then in September Richard Walker landed the forty-four pounder. This fish, tremendously important though it was as a symbol of the

(right) *Tim Goode with a catch of four carp in excess of 12lb, taken in one night's fishing*

new approach, caused people not closely involved in the capture of Walker's 'Clarissa', to lose their sense of proportion.

Walker, with Maurice Ingham, had already made a notable addition to angling literature with *Drop me a Line*; but in 1953 the seminal book of the period emerged—the first edition of Dick Walker's *Still-Water Angling*. This, together with a new mass-circulation angling periodical, *Angling Times*, promulgated the ideas of planned catching of big fish far more widely than ever before.

The new confidence in big-fish catching was not generally accepted, and it was scepticism which led to the three-match confrontation between Tom Sails and Richard Walker. Walker won and in doing so landed a barbel big enough to make again the point that the achievements of the new approach were not limited to carp—as had already been demonstrated by the *Daily Mirror* contest. The shackles which had bound conventional angling had been cast off, and with a flourish, but before long some members of the new specimen-hunting fraternity began to bind themselves in new ones apropos record fish.

It was, in a sense, unfortunate that so much attention was focused on 'Clarissa' for the achievements of the new approach would have been just as valid had she swum on undisturbed in Redmire, and some of the myopia which afflicted anglers might have been avoided. Specimen hunting, as it was then and still is, has little to do with record hunting and the newcomer to the search for big fish would do well to disregard the records-orientated sensationalism of the angling press. For most of us, setting sights too high only leads to disappointment. Records are inevitably rarities, and most anglers never fish a water which even holds a record fish.

How then can the history of specimen hunting guide the newcomer? Initially, provided realistic targets are set, success is attainable for those with the right approach, because good fortune is not the deciding factor in the long run, and the angler will get the fish he wants if he works on the right lines. But what are they?

The first observation applies equally well to aspiring bank robbers or tiger hunters—once the angler has decided on his quarry he must find out where it lives. The carp record did not jump from 26lb to 44lb in the space of eleven months because the CCC were better anglers than their historical forebears, but mainly because access was gained to waters holding bigger carp than had hitherto been available and where the skill gained in pursuit of less monstrous fish could be exploited.

Having ascertained what he wants to catch and where those fish may be found—and in modern big fish hunting the pursuit of waters can often be almost as fascinating as the pursuit of fish—it is imperative for the angler, new to big fish, to have some quick success. This prerequisite should be taken into account when the choice of species is made; perhaps bream, chub and pike offer the easiest way up the first steps of the ladder.

The tyro big-fish catcher needs initially to establish a set of priorities clearly in his mind and to map out the progress he

wishes to make, not just in terms of species but in terms of sizes. It is easy to make the mistake of aiming too high, of thinking 'This season I shall catch a 2lb roach, a 20lb carp and a 20lb pike' and ending the season disappointed and frustrated; aiming too high does more than invite frustration—it devalues real success deserving appreciation. Setting up arbitrary figures for success or failure can lead to the dismissal of 1lb 15oz roach and 19lb 15oz carp and pike—which is absurd. This exaggerated self-set target is encouraged though by the weekly angling press which, to boost circulation, focuses, albeit inadvertently, too much attention on fish that are taken by only very few people. I believe that the newcomer should ignore this sensationalism and just aim to improve on his own personal best for each species.

Geography is another reason for this approach, for some areas are potentially richer in big fish than others. Some of us prefer, either for solitude or pleasant surroundings, not to travel and successes should not be belittled by measuring them against some national yardstick. There is the case of a very good carp angler in Yorkshire who had taken only one carp over 20lb from a lake near his home. Then he came to a top-class carp lake in the South and his first half-dozen fish included two of that size. Had he measured his success in the North by southern standards, he would have been less satisfied with his twenty-pounder! The waters you are fishing must be realistically assessed and then expectations formulated accordingly. Retain a sense of proportion and don't underestimate achievement.

Graham Booth with a carp that weighed more than 20lb

239

Graham Booth with an eel of 5lb 10oz from a Yorkshire water—a huge eel by national standards

Concentration on a 'personal best' series of catches gives satisfaction and contentment enough.

A conspiracy of silence has grown up about big-fish catching which could almost be interpreted as hostility towards newcomers. The 'conspirators' are usually men of rather limited experience who live in a world of fantasy, becoming as keen on creating cliques and secret societies as on catching fish. The newcomer should not be dismayed, and be grateful for his sense of proportion.

The first commandment of the pioneer specimen hunters is that catching big fish should be based on being in the right place, at the right time with the right tackle. The right time because, although fish may feed sporadically all day, certain times are better than others—particularly dawn and dusk. All manner of factors influence feeding: water temperature, light intensity, water clarity, depth and speed are some of them. All these must be taken into account.

Place is important because big fish are not spread over a lake like the pattern of a curtain fabric: they are creatures of habit and stick to it. They are influenced by fear and by weather as well as hunger and it is up to the angler to ensure they are also influenced by his ground-bait.

Fish location is a fascinating topic—as absorbing as any other aspect of the sport; and, like so much of the science of big-fish hunting, a matter of detail. The angler needs to assess many factors affecting the whereabouts of his quarry, at the same time keeping his mind open enough to disregard all the

240

generally accepted factors when he sees the fish he wants feeding somewhere else—contrary to all expectations. Having measured wind, water temperature and light intensity, the angler painstakingly builds up a picture of where he believes the fish may be.

Take the case of gravel bars in carp fishing—vogue-swims at present, and not as simple a matter as it seems. Success is not just a matter of casting a bait on to the bar, sitting back and waiting. The nature of bars varies enormously and they need to be identified whether they are shale, chalk, gravel, or sand for they all have different fish-attracting characteristics. The same applies to lake-beds with their different rates of reaction to temperature changes in the water. In some conditions parts of the bottom remain warmer than the rest of the lake-bed after the temperature falls, creating a ready-made hotspot. Find a gravel bar with a spring percolating up it and you really are in business! The same meticulous thought must be given to dress and behaviour: the angler should not appear an alien to the fish and, if he blends in with his background and keeps quiet, he will be a better fisherman.

Unless the design and strength of tackle is right all the angler's observation and planning will be in vain. Great strides were made in the early days of specimen hunting in tackle design and there is a great selection of specialist tackle available. With time he will probably wish to make some of his own to meet his specific needs. Tackle can become an addiction.

Bait has been elevated in the last few years from being a secondary matter to one of prime importance. There are two reasons for this—one self-evident, one more open to debate. Once a fish has been caught on a bait he remembers it and has a tendency thereafter to avoid it—this has been proved by experiment and experience. The belief in 'mug fish' which are taken repeatedly only confirms the validity of this theory of a fish's memory because it is a rare phenomenon. No matter how good the conditions and preparations are, if the bait has been seen twice before by the fish it only serves to send it bow-waving up the lake. A wise angler will know what bait are being taken at a particular venue and what has been used before, and make a point of using something else. Some baits last longer than others; sweet-corn, now so popular, serves better in this respect than some others, particularly paste baits which seem to 'blow out' very quickly. Make sure, then, that your bait will not reduce your quarry to a nervous wreck, and drive him off to the opposite end of the lake.

The second part of the bait debate is less simple. It is the contention that some baits are intrinsically better than others and, given a choice, it is possible to predict that the fish will take the 'better' bait. This is the 'super bait' syndrome which started with 'exotic' carp baits and has progressed onwards through high-protein baits to amino-acids and high powered chemical-packed concoctions. The proponents of the super bait believe, explicitly or implicitly, that a fish takes one of their baits either because it knows it will do it good or merely because it cannot

Safely netted. The distended top lip of this specimen bream gives it a strange look (Ernest Merrit)

241

resist it—the feeding responses being stimulated to such an extent that natural caution is reduced. The thinking behind the most advanced of these baits is so sophisticated that it need not concern the newcomer. Those who are unconvinced by the super bait point out that the spectacular successes of the last few years could equally well be due to more good anglers doing the basic things correctly and more often—to the advent of what is in fact full-time angling.

The argument about these complex baits must make some of us believe that, unless we have one possessed with a touch of magic, no big fish can be caught. This is very mistaken, and I advise paying more attention to not scaring fish (at the initial stage at least, and perhaps for a long time afterwards) than making a needless search for a magic wand. The right bait is a great aid to success but it gets a chance to be effective only if the basics are observed first.

My philosophy in the pursuit of big fish is to be unafraid of following instinct even if it means disregarding all advice that has been offered and not to be afraid of being unorthodox. History is full of men who make great discoveries by thinking the unthinkable. Angling is like that, and the man on the spot should keep confidence in his own judgement for he may be superior to the man with all the theories. Catching big fish is not easy, but it is not so difficult as to deter any competent angler from achieving a very satisfying level of success.

Richard Walker's record 44lb carp, taken at Redmire Pool in September 1952. Its supporter is Peter Thomas (Richard Walker)

The Pleasures of
Dressing Your Own Flies

31

David J. Collyer

Fly-dressing is a craft that anyone can learn—that is not to say that everyone can become an expert but certainly a perfectly presentable fly can be produced after only a short amount of practice. A fly which will not only give the creator a great sense of achievement but which will also deceive a fish.

Perhaps after having been involved in fly-dressing and fly-fishing for over twenty years you tend to forget that first great thrill of taking a trout on a fly that was tied by your own hand; I'm sad to say that I can no longer remember that first fish to my own fly, I feel as if I ought to. . . . Now my greatest sense of achievement comes from inducing a fish to take a fly that I've not only tied myself but also one which I've invented. This is where my blood begins to stir and my pulse to race. This particular aspect of fly-dressing—the inventing and testing of new and therefore interesting flies—is something to which I am addicted, to see the leader gently twitch under to the take of a trout to a nymph or to feel everything come up hard as he strikes into a new lure, this to me is what my fly-fishing is all about. The beauty of it is that it can happen quite often—the trout that takes your first fly is only one fish and that feeling can never be repeated, unless of course you count the feeling you get when your first fly is taken by a salmon. . . .

I did not know it at the time but, without doubt, this was the reason I first took up fly-dressing. I had all sorts of reasons in my mind; I was going to get my flies much cheaper than I could buy them in the shops (if this is your prime reason for tying flies forget it, there is no way your expenditure on fly-tying materials and tools can be justified financially). The quality of the professionally dressed flies was very poor twenty odd years ago and, after looking at some of them closely, I decided that even a fellow like me who had a bunch of bananas for fingers could do better than this. I then thought of all the times I'd read about the killing powers of a certain pattern but my tackle shop just never seemed to have that particular fly in stock. I would now, with my new-found skills, be able to produce unlimited quantities of whatever patterns I liked—this of course was true but unhappily, when you first start fly-dressing, your materials tend to be somewhat limited both in quantity and variety and this can be a very restricting factor. I was fortunate in one way because I happen to live relatively near to one of our major supply houses for these materials so I could get more or less

Sinfoil's Fry

Collyer Nymphs

Muddler Minnow

what I wanted when I wanted it. The only minor problem was finance: everytime I went in there I found that a five pound note had mysteriously vanished from my wallet! A fiver buys an awful lot of flies you know—or at least it did twenty years ago.

It was only after I had acquired a certain amount of expertise that my thoughts began to stray from the standard dressings and I found that I wanted to produce 'a fly of my own'; not just *any* fly you understand but a fly which could stand alongside the older patterns and, figuratively speaking, hold its head up high. I wanted not only a new fly but a good fly as well—and that, let me tell you, is not easy. Any idiot can invent a new fly, it's dead simple, all you do is make it very complicated! If it's an involved dressing then the odds are rather like the football pools against anyone having come up with the same combination of colours and materials before. What takes skill, patience, practice, observation and a large amount of know-how is to invent a new fly which is both simple to dress with easily obtained materials and which is also a real killer. *That* is where the expertise comes in and it is also where the fascination and the satisfaction to be gained from dressing my own flies have led me.

How shall we begin to dress our first flies then? Without doubt the best method is to place yourself in the hands of an expert. Most local authorities run adult education evening classes in fly-dressing and most of the chaps who run these classes are very competent fly-tyers. What you want is a man who has run a successful evening class for at least two years. I know we all have to start sometime and all tutors have to run their first class at some time but, if the class has run for two full sessions at least, then you can be sure that he knows what he is talking about because otherwise word would have gone round and the class would have folded.

Place yourself in your tutor's hands and be prepared to dress flies as he does and not according to any methods you may have learned elsewhere. Nothing is more frustrating than trying to teach someone who thinks they know better than teacher—the fact that they may indeed know better is not really the point! The tutor is paid to do his job efficiently so give him a chance to do it. Attend every class you possibly can because most classes work to a curriculum which progresses through the various stages of dressing and to miss out one or two in the middle can be most frustrating, both for the pupil and the tutor. If you know you can't make it one evening, tell him.

There are other ways of learning to dress flies but I have no doubt that the evening class is by far the best method. You can learn an awful lot from books and from articles in the angling press. It will help if you join a group of people with similar interests to your own; the Fly-dressers Guild springs to mind. The local branches run evenings in the winter with film shows of fly-dressing and fly-fishing, there are visits from angling personalities to lecture and there are usually clinics and demonstrations so that your techniques can be sharpened. Aside from all this—they're also a grand bunch of lads and there is

244

always someone available to help you over any problems you have with your fishing or fly-tying.

However you learn to dress your flies remember that there is only one way to get to be good at anything and that is to practise; you must put in the time. It's no good at all spending half-an-hour a week tying a few nice easy flies—you wouldn't expect to get to be good at tennis or golf with just a short time to practise your strokes. Like anything else that's worthwhile you must spend time on it. Also it is not a good idea just to keep trying to tie different patterns: practise one or two until they are perfected and then progress on to others. If you experience a particular difficulty with a certain operation—for instance applying wings is something we nearly all have problems with in the early stages of our fly-dressing careers—practise that one operation until you have perfected it. Don't bother with tying complete flies; just wind a neat bed of silk on to the hook shank and tie in your wings or hackles, or whatever else you're experiencing difficulty with, and then run a sharp blade along the shank to strip it off each time. Suddenly you will find it all going right and that is the time to start tying the complete fly—not before.

Now you've got your flies, your tying skills are proficient if not exactly expert, you now have to apply those flies to their true purpose, the final test, the fish.

A fish, generally speaking, is reckoned to be pretty stupid (that is always excepting the one that you happen to be fishing for at this particular moment—he has an IQ only slightly below Einstein). I have heard it said that most fish exhibit an intelligence of about one tenth of a hen's; chickens are not exactly the brightest of God's creatures. How is it then that these fish that we try so hard to deceive give us so much of a contest? It is because they have the use of an inherited instinct that warns them of our attempts to deceive them and this is one reason why we constantly attempt to find new flies and methods of presenting them. Make no mistake about it, fish may not be very bright but they can and do learn, not just from their own mistakes (which in case of trout anyway tend to be in the singular and rather final) but from the errors of their fellows. You will find that, if you hook and lose a fish on a particular fly, the fishing will often slacken off until you change your fly and then suddenly they show interest again. I find this to be particularly true in the case of shoaling rainbows. Browns tend to be more solitary characters and to retain a territory of their own whereas the rainbow shoals will roam over a wide area.

I have found that one of the best ways of creating new fly patterns is to go out with a plankton net and catch up specimens of the nymphs and larvae I am trying to imitate. These are then taken home and studied at the fly-tying bench. Remember that when you are trying to create a new or better fly pattern what is as important—if not more so than the correct size and colours—is the action that the dressing will impart to that pattern. It is no good for instance tying a surface fishing

'David Collyer is not only one of the best professional fly-tiers in the business, he is also an exceptionally capable angler'— Richard Walker

chironomid pupa and expecting it to work well with a lead underbody, or making a deep fishing shrimp pattern that takes an age to sink to the bottom because of flaring hackle fibres that slow its fall through the water.

You are not of course restricted to producing just imitations of the natural insects; there is even more scope in the production of the fancy patterns and the lures. Your only limitation when inventing new lures is your imagination or your stock of materials.

Fly-dressing is a craft which offers real scope to any artistic talents you may have and at the same time provides a real and lasting interest with an end product to it. It is a skill you will never regret learning.

Tying a good knot

Richard Walker has said that reliable knots can make the vital difference between landing or losing the fish of a lifetime.

In Fig A this commonly used knot for spade-end hooks is less reliable than the knot in Fig B. The first knot is liable to slip and pull free under pressure. In Fig C the reliable knot is tightened and slid along the shank. The more pressure applied to the line the more tightly the knot will grip the hook shank.

Fig D shows an equally reliable knot for tying eyed hooks or swivel eyes. Eyed hooks are commonly used in the larger sizes with thick nylon to match. This knot gives far more grip and reliability than a tucked half-blood knot.

Fig E shows a similar knot for joining two strands.

A   A common but unreliable knot for spade-end hooks

B   A thoroughly reliable knot for spade-end hooks

C   Knot B tightened. It is then slid up to spade

D   Grinner knot (to hook or swivel)

E   Double grinner knot (joining two strands)

Fish Behaviour

32

Richard Walker

Far more important in successful fishing than good tackle or skill is knowledge of the fish the angler is seeking to catch. No man can be a good angler unless he is also a good naturalist, especially in respect to the life in and around the water.

Fish are greatly affected by their environment. Their body temperature is approximately the same as that of the water in which they live. Within limits, the lower the temperature, the more slowly they move, the less food they eat and the longer they take to digest it. Water, however, dissolves less oxygen as its temperature rises, until there is insufficient for the fish. At this point they cease to feed. For each species, therefore, there is an optimum temperature at which they feed best, and a range of temperatures outside which they hardly feed at all. This range is not the same for every species, and other influences may affect its extent, so that even for any one species, it may vary from one water to another. In fresh water, only grayling feed well when the temperature is below about 40°F, and few fish feed well if it rises above about 70°F. When the water temperature is approaching either of these limits, therefore, it is advisable to fish where the warming or cooling effect is least.

Commonly, in deep lakes in summer, fish will seek greater depths in hot weather because the water is cooler there. In shallow lakes, areas where the surface is rippled by wind will be both cooled by evaporation and better oxygenated because the surface area is increased, and fish are likely to be there. In rivers, waterfalls or rapids have a similar but greater effect. A thermometer for measuring water temperature is a most useful aid to the angler.

As everyone knows, different kinds of fish have different food preferences, though there is much overlapping. Good baits are discussed in other chapters; here we are concerned with general feeding behaviour. A fish may be unwilling to feed through low temperature, lack of oxygen, fear, preoccupation with spawning, or some other reason. Or it may be willing to feed on anything edible that it has not learned to avoid. A third condition is when it is willing to feed only on some particular sort of food, and this commonly occurs when there is present in the water large numbers of small, identical food items. Great numbers of a particular kind of insect, mollusc or crustacean will usually induce this selective feeding by fish, or preoccupied feeding as it is usually called.

(overleaf) *Richard Walker lands a big tench* (Richard Walker)

247

In fly-fishing, it becomes necessary to use an artificial fly that bears some points of resemblance to the insect that the fish are eating selectively. Fortunately, if enough points of resemblance are incorporated in the artificial, the fish usually overlook the inevitable points of difference.

There are some species of fish which are unsuitable for fly-fishing, and their selective feeding on organisms that are usually too small to use as bait poses problems. The answer is to attempt to wean these fish away from eating natural organisms and on to eating something suitable for baiting a hook. This is done by throwing plenty of bait into the water. It is called ground-baiting; most anglers think its purpose is to attract fish to a particular area, but in fact by far its most important function is to educate the fish so that they begin eating what the angler wants them to eat. There are three golden rules for ground-baiting: the first is that the hook-bait must relate to the ground-bait in its nature; the second is that the hook-bait and the ground-bait must be in the same place, or at least follow the same line of current or drift. The third rule is to use the right quantity—enough educates and may attract—but too much fills the fish so that they stop feeding eventually.

It is important to be aware of the senses of fish. In childhood I was advised by my grandfather to pretend that every fish had a gun and would shoot me if it saw me. The great majority of anglers handicap themselves by frightening the fish they wish to catch, so that they either flee or stop feeding. There have been many learned treatises on how much fish can see and what limitations their vision has, but my grandfather's advice remains sound. Despite what scientists may say, fish can see an angler on the bank at a considerable distance if he lets them, and specially if he moves between them and the sky. That applies even when the water is muddy. All the light that reaches the fish comes from the sky. Anything that moves between fish and light-source must be noticed by those fish.

Fish cannot, however, upset the laws of refraction. Any ray of light that strikes the surface of the water at an angle of less than about 10° is totally reflected. Therefore, if the angler keeps below an imaginary line, making an angle of 10° to the surface above the fish, he can neither see nor be seen by that fish. However, even then he may scare the fish by starting a panic among nearer, often smaller fish. Panic spreads rapidly among fish. One cannot therefore be too careful to avoid scaring them. Drab dress, slow deliberate movement, making use of bankside cover, avoiding being silhouetted against the sky, are all important precautions to take.

Fish are also extremely sensitive to vibrations, which they detect via sensitive nerve-endings in their lateral lines and elsewhere. A heavy footfall on the bank, the dropping of a hard object in a boat, careless wading; all these and many other sources of vibration can alarm fish over a wide area, as also may the splash of one's tackle alighting on the surface or, in the case of leger and paternoster rigs, the lead hitting a hard river- or lake-bed.

How acute is a fish's sense of smell, or taste, we do not know, but some kinds of fish are able to detect flavours in the water at great distances. Place a freshly killed small fish in any water where there are eels and sooner or later an eel will find it, if a pike doesn't find it first. The scent or flavour of baits is therefore important, but this does not mean that you can buy any magic essences from the chemist's shop that will make baits irresistible to fish, or that tobacco scent, if you smoke, will deter fish from taking your bait. Fish find baits by seeing them, feeling vibrations from live-baits, and by detecting natural scents; if a fish is seeking a worm, it expects a smell or flavour of worm, not of oil of aniseed or geraniums. One might suppose that alien smells like tobacco or of the human hand would repel fish, but in practice these two seem to have no effect; other scents, like oil and petrol, sometimes do.

In Britain, great numbers of anglers regularly fish a limited number of waters. Coarse fish are nearly all returned alive, and even in trout fisheries, some fish are hooked and lost. There can be no doubt that fish of all kinds can communicate alarm or suspicion to others. On seeing a bait or lure that previous experience has taught it to fear, a fish will usually flee. Other fish, observing this, will follow suit. In most well-fished waters, many fish will have learned to fear the most commonly used baits and lures. Match-angling in particular teaches great numbers of fish to avoid being caught. If a scientific researcher wished to teach as many fish as possible to avoid being caught on rod and line, he would be hard put to devise a more effective means of doing it than by distributing anglers at 15yd to 20yd intervals along miles of river or canal every week, and setting them to fish for several hours, using only a small selection of baits and returning alive all the fish they catch.

To succeed in catching fish of good size, therefore, it is important to seek new baits and lures that few fish have learned to fear. It is so tempting for anglers to use baits that have been very successful in the past, long after their effectiveness has greatly diminished. It is also very tempting to blame failure on lack of fish and to demand restocking, when in fact fish are plentiful, but have learned how to avoid capture.

Beyond any doubt, the successful location of the fish one wishes to catch is by far the most important step towards catching them. In some waters that are clear and of limited extent, it is possible actually to see the fish. More commonly, that is difficult or impossible, though some species may betray their whereabouts by leaping, rolling at the surface, sending up bubbles characteristic of their species, or by stirring up mud. Failing such clues, recourse must be had to knowledge of their behaviour in relation to current, temperature, wind direction, nature of river- or lake-bed, availability of food, and such other factors as may relate to the problem.

Water is at its heaviest at a temperature of 39.2°F. This means that in lakes and ponds, whenever the temperature at the surface is below 39.2°F, the deepest water is also the warmest. Conversely, if the surface temperature is above

39.2°F, then the deepest water is the coolest. The effect of wind is to increase the oxygen content of water, and except when a very warm wind is blowing on very cold water, wind cools. The stronger the wind and the more it disturbs the surface, the greater these effects are.

River water is usually fairly constant in temperature from top to bottom, except where it may be influenced by warm water discharges from factories or power stations, or by the presence of springs in the river-bed. The latter can be of great importance in cold weather because they produce a relatively small warmer area of water in which great numbers of fish may be found. Temperature is of such great importance in fishing that a cased thermometer of the slow-registering kind is of the utmost value to the angler. Depths can be ascertained by the normal method of plumbing, but on large waters an electronic echo-sounder is very much better. An effective model is no more expensive than a good fishing rod.

Above all, it is important to realise that a fish is a wild animal, and to be successful in angling, this must never be forgotten.

Acknowledgements

Unless different credits are given in the captions, photographs are the contributors' copyright with the following exceptions: Chalkstream Trout, *Graham Swanson*; Dace, *Angling Times*; Grayling, *J. Barry Lloyd*; Rudd, Roach and Tench, *Angling Times*. In the Sea Angling section, where individual credits are not given, the photographs are Leslie Moncrieff's copyright and the publishers are additionally grateful to him for collecting the bulk of the pictures for this section.

The drawings of the Gold Ribbed Hare's Ear fly are by Freddie Rice from his *Fly-Tying Illustrated* and are his copyright. All other drawings of flies are by Derek Bradbury and are his copyright.

The publishers wish to thank all concerned with a special word of appreciation to Peter Maskell of *Angling Times* for his help.

Index

Page numbers in italics refer to illustrations